D1479150

The Elegiac Passion

Emotions of the Past

Series Editors
Robert A. Kaster | David Konstan
This series investigates the history of the emotions in pre-modern societies, taking 1500 CE as the conventional threshold of modernity. In addition to new work on Greco-Roman and medieval European cultures, the series provides a home for studies on the emotions in Near Eastern and Asian societies, including pre-modern Egypt, India, China, and beyond.

The Elegiac Passion
Jealousy in Roman Love Elegy
Ruth Rothaus Caston

The Elegiac Passion

Jealousy in Roman Love Elegy

RUTH ROTHAUS CASTON

OXFORD
UNIVERSITY PRESS

OXFORD
UNIVERSITY PRESS

Oxford University Press is a department of the University of Oxford.
It furthers the University's objective of excellence in research,
scholarship, and education by publishing worldwide.

Oxford   New York

Auckland   Cape Town   Dar es Salaam   Hong Kong   Karachi
Kuala Lumpur   Madrid   Melbourne   Mexico City   Nairobi
New Delhi   Shanghai   Taipei   Toronto

With offices in

Argentina   Austria   Brazil   Chile   Czech Republic   France   Greece
Guatemala   Hungary   Italy   Japan   Poland   Portugal   Singapore
South Korea   Switzerland   Thailand   Turkey   Ukraine   Vietnam

Oxford is a registered trade mark of Oxford University Press
in the UK and certain other countries.

Published in the United States of America by
Oxford University Press
198 Madison Avenue, New York, NY 10016

Library of Congress Cataloging-in-Publication Data
Caston, Ruth Rothaus.
The elegiac passion: jealousy in Roman love elegy /Ruth Rothaus Caston.
pages.   cm.
Includes bibliographical references and index.
ISBN 978-0-19-992590-2
1. Elegiac poetry, Latin—History and criticism. 2. Jealousy in literature. I. Title.
PA6059.E6C37   2012
874'.0109—dc23   2011048703

1 3 5 7 9 8 6 4 2

Printed in the United States of America
on acid-free paper

To my mother and the memory of my father

CONTENTS

PREFACE

The present book is both about a passion, jealousy, and about a genre, Roman love elegy. The intersection of these interests is in many ways a natural one: while Roman love elegy is most obviously about love and the narrator's various erotic relations, it is equally concerned with rivalry for affection and jealous responses. But I argue that the connection runs even deeper. Many of the distinctive characteristics of Roman love elegy—its obsessive detailing of events, anxiety over trust or *fides*, and interest in role-playing—are features that derive from the pathology of jealousy and explain many elements of the genre that have to this point not been adequately understood. The centrality of jealousy in Roman elegy is also unmatched elsewhere in ancient literature, pointing to a special connection between content and form.

I knew that jealousy was going to be a fascinating subject right from the start. Whenever I told people what I was working on, they showed intense fascination and peppered me with lots of questions before declaring that, strangely enough, jealousy was an emotion that they themselves had never experienced. It is a peculiar fact about jealousy that we tend to feel ashamed to admit it. For while excessive suspicion is obviously a sign of one's own lack of trust, the basis for jealousy is a concern about the strength of a relationship and the commitment on which it relies. Were someone not to feel jealous when a special relationship was threatened, it would be a sure sign that the person did not value it as highly as he or she should. Though a negative emotion, then, jealousy tells us a great deal about positive aspects of love, in particular the *fides* on which it rests. Yet the hesitancy to admit jealousy is also revealing of our insecurities and weaknesses, and in the specific case of love elegy, a crisis of confidence in the narrator that spreads to his other, non-erotic relationships.

It is a pleasure to be able to thank many people for their advice and encouragement during the course of writing this book, beginning from its early stages as a dissertation. First I would like to thank my committee at Brown, Michael Putnam, David Konstan, Martha Nussbaum, and Jeri DeBrohun, for their support and combined expertise in Latin poetry and the passions. Michael and David have continued to be part of the project as it developed and evolved, and I would like them to know how very grateful I am, both for what they have taught me and for their friendship.

A number of other people have read more recent versions and given extensive and valuable comments. The series editors, Bob Kaster and David Konstan, both provided substantive criticisms that have significantly improved this book. Marilyn Skinner and my colleagues Artemis Leontis, Celia Schultz, and Ruth Scodel all read the manuscript in its entirety and suggested many helpful revisions. My research assistant, Nicholas Geller, went above and beyond the call of duty in checking the final version and saved me from many errors. I am also grateful to the (formerly anonymous) reviewers for the press, Roy Gibson and Christopher Gill, for their detailed, perceptive, and constructive criticisms, from which I benefitted immensely, and finally to the Classics Editor of Oxford University Press, Stefan Vranka, for all his help. The standard disclaimer of course holds as well: any faults that remain are obviously all my own.

I would also like to thank fellow participants and audience at the conference on the emotions I organized at UC-Davis in 2003, as well as audiences of earlier versions of Chapters 1 and 2. The Loeb Classical Library Foundation generously funded a year of support at a crucial juncture in 2003–4. Thanks are due as well to *The Classical Journal* for permission to reuse material from my article "Love as Illness: Poets and Philosophers on Romantic Love," *CJ* 101.3 (2006) 271–98 in Chapter 1 of the book.

Last but not least, I want to thank my family for their patience and support: my mother and sisters who were always there with their encouragement; my daughters, Eva and Sarah, who were extraordinarily understanding and generous about the time I spent away from them, and always a source of good cheer (and whose occasional bouts of sibling rivalry added to my knowledge of jealousy); and my husband, Victor, who has been unwavering in his support and helped me see that what underlies it all is trust and loyalty.

The Elegiac Passion

Introduction

Today the passions are a subject claimed by many fields: psychology and philosophy, sociology and anthropology, neurobiology and ethnography, history and literature. In the ancient world, interest in the passions was also spread among different disciplines, as philosophers debated their role in a happy life, rhetoricians taught how best to employ them for purposes of persuasion, and literary critics discussed their therapeutic and educational role in literature. Ancient literature itself exhibits a fascination with the *pathē* from the beginning, with the very first word of the *Iliad*, *mēnin*, announcing anger as its theme. In Greek tragedy, the overwhelming passions of female characters like Medea or Hecuba come quickly to mind, but male characters like Ajax also display violent emotion. The *pathē* are just as prominent in Latin texts as they are in Greek. In epic, Aeneas' anger at the end of the *Aeneid* has especially stimulated scholarly debate.[1] But other emotions are prominent elsewhere in Roman literature, too: envy and grief in Ovid's *Metamorphoses*, for example, and fear in New Comedy and the historical writers.

The close examination of emotions in ancient literature is still a relatively recent phenomenon. Important groundwork was done in the 1980s by Stanford on Greek tragedy,[2] while the extensive contributions of Nussbaum, Sorabji, and Gill over the past two decades have revealed important connections between philosophy and literature.[3] More recently, there have been several detailed studies by literary scholars on a wide range of genres and individual emotions: a volume by Braund and Gill on Roman literature, Konstan's study of pity and now a broad study of 12 central emotions in Greek literature, Harris' work on rage, and Kaster's book on a cluster of related emotions (shame, envy, regret, and disgust).[4] These excellent studies have created a thriving discussion that has already had ramifications for the study of ethics and values as well as literature.

1. Cf. Galinsky 1988, Putnam 1990, and Gill 1997.
2. Stanford 1980.
3. Nussbaum 1990, Nussbaum 1994, Sorabji 2000, Gill 1997, Gill 2004.
4. Braund and Gill 1997, Konstan 2001, Konstan 2006, Harris 2001, and Kaster 2005. For other studies of the emotions in ancient literature, cf. Barton 2001, Braund and Most 2003, Konstan and Rutter 2003, and most recently Polleichtner 2009 on the representation of the emotions in select passages of the *Aeneid*. He discusses jealousy in ch. 6, though in my view it is envy, not jealousy, that is at issue; there on the distinction between the two emotions, see below.

Despite this recent surge of interest in the emotions in Greek and Roman literature, however, there has been very little focus on love elegy or its relation to contemporary philosophical positions.[5] This absence stems in part from a preoccupation with anger and pity and with "high" genres such as epic, tragedy, and history. Yet when we think about Roman love elegy, we realize that it depends crucially upon the passions: without love, anger, jealousy, pity, and fear, elegy could not exist at all. The poetry of Propertius, Tibullus, and Ovid traces the tangled relations of poet, mistress, rivals, and friends, and their varying affections and competition for attention, thus providing an account that stresses not only the particular history of the characters involved but also their beliefs about each other's motives and intentions.[6] As Gibson has recently said of the language there of madness, insanity, grief, and anger, "The elegist's repeated use of the terms reviewed above, including those associated with fear, anger and distress, suggests a degree of emotion which all the major philosophical schools, not just the Peripatetics, would find 'excessive' in various ways."[7]

Jealousy is arguably at the center of all these emotions in elegy. The poems are built upon the presumed existence of a love triangle involving poet, mistress, and rival,[8] fertile material for exciting suspicions and competition. The very structure of elegy thus creates an ideal scenario for the arousal of jealousy. Elegy also provides a multifaceted perspective on jealousy that gives us details and nuances of the experience of jealousy not found elsewhere in ancient literature. We learn of both male and female jealousy, and they are characterized quite differently, even if both portraits are conceived by a single poet.[9] Rivals come on the scene and are inevitably compared to lover or beloved, giving us some indication of their character and motivation.[10] In many cases the poems detail the progression of the emotional state over time. By following the narrative line of a poem, or sequence of poems, we are able to discern the various stages by which a character is eventually overcome by jealous thoughts and desires.[11] More

5. The only discussions I have found are Allen 1950a, 260–1, Brown 1987, 142–3, Booth 1997 on Catullus c. 76, and Cairns 2004. Booth's article is important in addressing philosophical influence on love poetry, though its conclusions are negative.

6. This is of course less true for Ovid than for the other two elegists and Catullus.

7. Gibson 2007, 44.

8. The rival is not a fixed character, but changes from poem to poem. Still, he conforms to a few standard types, such as the *dives amator* and the soldier.

9. Sulpicia provides an authentic female jealous voice but does not provide much evidence of jealousy, perhaps because of the brevity of the corpus.

10. Although the poet allows us to hear of the beloved's jealousy within his poems, he does not give the rival a voice.

11. Latin love elegy has often been read as the record of a relationship, however much this is a poetic construct, and the conclusions of Propertius Bk. 3 and *Amores* 3 purport to be a farewell to both the love affair and love poetry. But even on a smaller scale, we can trace mounting jealousy; this is especially clear in those *Heroides* that concern jealousy, such as Paris' letter to Helen (16) or Hero's letter to Leander (19).

potent still, the first-person, subjective voice of elegy means that we learn about jealousy most often from the mouth of the one in its grip. If we were to take these self-presentations at face value, the resulting representation of the onset and development of jealousy could almost be described as clinical.[12] The development of jealousy is such a central theme in the narrative of elegy that it provides a "red thread" into the emotionally chaotic life of the characters we meet there.

Why has the abundant evidence for elegiac jealousy been overlooked? One reason has to do with how jealousy manifests itself in the poetry. Tracing the emotions in ancient literature is a quest that has been framed more through word studies than in conceptual terms. Often philologists have not ventured further.[13] The advantage of a purely terminological approach is that the canons of evidence are clear-cut, but it risks overlooking rich and varied evidence that is not tied to a specific phrase (or phrases). This is true for jealousy where, in the majority of cases, the early signs of jealousy are not indicated by a word or even cluster of words, which tend to appear only when jealousy is in full swing. Instead, we must rely at early stages on references to other emotions like fear and anger, which are a crucial part of the jealousy complex, the poetic context, and characters' behavior. Terminology alone cannot detect jealousy, and that is perhaps particularly so in the case of an emotion that is admitted only with difficulty (more on which below).

Another reason for the neglect of jealousy in Roman love elegy has to do with the tendency to study this genre exclusively through the lens of love.[14] There is nothing wrong with such an approach, of course, so long as it is does not detract from other ways of examining the poems. But there has been an almost singular emphasis on this one passion in particular, and this has obscured the other emotional currents in the poetry. Even fear and the fear of death have been viewed under the rubric of love rather than in their own right, much less in connection with Epicurean theories with which the elegists would have had contact.[15]

In this introduction, I offer some general background on the emotions and jealousy and how I use these terms. To begin with, what is an emotion? How is it

12. The more extended *Heroides* especially resemble some of the patient narratives we read in psychology (e.g., those recounted in Lagache 1947, White and Mullen 1989, Baumgart [1985] 1990, Pao 1969).

13. Kaster 2005 and his use of scripts developing out of word usage is an important exception; see his p. 151, n. 17 for other examples of studies that rely on scripts or context.

14. Of course virtually every treatment of elegy has to consider love or the *topoi* that characterize it. What I want to criticize here is the exclusive emphasis on this one emotion to the neglect of others.

15. See for example Papanghelis 1987 on love and death in Propertius. On the Latin poets and Epicureanism, see Giuffrida 1940 and now Armstrong et al. 2004. Another way that love may have obscured jealousy is the fact that romantic love has certain similarities to erotic jealousy, such as the insecurity about whether we are loved as much as we love.

different from, say, a mood or feeling? What were the ancient theories of the passions, in particular those most influential on the Romans, Stoic and Epicurean? I then turn to definitions and methodology. How should we understand jealousy and its close associate, envy? How can we determine when jealousy is present? Are there any verbal clues? What else besides terminology is an indicator of jealousy? Finally, I address the issue of genre and why jealousy is so prominent in elegy in particular, when we might easily have expected it to appear in other genres as well, especially those with love as a central theme. After addressing these questions we will be in a better position to evaluate the evidence for jealousy and the interpretation of its role in the chapters that follow.

The Emotions in General

What is an emotion? As a first, rough answer, I offer some examples. One might get angry at an insult, or feel envious of a rival's recent success, or fear a car spinning out of control. There are often characteristic bodily feelings that accompany these emotions, for example the flush of shame, the throb of anger, or the butterflies of fear. But there also seem to be characteristic beliefs one must have in order to feel each emotion, concerning both what other people have said or done, and characteristic desires that lead one to respond. In fact, often there are certain fairly typical narrative situations or scenarios that belong to each of these emotions.[16] It is difficult to be more precise beyond this, not only because different cultures disagree on the basic list of emotions and the different nuances between them,[17] but also because the exact nature of emotions has been the subject of intense controversy from ancient times onwards. Some have thought that the emotions were forces beyond our rational control or even articulation, while others consider them thoroughly cognitive, the sorts of things that could be influenced by therapy and even philosophical argument.[18]

Nevertheless, there are some useful distinctions we can introduce at this stage. To begin with, emotions in the contemporary sense of the word seem to be distinct from moods and feelings. Examples of moods include anxiety or nervousness or euphoria. In contrast to emotions, they may be drawn out over stretches of time, and what they are "about" is less clear. Feelings include such things as itches, tickles, and shooting pain. They generally seem to be cases of bodily sensation, and while emotions often tend to have some bodily affect

16. See Wierzbicka 1999, ch. 2 on "cognitive scenarios," and White and Mullen 1989, 12.
17. On the cultural determinants of jealousy, see Davis 1935/6, Lutz 1998, Wierzbicka 1999, and Hupka 1981.
18. On the different types of theories of the emotions (sensational, physiological, behavioral, evaluative, cognitive), see the excellent introduction by Calhoun and Solomon 1984.

concurrent with them, this is by no means necessary. Even when these affects occur, there is clearly much more to the emotion involved.

In particular, emotions have content: they are of or about something. I do not just get angry, I get angry at what someone has said about me (or what I believe was said about me). And even more specifically, I get angry at remarks that I take to be a slight or insulting. When I feel envy, I do not just feel competitive, I feel envy towards someone whom I perceive as a rival and a possible threat, and I am envious of some advantage that I think he or she has acquired and that I would like for myself. The emotions thus display a highly articulate structure, involving a great number of beliefs about how the world is with respect to us. It is precisely because emotions have this content that they are evaluable. We can judge certain emotions to be appropriate or inappropriate, either because the associated beliefs may be ill-founded or false, or because our reaction and subsequent desires may be out of proportion to what the situation actually demands. Therefore emotions are not like blind drives or incoherent bodily sensations; they are highly articulate ways of seeing the world and reacting to it, and so in a certain way continuous with our rational thoughts rather than utterly beyond the reach of reason.

Many ancient Greek and Roman philosophers arguably held a cognitivist view of the emotions similar to the one I have outlined above, especially in the period with which I am concerned. According to the Stoics, for example, the *pathē* are impulses (*hormai*), a striving or endeavoring.[19] An impulse is defined as "a movement of the soul towards or away from something," but for the Stoics, this is not a blind force or drive but rather "an act of assent" (*sunkatathesis*)—that is, an endorsement of or commitment to some view of how things are in the world. It is this aspect that makes it a cognitive theory of the emotions and permits evaluation based on whether one's commitments are appropriate to the circumstances and well-founded. But in the Stoics' opinion, all emotions are excessive and irrational impulses since they all erroneously place excessive value on external "goods": wealth, possessions, power, relationships, and even life itself. These goods are not "up to us" (*eph' hēmin*) and are therefore hostages to fortune, things not entirely within our control. Since we should be entirely without error according to their moral ideal, the Stoics believe that all passions should be extirpated (*SVF* ii 443–55). The wise man should rely on nothing outside himself: he should value only internal goods—that is, his virtue and the state of his soul. It follows that the wise man will be *apathēs*, completely free of all passion.[20]

The Stoics divide *pathē* into four main types: desire (*epithumia*) and fear (*phobos*), pain (*lupē*) and pleasure (*hēdonē*). Desire and fear have priority, with pleasure and

---

19. Cf. Inwood 1985, ch. 5; Long [1974]1986, 175–8; Frede 1986; Annas 1992, chs. 5 and 9; Nussbaum 1993; Nussbaum 1994, chs. 9 and 10; and Graver 2007.

20. Though he can feel *eupatheiai* (see Annas 1992, 114–5) and *eros*, on which see next note.

pain contingent upon them: pleasure occurs when we obtain what we desire, pain when what we fear happens to us. Despite his adamant opposition to the passions, however, the wise man's life will not be empty of feeling. Insofar as all commitments and impulses involve an evaluative stance towards oneself and the world, the Stoic sage will have sound sentiments (*eupatheiai*) and will even love, although not in the passionate way that *eros* is normally understood.[21] The *eupatheiai* all depend upon a correct evaluation of what is genuinely of worth, and to this extent, his impulses, even towards the object of love, will be directed only towards moral good.

The Epicureans, by contrast, are adamantly opposed to *eros*, though here, too, this does not seem to exclude either intimate or sexual relations, as evidenced by the *mores* actually practiced in the Garden.[22] Such relationships are allowed in theory, provided one can withstand their difficulties, but Epicurus considers this to be virtually impossible.[23] The Epicureans are not in general as hostile to the emotions as the Stoics, however, since they believe the passions can be based on true beliefs as well as on false ones, and therefore can on occasion be the appropriate response. Thus there is nothing wrong with the emotions in themselves, so long as they stem from the right sorts of desires and occur in the right sorts of circumstances. Emotions are categorized under the two basic feelings, pain and pleasure, and the Epicurean's primary goal is to optimize the latter. To do this, one should avoid empty desires that are artificial and do not correspond to our nature in favor of those that we have by nature and that can be easily satisfied. The latter are only those that are necessary for the maintenance of our life and well-being, and not those that excite and so remove us from a stable natural condition. Only then can we secure the goal, freedom from disturbance (*ataraxia*).

The elegists do not of course formulate their views about the emotions in such technical terms, yet they were familiar to some extent with such theories. The contact of the Epicurean Philodemus with Horace and Virgil suggests an environment of shared intellectual ideas,[24] and at the very least they would have known boiled-down versions of many philosophical positions, the sort of thing we find served up in Horace's *Satires* and *Epistles*.[25] In the area of love, moreover,

---

21. Given the ordinary associations with *eros*, the Stoic conception is bound to cause confusion, which is evident in our sources for Stoic doctrine. Cf. *SVF* 3.650, D.L. 7.129–30, and for more evidence, Schofield 1991, ch. 2 and Appendix D. Cf. also Nussbaum 1995, 256; Inwood 1997, 63; Graver 2007, 185–9. This conception of love, which is directed at friendship inspired by beauty, is quite different from elegiac love, though it is significant that the Stoics call it *eros* and not *philia*.

22. Cf. Nussbaum 1994, 149–54 for a discussion of the evidence.

23. Note that Epicurus was against marriage (see Nussbaum 1994, 152–3), in contrast to Lucretius (*DRN* 4.1191).

24. I discuss the similarities between philosophical and elegiac views about love at greater length in the next chapter.

25. See Mayer 1986, Mayer 2005, and Muecke 1994.

all of the elegists show significant similarities with philosophers such as Cicero and Lucretius in their treatment of love as a disease (the subject of Chapter 1). Given Lucretius' and Cicero's use of literature as part of their argument against love, it would seem entirely appropriate for the elegists to use philosophical language as a foil for their own approach.

Definitions and Methodology

When we turn to jealousy itself, modern discussions are often hampered by the assumptions that we ourselves bring to the table. One of the most frequent questions that readers raise about jealousy concerns the exact difference between jealousy and envy. After considering that distinction briefly, I will look specifically at what I take jealousy to be.

Most contemporary psychological and philosophical studies of jealousy consider its relation to envy, with three basic differences emerging from the comparison. Jealousy tends to involve three parties,[26] while envy typically involves just two. Jealousy is most often over a person,[27] while envy is about a thing, position, or status. Jealousy arises when we fear we have lost, or are in danger of losing, someone from whom we have expectations to a third party, whereas envy arises when we desire something that someone else possesses.[28] This last distinction is especially important for understanding jealousy. In the case of envy, two people can own the same kind of sports car or win the same honor. Jealousy, in contrast, is a "zero-sum game" in which one person's gain is taken to mean another person's loss.[29]

But jealousy is better understood on its own, without reference to envy. "Jealousy," as I will be using it here, can be defined as follows. This formulation is particularly well suited to the elegiac depiction and captures what I think its salient features are there, as well as those that emerge from modern studies. A person *X* is jealous just in case he satisfies the following three conditions:

26. See, however, the schematization of jealousy as a square rather than a triangle in Davis 1935/6, 395, where he includes the role of the community and our worries about how we are evaluated by it. Kaster 2005 also well brings out the importance of the judgment of others in his study of emotions in Rome.

27. In the case of romantic jealousy, rather than, say, professional jealousy (for an example, see the case of the professional ballroom dancer or office promotion in Farrell 1980, 529, 540 and 555, and various borderline cases in Ben-Ze'ev 2000, 297–300).

28. On the difficulty of using words like "possess" or "possession" in connection with a beloved, cf. esp. Neu 1980, 442 and Farrell 1980, 554–7. Davis 1935/6 uses the term "possession" freely, though he distinguishes between "ownership" and "property" (395). See also the extremely helpful discussion in Ben-Ze'ev 2000, 289–97.

29. See Parrott 1991, 23 for another difference between jealousy and envy: the jealous person is often at a loss as to what the beloved sees in his rival, whereas the envious person knows the value of what the other person has.

I. *X* believes himself to have a claim to certain special attentions from another person, *Y*.

II. *X* believes that he has lost or is in danger of losing these special attentions to a third person, *Z*.

III. *X* desires to prevent *Z* from enjoying those special attentions and seeks redress for the injury believed to have been committed.

These conditions are all stated at a very abstract level but can be specified further, depending on the cultural context and circumstances. In the case of Roman elegy, for example, special attentions have to be exclusive and spontaneous. (Other forms of jealousy do not: sibling rivalry, for example, or erotic jealousy in other cultures such as that of the Mormons.) The threat, in elegy, as elsewhere, does not have to be real; it is often imagined. Preventing the rival *Z* from enjoying special attentions can mean working to regain the special attentions of *Y*, or alternatively, in the worst-case scenario, harming *Y* and/or *Z* so as to ensure that *Z* cannot have what *X* believes rightfully belongs to him.[30] What each amounts to in any particular period and culture may often be different.

My interest of course is in one highly specific group and time, the Roman elegists of the Augustan period. Throughout this book, however, I draw parallels with treatments of jealousy in modern texts. In doing so, I am not arguing for or assuming a reductive uniform account of jealousy across cultures. As Martha Nussbaum has argued about the virtues, it is possible to identify an abstract underlying structure, which nevertheless manifests itself in quite different ways in specific cultures and periods.[31] In addition, my interest is very much in the literary representation of jealous behavior, and this may have connections across cultures and time periods because of certain narratological dimensions of its expression (something I discuss in Chapter 5). But what constitutes those expectations, and the sense of loss, will be different in different cultures. As Kingsley Davis writes, "Whether as the obverse side of the desire to obtain sexual property by legitimate competition, or as the anger at having rightful property trespassed upon, jealousy would seem to bolster the institutions where it is found. If these institutions are of an opposite character to monogamy, it bolsters them nonetheless."[32] Thus, while recognizing certain common features, my interest is very much on the Roman context, in particular elegy's engagement with other texts and approaches to emotion and sexuality in the late Republic and early Empire.

---

30. The extreme version of the third step, the crime of passion, is rarely described in surviving ancient literature, though it is a frequent element in later literary representations of jealousy: cf. e.g., Shakespeare's *Othello*, Tolstoy's *Kreutzer Sonata*, Goethe's *The Sorrows of Young Werther*, Sabato's *The Tunnel*, and Nabokov's *Lolita*.

31. Nussbaum 1988.

32. Davis 1935/6, 403.

Returning now to the definition given above, there is no comparable character-ization of sexual jealousy from antiquity, either in Aristotle's *Rhetoric* or Pseudo-Andronicus' *Peri Pathēmata*.[33] The Greek terms *phthonos* and *zēlos* do not correspond to anything like what we mean by jealousy, nor to the situation we encounter in Latin love elegy. The definition offered in Cicero's *Tusculan Disputations* of *obtrecta-tio* seems to fall more in the spectrum of envy and rivalry than jealousy.[34] The closest term for sexual jealousy that we find, *zēlotupia*, typically has connections with violence that are explicitly avoided by the elegiac narrator (if not the mistress; see Chapter 4).[35] In fact, *zēlotupia* appears very rarely in Republican and Augustan Latin, and not at all in elegy.[36] We might ask, then, whether there is a Latin word or set of words that refers to the kind of scenario described above.

Some vocabulary does reappear in contexts involving jealousy, especially *livor* and *laedere*.[37] These words appear especially often in connection with jealous rage, and their association with bruises and blows suggests they may be the Latin equiv-alent of *zēlotupia*.[38] More often than not, however, jealousy is represented without any one verbal marker. This pattern is consistent with the representation of jeal-ousy in literature more generally, as I discuss below. The Propertian lover and the Ovidian lover in fact explicitly advise the lover not to reveal his jealousy to the mistress (Propertius 2.18A, *Ars Amatoria* II.539–40). Accusations and suspicions will drive women away, they warn: better to keep quiet if you want to hold on to the mistress. Still, recommendations of this kind are isolated, and advice to others does not presuppose a policy that the narrators necessarily follow themselves.[39]

There are as well a few cases where a character explodes in jealousy and it is labeled as such, either by the jealous figure himself or by the narrator. In *Amores* 2.7, for example, Corinna suspects the narrator of infidelity (rightly, we discover in the following elegy), and in Propertius 2.6, the lover is so overcome that he is jealous even over paintings of young men and baby boys still in the cradle (9–10).

---

33. Aristotle's definitions of *zēlos* and *phthonos* (*Rhet.* II. 9.3, 10.1) describe emulation and envy rather than jealousy, and the definitions of Ps.-Andronicus also fail to make the proper distinctions (*Peri Pathōn*, II.2–4). *Zēlos* gets picked up in the romance languages as the basis for our modern word jealousy: cf. the etymological study in Grzywacz 1937.

34. Translated as "jealousy" in Graver 2002 (see pp. 55, 59, 143, 144, on *TD* 4.20.46 and 4.26.56), in my view incorrectly.

35. See the important study of this term in Fantham 1986, and now Billault's study of both *zēlotupia* and *pthonos* in the ancient novel (2009).

36. Ultimately studies like Fantham's that rely on word searches will not adequately come to grips with the full range of the emotion. In fact, Fantham's study dismisses Roman elegy as a site of jealousy because the poets do not use the word *zēlotupia*.

37. See Paschalis 1986 on a use of *laedor* in Ovid's *Met.*, though he connects it more with infidel-ity and being wronged than with jealousy.

38. See especially Chapter 4 for evidence of *livor* and *laedo* in connection with violence stemming from jealousy.

39. Ovid actually admits he cannot follow his own advice in *AA* II.547–54.

These identifications of jealousy are startling, though, because of how rare they are. Only twice in Propertius and once in Ovid's elegiac works do we find such overt admissions by the jealous person himself. The reason for this infrequency, I suggest, has to do with the complexity of jealousy we have been speaking about. Characters may experience one or more of the component emotions in jealousy early on[40]—fear and anger are almost always present at the beginning—but the phenomenological experience of jealousy is so intricate and contorted that it takes time and the accumulation of insights before anyone can put a name to precisely what he undergoes. Characters who experience jealous feelings are obsessed with their conviction of infidelity and the symptoms of their own suffering. Yet only rarely do they describe their overall condition with the word "jealousy," whether because of shame, vulnerability, or a lack of self-awareness.[41] This may be in part what makes the revelations of jealousy in *Othello* and Proust's writing so remarkable: there are very few admissions like those elsewhere in literature. We cannot therefore rely on a single word, or even cluster of words, to help us locate jealousy. Instead it will be a concurrence of several factors that inform the reader of a character's affective state: a loss or perceived loss of special attentions and intimacy together with some kind of action, whether that involves threats, verbal abuse, or violence. In what follows, then, we will need to pay attention not just to the language and the context, but the literary devices that are used to effect this representation, all of which militates in favor of using close readings as an approach. By looking carefully at the ways in which the elegiac poets construct these representations, we can get a fuller appreciation of the way in which jealousy is represented and the ways in which it has influenced the genre.

The Disease that Cannot Be Named

This inability to name one's own jealousy is a feature of many literary representations of jealousy outside of love elegy, even though *we* indisputably have the concept, and the words, for jealousy.[42] We see this in a passage from Maupassant's novel, *Pierre et Jean*:

> He felt ill at ease, listless and miserable as people do when they have had some upsetting news. He was not distressed by any particular idea,

40. On jealousy as a composite emotion, see White and Mullen 1989 and Konstan 2006, 220–1.

41. See La Rochefoucauld, Maxim #472: "L'orgueil a ses bizarreries, comme les autres passions: on a honte d'avouer que l'on ait de la jalousie, et on se fait honneur d'en avoir eu, et d'être capable d'en avoir" (*Pride has its peculiarities just like other passions do: we're ashamed to admit that we're jealous, and we're proud of having experienced it and to be capable of having it*).

42. Troubadour poetry, in which one of the characters is called the *jaloso*, is an exception.

and he could not have found a reason at first for this heaviness of spirit and numbness of body. He felt a pain somewhere but could not say where. There was within him some little place that hurt, one of those almost imperceptible bruises that cannot be located, yet fidget, tire, depress and irritate you, an unidentifiable, trifling pain, a sort of seed of unhappiness.[43]

This excerpt comes from the book's second chapter and shows how Pierre himself is unable to pinpoint either the location of his pain or the precise cause of it. The reader, however, is not as uncertain. Jean, Pierre's brother, receives the favor of his father, the attention of a beautiful widow who is spending more and more time with the family, and suddenly, at the end of the previous chapter, a large inheritance from a family friend who had in fact been close to both boys. Pierre does not realize what exactly he is suffering, but his tormented feelings lead him to formulate certain ideas about his mother's fidelity as a way of explaining the situation in which he finds himself. Pierre's inability to identify his own emotional state raises questions about his authority as a narrator, yet we have no one else to rely on for the story of his mother's past. As I argue in Chapter 5, an author often uses a jealous character's suspicions and suffering to draw readers into the world of doubt and uncertainty as well.

This inability to identify one's own jealousy is not peculiar to modern novels but a continuous feature of a much older tradition. In Shakespeare's *The Winter's Tale*, for example, King Leontes grows mad with jealousy over the attention he believes his wife shows to Polixenes. He never describes his state in that way, however, referring only to his physical upset (I.ii.109–12; 139–47):

> Too hot, too hot!
> To mingle friendship far is mingling bloods.
> I have *tremor cordis* on me: my heart dances;
> But not for joy, not joy.
> Affection! thy intention stabs the centre:
> Thou dost make possible things not so held,
> Communicat'st with dreams;—how can this be?—
> With what's unreal thou co-active art,
> And fellow'st nothing: then, 'tis very credent
> Thou mayst co-join with something; and thou dost,
> And that beyond commission, and I find it,

---

43. Translation by Tancock 1979, 60.

> And that to the infection of my brains
> And hardening of my brows.

Even as King Leontes himself and the other characters begin to perceive his jealousy, there is an unwillingness to call it by name. Speaking about how a man feels about his wife's infidelity, King Leontes mentions only "the disease" (198–207; emphasis mine):

> Should all despair
> That have revolted wives, the tenth of mankind
> Would hang themselves. Physic for't there is none;
> It is a bawdy planet, that will strike
> Where 'tis predominant; and 'tis powerful, think it,
> From east, west, north, and south: be it concluded,
> No barricado for a belly: know't;
> It will let in and out the enemy
> With bag and baggage. *Many a thousand on's*
> *Have the disease, and feel't not.*

Camillo similarly refuses to use the word jealousy (384–7; emphasis mine):

> There is a sickness
> Which puts some of us in distemper; but
> *I cannot name* the disease, and it is caught
> Of you that yet are well.

It is mentioned finally only at line 451 by Polixenes himself, the object of King Leontes' jealousy, who has the clarity of mind and the benefit of longer observation to recognize the king's mental condition.

We find another case in Malory's *La Morte d'Arthur*, in a scene in which Queen Guenever has a fit of jealousy at discovering that Launcelot is not in his bed. Her fear that he might be with Dame Elaine causes her to be, in the words of the narrator, "nigh out of her wit, and then she writhed and weltered as a mad woman, and might not sleep a four or five hours."[44] The context of her reaction makes it clear that Guenever is jealous, but there is no identification of her feelings as such, either by her or the author. These and other similar examples reveal that a person's own reluctance to recognize and admit one's jealousy is not unique to elegy, but rather part of a common feature of representing the jealous experience, at least in drama and first-person narrations where an external narrator does not intercede.

44. Book XI, ch. 8.

Why Roman Elegy Is Distinctive

The preceding examples suggest that, as far as later literature is concerned, jealousy appears in a wide range of forms, including drama, the romance, the short story, and the novel; we could add numerous examples from poetry and opera to this list as well. The representation of jealousy is not vitally linked to period or genre, then, in the way that seems to be the case in antiquity. In David Konstan's provocative treatment of jealousy,[45] he argues that we do not find jealousy in Greek literature at all, and that its beginnings in ancient literature can be traced to Horace *Odes* 1.13, where for the first time a poet describes what can without hesitation be called jealousy.[46] Other works, even those where we might suspect jealousy is at work (in Euripides' *Medea*, for example, or Sappho c. 31 and the Catullus adaptation c. 51), in fact describe resentment and love on his view, and not jealousy proper.[47]

Yet there are other examples in Greek literature where it seems difficult to deny the presence of erotic jealousy: Hera's response to Zeus' amatory adventures, for example, or the effect on Deianeira in the *Trachiniae* when Herakles returns with Iole, or the rivalrous situation that ensues in Plato's *Symposium* when Alcibiades arrives at Agathon's house and finds Socrates sharing the latter's couch.[48] The abundance of spells in Greek magic for "binding" a rival also points to an acknowledgement of jealous feelings and the need to find ways to direct jealous feelings towards revenge and perhaps recovery of the beloved, the very sort of scenario depicted in Theocritus' *Idyll* 2.[49]

I would agree with Konstan to this extent: outside of elegy, jealousy in ancient literature often seems underdeveloped or imperfectly articulated, without the necessary details to establish definitively that feelings of loss stem from a loss of affection in particular, rather than something else, such as a loss of status or reputation (as Konstan for example argues in the case of the *Medea*). My own view is that even if we do allow that cases of jealousy appear in ancient literature prior to elegy, it is not *thematized* there in any major way. There may, for example, be a provocation of jealousy at the end of the *Odyssey* when Penelope

45. Konstan 2006, ch. 11.

46. See Konstan 2006, 238ff, and also Knorr 2006 on *Odes* 1.14 and a sequence of love triangles in *Odes* 1.

47. In the case of Medea, however, it is significant that Jason attributes her rage to jealous feelings, even if Medea herself has other motives.

48. We might also think of Antiphon 1 and Menander's *Perikeiromone* as sources for jealousy in Greek literature, as Ruth Scodel suggests to me. On jealousy in archaic Greek literature, see Pizzocaro 1994. For a corrective on Konstan's views about the absence of jealousy in Greek literature, see the review by Robert Kaster in 2006.

49. See Faraone 1999, esp. ch. 3.

suggests in front of her husband that someone has moved their marriage bed. Roman poets will later develop this theme and the possibility of Penelope's own jealousy.[50] Yet in Homer's poem, this opening is never exploited.

Jealousy does occur in comedy, too, where the function of humor and audience would allow for more freedom in representing humiliation, shame, and insecurity, but here, too, it is without the emphasis we might have expected. In one case, Terence's *Eunuch*, the play depends upon the conflicts caused by a love triangle between the overbearing soldier Thraso, the naïve young lover Phaedria, and Thais. The situation, which might seem perfectly designed for exploring jealousy (another triangle arises when Thraso mistakenly believes Chremes is a rival), in fact disappoints and jealousy is not further developed here either.[51] By the play's end, rivalry gives way to acceptance and the notion of gain takes precedence over any feelings of loss.[52] The playwright, and perhaps the audience, appears less interested in jealousy and rivalry than in exploring different kinds of love relationships: emotional, physical, familial, and supportive (financial). A closer precedent perhaps is Meleager, whose poems reveal the lover's jealousy over unnamed rivals. Yet the poet does not describe his relationship with these rivals or with aspects of his contemporary society at large. Thus unlike Roman love elegy, jealousy here is integrated neither into the literary identity of the narrator nor into a social commentary.

Apart from the poetry of Meleager, one striking feature of all the examples mentioned thus far is that they do not come from a unified first-person voice in the way that elegy does. As I argue in Chapter 5, the familiarity of the narrator, and the lack of any other voice that might provide independent evidence with which to contradict or corroborate what he or she says, has a significant effect on our engagement with jealousy as readers. Since the narrator in elegy is one of the characters directly involved, he will often be blind to his own jealousy while revealing and exposing it through his diction and actions. These structural features of elegy—the first-person voice, the limitation to a single voice over a large body of poems, and the triangular relationship of characters present in so many poems—explain why jealousy becomes such a prominent presence in this genre. Other genres, with their more varied themes and voices, do make mention of jealousy, but never in as developed a way.[53]

---

50. Cf. e.g., Ovid, *Her.* 1.

51. Konstan may then be right to deny that jealousy is to be found here (Konstan 2006, 236).

52. On this ending, see Pepe 1972, who views the end as a reassertion of old values. He argues that despite the agreement of the male lover's father to support Thais, the play nevertheless accepts Thraso's backing for the affair as well, thus encouraging the "pejorative, stereotyped picture of her" (144). Konstan 1986 offers a less negative and more nuanced interpretation.

53. See the suggestion in Bertaud 1981 that there is a connection between literary interest in jealousy and the politics of a given period. Her study of jealousy focuses on literature written during the reign of Louis XIII but notes a decline of similar interest during the reign of Louis XIV.

Chapter Overview

I turn now to a brief outline of the chapters and main argument of the book. In the first chapter, I establish some background for the study of jealousy by examining the differences between the elegiac treatment of love and that of philosophy, whether Stoic or Epicurean. The poets' insistence on a life of love, whatever the costs, stands in stark contrast with the Stoic and Epicurean strictures against the emotional life. The elegists, like the philosophers, describe love as illness and search for a cure, in precisely the same language. Yet in the end the poet-narrator persists in love and opts instead for what can only be described as a poetic remedy, seeking solace in his love poetry. This chapter shows the elegists' view of love as problematic and their interest in demonstrating their expertise in handling emotions in comparison with that of other authorities, especially philosophers, a rivalry that reappears in subsequent chapters as well.

In the next three chapters, I address the depiction of jealousy in the love relationship. In Chapter 2, I turn my attention fully to examples of jealousy in the elegiac corpus. In the core cases I examine, we find not only descriptions of jealousy but also judgments about when jealousy is appropriate or not, and how we should either own up to it or control it. By examining in detail several examples of excessive jealousy in the poems, we can identify the suspicions, accusations, and fantasies that typify the jealous experience in elegy. Each case illustrates the characteristic beliefs and desire of the jealous person: the belief that one is owed special attentions, the belief that these affections are jeopardized by a rival, and the desire to protect and avenge one's interests. One of the striking features of the narrator's judgments is the way in which he criticizes not only too much jealousy, but also too little. The poets imply that anyone who is human and deserving of these attentions should feel jealousy at such betrayals of trust. Yet the narrator's position is complicated by the fact that he himself is engaged in adulterous relationships that depend upon a husband's inaction. His outrage thus teeters on a double standard.

Chapters 3 and 4 explore in greater detail two topics that are prominent in the examples in the previous chapter: the role of the senses and the use of violence as a response to jealousy. Signs of betrayal picked up by sight or hearing are among the most common triggers of jealousy: seeing the beloved in a new dress and overhearing whispers and rumors are common fare in these poems. The senses are crucial to the arousal of jealousy and provide an opportunity for the poet to focus on the initial stages of the emotion. Yet there is a marked difference here between male and female characters: women are portrayed as hesitant to believe the truth of the betrayal, while male lovers need no convincing. The poets also give attention to the subsequent stages and the reactions to jealousy, where we find another distinction between male and female behavior. Women are almost always represented as using physical blows, while men explicitly avoid brute aggression, resorting to verbal abuse instead. The elegies I examine make a point of distinguishing these responses, emphasizing the male lover's self-restraint in contrast to the mistress' wild and ineffective behavior. Even the exceptions to this pattern, poems in which male lovers lose their self-control, corroborate a pattern of male lovers identifying with the man who is self-possessed over the one who has lost all control. The avoidance of violence points not only to the poet's promotion of a life of love over a life of politics, or of love poetry over epic, but to the way in which the lover has once again appropriated a kind of philosophical attitude, yet modifies it to suit his own interests.

In the remaining chapters, I consider the broader ramifications of this elegiac conception of jealousy. In Chapter 5, I look at the way that distinctive features of the genre lend themselves so effectively to the theme of jealousy. In particular, I examine the role of readers, both those internal and external to the poems. In a number of key elegies, the narrator's rival is another love poet, and so a more sensitive reader, unlike his more typical rivals who are wealthy military or political men presumably uninterested in this sort of poetry. In these cases, too, we find a great deal of ambivalence, including sympathy and even forgiveness. But the rivalry, both erotic and poetic, never entirely disappears.

External readers are also drawn into the jealous triangles represented in elegy. The first-person account of jealousy recreates within the reader the experience of suspicions and fears, playing on the reader's own vulnerabilities. The suspense as the jealous figure obsessively hunts down clues about the beloved's infidelity leads readers to try to sift through what is often an inconsistent and uncorroborated account. The narrator's obsessive visualization is also an indulgence of the reader, who savors those details as part of the experience of reading. By making us aware of these parallels between reader and jealous figure, the love poets create greater sympathy for their narrators at the same time that they stimulate skepticism and disbelief.

In Chapter 6, I consider the root concern behind all this interest in jealousy, and the way in which the Propertian narrator in particular sees it as a larger problem in society and not simply a feature of his individual love relationships. I examine the importance of *fides*, which is often translated as "trust" or "loyalty" but has a much broader and richer meaning. The use of the term reveals a complex network of reciprocal expectations and obligations, both personal and political, that are specific to the Roman context. I argue that jealousy turns centrally on the question of *fides*. The fear of broken obligations and the consequent lack of trust are relevant not only to the love affair that forms the subject of these poems but to many other relationships represented in elegy as well. In this way, the problematic experience of jealousy in Propertius reflects a more widespread breakdown of obligations in other social and political spheres.

Finally, Roman love elegy is not simply preoccupied with the kinds of relationships that are prone to jealousy, or even just preoccupied with jealousy itself. In the conclusion, I argue that many of the features characteristic of jealousy are actually responsible for some of the more distinctive elements of Roman elegy itself. Jealousy is not merely the subject matter of elegy: it creates and structures elegy's various generic features. Jealousy thus provides a much more satisfying explanation for the specific character of Roman elegy than the various theories about its origins that have typically been put forward.

1

Rival Authorities

Elegy and Philosophy on Love

Although jealousy may involve feelings of hatred, pity, fear, and other emotions, fundamentally it derives from feelings of love.[1] In antiquity, love was seen as a problem that was rife with harmful dimensions, including longing, frustration, the disruption of one's life and pursuit of longer-standing goals, not to mention other difficulties. Because jealousy is part of this negative dimension of love, it needs to be understood against this larger backdrop. In this chapter I focus on the philosophical tradition with its critique of love and its negative effects, which provide a useful foil against which to understand elegy's own stance.[2] Although the two approaches to passionate love are fundamentally opposed, the philosophical and elegiac characterizations of the lover share a great many traits. Among other things, the elegists describe love as an illness, one of their favorite motifs and an analogy critical to Hellenistic therapeutic argument. This motif is not peculiar to these two genres: we find earlier instances of it in tragedy and Hellenistic poetry, for example, and in Roman comedy as well.[3] But it would be a surprising accident if the elegists' use of this motif was developed completely independently of Cicero and Lucretius' very public denunciations in the recent past.[4] More likely, the two traditions are intertwined here and form part of a common debate over the passions in Rome at

1. Aquinas makes this dependence clear at *Summa Theologica* Ia.2ae.28,4.
2. See Nussbaum 1990 for an illuminating and far-reaching treatment of philosophy and literature on love.
3. See most recently Williams 2010. For other studies of love as illness in ancient literature, cf. Crohns 1905, Preston 1916, 3–14, Fantham 1972, 14–18, and especially 82–91, Pigeaud 1981, Schadewaldt 1985, Stemmler 1990, 7–9, Griffiths 1990, Maehler 1990, Toohey 1992, Cyrino 1995, and on the medical metaphor in Cicero, Koch 2006. Galen offers a vivid description of an actual diagnosis of a case of lovesickness in *On Prognosis* 6.1–10. For a modern treatment of the theme, see Sontag 1979.
4. Lucretius' poem and Cicero's philosophical writings were published in the middle part of the 1st c. BCE and it is likely that the elegists had access to them. The ideas formulated in the works of these two authors were also part of the intellectual atmosphere of the period. On the prominence of popular philosophy in Roman life, cf. Giuffrida 1940, Boyancé 1960, Castner 1988, Griffin 1989, Erler 1992, Manning 1994, Barnes and Griffin 1997, and Armstrong et al. 2004.

this time. The broader intellectual context in which these discussions take place has generally been overlooked but adds an important dimension to the elegists' portrayal of love and jealousy. I will examine other points of contact between elegy and philosophy in subsequent chapters, where we see that the elegiac narrators have a pattern of adopting positions held by other authorities, only to diverge from them in ways that seem intended to display their own superiority. These shifts promote experience and feeling over theory and distance and display a coherent response to philosophical recommendations about eliminating emotions.

In this chapter, I examine three points of correspondence between elegy and philosophy: the plight of the lover, the description of love as an illness, and the emphasis on finding a cure. Not only do both portraits describe love as a disease, both also attempt to provide a cure. This is made explicit in Lucretius' *De Rerum Natura* and Cicero's *Tusculan Disputations* and is even made the aim of one elegiac work in its entirety, Ovid's *Remedia Amoris*.[5] But the Propertian and Tibullan narrators also look for a cure in the course of the poems. Their pleasure in their symptoms varies, and they both luxuriate in their misery and complain. As a result, they experiment with a wide range of remedies, including those recommended by Lucretius, Cicero, and Ovid.

Yet as often as the elegiac lover claims to desire relief from his love, he insists that he would not value a life different from the present one.[6] The philosophers might allege that this is just weakness on their part. But it is worth asking whether love for the elegiac lovers is something to be chosen, whether to their minds it forms part of a happy and fulfilling life or if not, whether they suggest any alternative. As we shall see, first in the characterization of the lover and his illness and then in his attitude towards a cure, the narrator insists on the inevitability of romantic love. And while he is aware of the types of cure offered by philosophy, he offers the makings of his own, poetic solution for all of love's difficulties. In elegiac poetry, writing poetry is essential for understanding and enduring the tumultuous elegiac affair, and this choice is formulated pointedly in contrast to what philosophy has to offer.

The Lover's Plight

Lucretius' famous discussion of love comes at the end of Book 4 of the *De Rerum Natura* (1030–1287). Falling in love is described as physical and psychological ruin: a "dreadful craving" (*dira lubido*, 1046) leads to painful consummation, and

5. This connection between the *De Rerum Natura* and the *Remedia Amoris* is made less often than one would expect. Cf. however the commentary by Henderson 1979 on the *RA* (xvi–xvii), Sommariva 1980, Pinotti 1988, and Conte [1991] 1994, ch. 2.

6. I use the masculine pronoun for the elegiac narrator here and in what follows, since Sulpicia's corpus does not provide sufficient evidence: while she does describe the symptoms of lovesickness in 3.17 and 3.18, the poems are very brief and there is no discussion of a cure.

from there, ominously, to "chilling anxieties" (*frigida cura*, 1060). The lover's life is passed unproductively, worthlessly, at the will of someone else, his money wasted on Eastern fineries like perfume and silken clothing (1123–30). But all this is in vain. The object of his love has unrealized flaws from which he will later suffer. She will be unfaithful, talking ambivalently about him and flirting with other men (1135–40). He will weep, locked outside his mistress' door (1177–9), and become the laughingstock of other men. Lucretius expects his reader to see this sequence of events as obviously harmful and so hopes to dissuade him from romantic love.

The elegiac lover falls into precisely the same traps as the lover Lucretius describes. According to his own account, the narrator is removed from public life, having given up a political career for his mistress and his love poetry. He is always fighting to keep his fortune, for his mistress craves the costly gifts and excursions that his rival, the *dives amator*, can offer. The mistress has flaws (which, however, the lover believes he can overlook, all the while still mentioning them), and the lover often accuses her of infidelity. We hear that he spends many nights locked out of her house and has lost his standing with friends as well as with the public at large.[7]

Yet we also see other, less debasing features of the lover's passion, like the hopes he has for his love. He longs for the fidelity of his mistress and a modesty unaffected by other men's attentions. His most profound desire is that their love be mutual and exclusive and that they be united in both love and death.[8] The elegiac mistress is not entirely unworthy of these hopes and desires either (as Lucretius' rhetoric might suggest): her beauty is unrivalled and she is learned, writing poetry in addition to playing the lyre. Nor has his love for her rendered the narrator's life entirely unproductive: he has, after all, produced several books of accomplished poetry and claims a following among youthful readers as well as lasting fame. We are presumably meant to see these positive aspects of elegiac love as sustaining the lover and explaining his decision not to destroy his love entirely, as the philosophers would like.

Some of these similarities between elegy and philosophy stem from what is clearly a shared set of concerns about love that was prevalent in the culture of the time.[9] But while the narrators frame their discussion of the harmful effects of love in the philosophers' own terms, we will see them diverge from Lucretius' and Cicero's accounts in the acceptance and even embrace of their condition and the distinctly poetic ways in which they cope with the inevitable costs of love.

---

7. For a fuller treatment of these characteristics of the elegiac lover, cf. Luck 1959, Boucher 1965, 13–35, and Lyne 1980.

8. This is especially true of Propertius, on which see Papanghelis 1987.

9. See Brown 1987, 139–43 on the thematic and linguistic similarities in Lucretius' and Catullus' depiction of the lover. On Cat. c.76 and its relation to the themes of illness and cure, cf. Moritz 1968, von Albrecht 1977, 80–94, Skinner 1987, and Booth 1997.

To begin with, one of the most damaging effects of devoting oneself to love is the resulting loss of independence within the relationship and the loss of reputation outside it. Lucretius links the two explicitly (*DRN* 4.1122, 24):

> *adde quod alterius sub nutu degitur aetas,*
> *languent officia atque aegrotat fama vacillans.*[10]

Add that their life is spent at the will of another,
their obligations are neglected and their shaky reputation grows sick.

In Lucretius' view, it is because the lover is at his mistress' beck and call that he no longer has the time to keep up with duties to friends and country. Thus his reputation "grows sick," just as he does. The Tibullan lover makes a similar connection between the demands of a mistress and his *fama*, though here it is put in a more personal and desirable light (1.1.55–8):

> *me retinent vinctum formosae vincla puellae,*   55
>   *et sedeo duras ianitor ante fores.*
> *non ego laudari curo, mea Delia: tecum*
>   *dum modo sim, quaeso segnis inersque vocer.*[11]

The chains of a love girl hold me captive,
and I sit, a doorman, before unyielding doors.
I have no desire to be praised, my Delia:
so long as I am with you, I beg to be called lazy and slow.

The lover cheerfully admits he has become a slave to his mistress, one of many examples of his *servitium amoris*.[12] He does not care for public honor so long as he can be with Delia. He is willing to sacrifice everything for his love: autonomy, reputation, and health. But he clearly relishes the sacrifice. Being chained to a lovely girl does not come off as unpleasantly restrictive. As *quaeso* shows in the last line, there is something appealing to him about his bondage, despite his mistress' disinterest. The lover cares nothing about what others think of him or his choice of lifestyle; he even wishes to flaunt it. The pursuit of Delia makes it all worthwhile. As the narrators make clear elsewhere, love without this sort of

---

10. All quotations of Lucretius are from Bailey's Oxford edition (1922), which prints 4.1124 immediately following line 1122. All translations of Latin are my own.

11. All quotations of Tibullus are from Postgate's Oxford edition (1980).

12. On the loss of public repute associated with *servitium amoris*, cf. Copley 1947 and Lyne 1979. More commonly the lover complains about a *ianitor* who keeps him out of his mistress' house, while here Tibullus is himself the doorkeeper.

constraint is simply not worth the name.[13] The best kind of love, they think, is one that has a dominant role in our life and so reorders other priorities according to its demands, even if this makes them look obsessive and masochistic to our eyes.

The Propertian and Ovidian narrators, too, describe the enslavement of lovers, their friends and themselves, and both choose to give up political life and standing. At the end of a poem in which he has turned down a journey with obvious political benefit, the Propertian lover concludes by stating his natural preference for love over war (1.6.25–30):

> me sine, quem semper voluit Fortuna iacere,   25
>   huic[14] animam extremam reddere nequitiae.
> multi longinquo periere in amore libenter,
>   in quorum numero me quoque terra tegat.
> non ego sum laudi, non natus idoneus armis:
>   hanc me militiam fata subire volunt.   30

> Allow me, whom Fortune always wished to be despised,
> to give my final breath to this wickedness.
> Many have perished willingly in a prolonged affair.
> May the earth cover me, too, in their number.
> I was not born for praise, nor for arms:
> the fates want me to undergo this type of warfare.

The lover imagines himself at the mercy of forces outside his control, fate and fortune, and feigns resignation. He blames external forces, as if unaware of his own role in producing emotional excess. His attitude is thus in opposition to the philosophical view that holds a person responsible for his own emotional state. Wedded to his complaint, however, is his clear desire and rationale for such a lifestyle. Both the military metaphor and the claim of belonging to a large group of others who are devoted to love ennoble his choice.[15] The Propertian lover also attempts to excuse his lack of involvement by invoking his fear of Cynthia's temper. While the decision to write love poetry is itself the obstacle, it is significant for us here that he isolates Cynthia's ill humor as the

13. Cf. e.g., Prop. 1.6.12, Tib. 2.4.7–10.

14. *Huic* is Housman's emendation. All quotations from Propertius are from Fedeli's 1994 Teubner, though I will indicate different readings in Heyworth 2007a (except for those involving punctuation).

15. The choice of love over war is also a generic decision to write love poetry rather than epic. The avoidance of military campaigns is something the elegists share with the Epicureans, who tended to stay away from politics; cf. Momigliano 1941, Boucher 1965, 30, and Griffin 1989, p. 2, n. 3.

cause. As in Tibullus, in Propertius the lover does not find his mistress' adversity entirely disagreeable. Obstacles are, in fact, a stimulus to love, even when it is a rival who provides them.[16] As we shall see, the jealous lover in particular prizes these setbacks, thriving on love's problems as a way of nourishing and justifying his jealousy. What could be considered a rejection by Delia or a character flaw in Cynthia is, to their lovers, a challenge and so a greater enticement to pursue love.

The lover's tendency to overlook his mistress' flaws concurs with the philosophical diagnosis. According to Lucretius, the lover's desire blinds him to his beloved's faults and inflates her with qualities she does not in fact possess (*DRN* 4.1149–54):

> *et tamen implicitus quoque possis inque peditus*
> *effugere infestum, nisi tute tibi obvius obstes*   1150
> *et praetermittas animi vitia omnia primum*
> *aut quae corpori' sunt eius quam praepetis ac vis.*
> *nam faciunt homines plerumque cupidine caeci*
> *et tribuunt ea quae non sunt his commoda vere.*

> And nevertheless even when entangled and shackled,
> you can escape the risk of passion, unless you get in your own way
> and overlook all the vices of mind
> and body in the woman you eagerly desire.
> For most men do this, blinded by desire,
> and they attribute charms to women that they do not in fact possess.

Cicero's report emphasizes that this blindness is even more pervasive, for in the Stoics' view the sick person, here not just the person in love, is deceived not merely by flaws, but by the situation as a whole, including his evaluation of what is important and valuable (Cic. *Tusc. Disp.* IV.xi.26):

> *Definiunt autem animi aegrotationem opinationem vehementem de re non*
> *expetenda, tamquam valde expetenda sit, inhaerentem et penitus insitam.*[17]

> They define sickness of the soul as a powerful belief, persistent and
> deeply rooted, about something that is not desirable, which they consider as though it really were extremely so.

---

16. See Seneca, *De Ira* 2.28.7, cited in Cohen 1991, 121, about why those with competitive spirits are drawn to commit adultery.

17. The text is Pohlenz' Teubner edition. Cicero goes on to list the types of sickness he means, which include *mulierositas* or love of women. Cf. also Lucretius 4.1160–70, Hor. *Sat.* 1.3.38–66, and Ov. *AA* II.657–62.

Cicero also tells us that the Stoics emphasize the persistence of this belief, that they will continue to regard such things as important in various ways over time, while Lucretius seems to imply by *primum* (1151), "at first," that the illusion will pass. Propertius wants to have it both ways, we shall see. At the end of his relationship with Cynthia, the Propertian lover comes to realize his previous obliviousness (3.24.5–6):

> ... *mixtam te varia laudavi saepe figura,*[18]
> *ut,*[19] *quod non esses, esse putaret amor;*

> I often praised you for embodying a variety of beautiful features,
> so that my love thought you to be something that you were not.

Still, even a more realistic view of the beloved is not always sufficient to destroy love. It is evident that he still has strong feelings, despite his claims to see things in a more dispassionate way. Cynthia will, of course, reappear twice more in Book 4: in poem 7 (only as a ghost, though a verbose one) and again in poem 8. The mistress' game-playing, ill temper, and infidelities make her not repellent, but in fact more desirable to her lover.

One last correspondence between the elegiac and philosophical portrayal is the mockery of the lover. In Lucretius, those doing the ridiculing, though they do not realize it, are prey to the very same ills (*DRN* 4.1157–9):

> *atque alios alii irrident Veneremque suadent*
> *ut placent, quoniam foedo adflictentur amore,*
> *nec sua respiciunt miseri mala maxima saepe.*

> And one lover mocks another, and persuades him
> to conciliate Venus, since he is tormented by an unseemly love.
> Yet often, miserable, he does not take note of his own terrible suffering.

These men, all of them afflicted, tease each other and egg each other on to amatory exploits. While the Lucretian narrator is clearly critical, the lovers he depicts do not seem to be either moralistic or judgmental in their mockery. If anything, they are trying to implicate others in their own activities.

The elegiac lover, too, is often subject to the derision of others. But a number of points distinguish the *topos* here. In elegy, the person doing the mocking is

---

18. On the difficult phrase *varia figura*, see the suggestions of Camps 1966b *ad loc*. Another possibility not suggested by Camps would be to take *figura* as "a manner of speaking or writing" (*OLD* s.v. #9c).

19. Heyworth 2007a prints *cum* here.

not himself in love, at least not yet. More significantly, the lover answers the ridicule: he condemns and admonishes his critic with a triumphant *tu quoque*. We find examples in Tibullus and Propertius:[20]

> *at tu, qui laetus rides mala nostra, caveto*
> > *mox tibi: non uni saeviet usque deus.*
> *vidi ego qui iuvenum miseros lusisset amores*
> > *post Veneris vinclis subdere colla senem*   90
> *et sibi blanditias tremula componere voce*
> > *et manibus canas fingere velle comas:*   (Tib. 1.2.87–92)

But you who readily laugh at my troubles, look out
presently for yourself: the god will not torture just one man forever.
I have seen one who mocked the wretched affairs of the young,
later as an old man submit his neck to the chains of Venus,
and compose soothing words to himself in a shaky voice,
and arrange with his hands his white hairs.

> *Dicebam tibi venturos, irrisor, amores,*
> > *nec tibi perpetuo libera verba fore:*
> *ecce iaces[21] supplexque venis ad iura puellae,*
> > *et tibi nunc quaevis[22] imperat empta modo.*   (Prop. 1.9.1–4)

I used to tell you, when you mocked me, that you would fall in love,
and that your words would not always be so bold.
Here you are, fallen, behaving like a suppliant towards your girlfriend's
    wishes,
and some girl, recently bought, orders you around.

What we see in both of these examples is the revenge of Eros. Whoever is critical of love or tries to ignore it will end up eating his words. He, too, will suffer the fate of the ones he ridicules. In late antiquity, this revenge was even practiced on Lucretius, for according to a story told by Jerome, Lucretius himself fell victim to the workings of a love potion.[23]

The elegiac narrator's tone is moralistic. And for his readers the comeuppance does not consist in falling in love, but rather in realizing how vain the belief is

20. Cf. also Cat. 50.18–21, Tib. 1.8.71–76, Prop. 1. 7.25–26, 1.9 *passim*, Hor. *Od.* 4.10, Ov. *AA* I.83–88.

21. Heyworth 2007a reads *taces* instead, though this does not fit as well with *supplex*.

22. Heyworth 2007a prints *quidvis*, but *quaevis* better emphasizes the woman's low status and thus the man's subjection.

23. See Eus. *Chron.* for the year 94; the story is almost certainly false, but the impetus (revenge will come to non-lovers) is consistent with the sentiment expressed in the other examples.

that one could avoid this fate. Though the elegiac lover is on the defensive, he knows he is better informed. For him, love is not a weakness or a temptation only for the more susceptible. It is something that everyone will undergo at some time or another, regardless of age, class, or training. In the *Ars Amatoria*, Ovid warns men (and goes on to reassure women) that even the one who feigns love will eventually succumb (Ovid, *AA* 1.615–6):[24]

> *saepe tamen vere coepit simulator amare;*
> *saepe, quod incipiens finxerat esse, fuit.*

> Often he who faked it nevertheless really begins to be in love;
> often he becomes what he had initially pretended to be.

One cannot completely avoid love or take precautions against it, as the philosophers would like. The philosophers' diagnosis is predicated on the assumption that it is possible to be free of love, at least damaging love. But for the elegiac narrators, if we are human, we can only learn to cope with love or limit its harm. How to cope is precisely what the elegiac lovers are struggling to discover.

So far we have seen that the elegiac lover conforms in many respects to the lover portrayed by Lucretius and Cicero. Submissive, removed from Roman public life, blind to his mistress' faults, subject to the mockery of others, this lover seems to be exactly the sort of case the philosophers are worried about. Both groups address a single set of phenomena and frame it in similar terms, yet they reach radically different conclusions as to what should be done. The shared features and language of both approaches only heighten and sharpen their disagreements. The lover's simultaneous acknowledgement and acceptance of love's dangers signal an attitude to the emotion that diverges from the earlier philosophical account. The elegiac lover takes love to be an inescapable part of the human condition and something he cannot live without. The poetic application of the medical analogy will show just how far this extends.

The Diagnosis: Love as Illness

The philosophers compare love to an illness because they believe it needs treatment, a treatment only philosophy can provide. This took the form of therapeutic arguments, whose importance in Hellenistic philosophy has been well

---

24. See *AA* 1.183–86 for another case in which the supposedly disinterested advisor succumbs to love.

demonstrated by Martha Nussbaum.[25] The therapy is designed to alleviate the "illness" of the person afflicted with the emotions, as psychotherapy does, except that philosophical arguments are used instead. The arguments that remove the troubling emotion are described as "cures" or "remedies," and the passions are said to be "torn out" or "cauterized" from the body.

We find a developed use of this medical analogy in Lucretius and in Cicero's *Tusculan Disputations*. Lucretius' honeyed rim image in Book I and IV of the *De Rerum Natura* is perhaps the most familiar example of philosophy's appropriation of medical imagery and the shift from physiological to psychological language (cf. 1.936–950 and 4.11–25). The discussion in Book IV (1030–1287) pinpoints several crucial aspects of lovesickness for us. First, the lover's pain is like a sore, *ulcus*, or a wound or blow, *vulnus*, and *ictus*.[26] His desire is unquenchable and is compared to an undying flame or thirst. He experiences two contrasting moods, one passive and miserable, and characterized by terms like *cura*, *miser*, *dolor*, and *vinctus*. The second is more active and wild, and is denoted by *insania*, *demens*, *rabies*, and *furor*.[27] When under the influence of the second of these two moods, the lover is also described as "lost," literally "wandering" (*errans* or *vagans*).[28]

Cicero also draws the parallel between medicine and philosophy at the beginning of *Tusculan Disputations* III and throughout Book IV. Inquiring whether or not there is a treatment for those who show unsoundness of mind, he asks (3.3.3–5; cf. also 4.23, 27):

> *quibus duobus morbis, ut omittam alios, aegritudine et cupiditate, qui tandem possunt in corpore esse graviores? . . . est profecto animi medicina, philosophia; cuius auxilium non ut in corporis morbis petendum est foris, omnibusque opibus viribus, ut nosmet ipsi nobis mederi possimus, elaborandum est.*

> Leaving aside others, what illnesses of the body can be more serious than the two diseases of anguish and desire? . . . There is indeed a medicine for the soul: philosophy. Its help must be sought not outside of ourselves, as in the case of physical disease, but we must strive with all our resources and strength to be our own doctors.

Cicero, too, dwells on the submission into which the lover has fallen and the passive characteristics mentioned above. He also identifies physical symptoms: the voice

---

25. Nussbaum 1994. Cf. also Rabbow 1954, Pigeaud 1981, 441–522, White 1995, Sorabji 1997, and Sorabji 2000. See, too, the response to Sorabji 1997 by Bernard Williams in the same volume (1997).

26. Cf. also forms of *saucius* for the wounded person, for example in Tib. 2.5.109, quoted below.

27. On the two moods, cf. Toohey 1992 and Booth 1997, 153.

28. Cf. Tib. 1.2.25; Prop. 1.9.33, 1.13.35; Cic. *TD* 4.15.35, 4.38.83.

will tremble, the complexion will pale or yellow, and the breath becomes difficult to draw. The eyes, too, may be watery. Cicero gives an unusually thorough list of physical symptoms, though he does not mention loss of weight, a disorder to which the lovesick figure is usually prone.[29]

Lovers also experience the sensation of a burning heat or flame that cannot be allayed. Foolishly, Lucretius tells us, they think it can be removed, that they can cool their passion. But in fact, the more they have, the more they want (*DRN* 4.1086–90). Any relief from the burning is only temporary (4.1115–20), and madness, *rabies* and *furor*, afflicts the lover unable to find alleviation. We find just such a lover in Tibullus' elegies. In 2.6, the narrator prays that he might see love's torches extinguished (*extinctas faces*, 16), for he has been driven mad (*insana mente*, 18) by Nemesis' locked door.[30] He has considered death as an escape, but hope keeps him going in the expectation that tomorrow will be better. The lover desperately wants an end to his bondage but is deceived by his optimism.

Some of these symptoms are part of a much older poetic vocabulary for love where they had nothing to do with illness specifically. The wound, for example, is of course also associated with war and hunting, connections still dominant in Lucretius and the elegists.[31] For example, in a bloody image, Lucretius describes the lover's wounds from Venus in terms of a blow received from an enemy, *hostis* (*DRN* IV.1048–52). And in the elegists, wounds can come from Cupid's arrows or result from love's warfare (in Prop. 2.9.9–12 and 2.25.45–6, for example). But wounds take on a different significance when positioned near other words denoting sickness, as an example from Tibullus shows (2.5.109–12):

> . . . *iaceo dum saucius annum*
> > *et faveo morbo, cum iuvat ipse dolor,*   110
> *usque cano Nemesim, sine qua versus mihi nullus*
> > *verba potest iustos aut reperire pedes.*

> While I lie here for a year now, wounded
> and giving in to my illness, since the pain itself helps,
> I sing continuously of Nemesis, without whom my verses
> cannot find the right words or meter.

---

29. In Greek literature, cf., e.g., Hom. *Od.* 4.788, Eur. *Med.* 24, Eur. *Hipp.* 274ff., Eur. *Or.* 39–41, Theocr. *Id.* 2.88ff. In Roman lit., cf., e.g., *DRN* IV. 1120; Prop. 4.3.27, Ov. *Am.* 1.6.5–6, *Her.* 21.15–16, 21.213–20, *AA* 1.733–36, and *Met.* 3.339–510.

30. See Maltby 2002 on the imagery of arrows, torches, and madness in lines 15–18.

31. On hunting in the Greek world generally, cf. Barringer 2002. On Roman literature and art, cf. Anderson 1985 and especially Green 1996 on the connection between Venus and venery in *Ars Amatoria* I.

Here the love-wound is coupled with disease and pain, not war or the hunt.[32] Despite his illness, the Tibullan lover experiences pleasure and benefit.[33] He is actually favorably inclined towards his disease, for it is necessary for his writing. Nemesis, the mistress of his second book, gives both inspiration and shape to his poetry. So in the next poem, 2.6 (discussed just above), the lover does not name any satisfaction or benefit from his suffering. But its placement immediately after 2.5 implies that we should understand the production of poetry generally as resulting from love's wounds. These poems, as well as all the others in the book, it is suggested, result from love's cruelty.

The Propertian lover makes the same claims about Cynthia's effect on him in the opening poem of Book II. Not the muse but his *puella* is responsible for his poetic output, whether because of her physical appearance (5–8), her lyre playing (9–10), her sleepy face (11–2), or her lovemaking (13–4)—whatever she does or says, in other words: *seu quidquid fecit sive est quodcumque locuta/maxima de nihilo nascitur historia* (15–6).

Many of the other physical and emotional symptoms of the elegiac lover turn up conveniently in a single poem of Propertius, the fifth in his first book (a poem I return to in Chapter 5). This poem recounts the lover's early history with Cynthia in the form of a warning to Gallus, who has expressed an interest in Cynthia. It is stocked with the ailments the Propertian lover himself suffered from and which he now predicts are in store for Gallus (11–30), and so merits being cited at some length:

> non tibi iam somnos, non illa relinquet ocellos:
> 　　illa feros animis alligat una viros.
> a! mea contemptus quotiens ad limina curres,
> 　　cum tibi singultu fortia verba cadent,
> et tremulus maestis orietur fletibus horror, 　　　　15
> 　　et timor informem ducet in ore notam
> et quaecumque voles fugient tibi verba querenti,
> 　　nec poteris, qui sis aut ubi, nosse miser!
> tum grave servitium nostrae cogere puellae
> 　　discere et exclusum quid sit abire domum; 　　　20
> nec iam pallorem totiens mirabere nostrum,
> 　　aut cur sim toto corpore nullus ego.
> nec tibi nobilitas poterit succurrere amanti:
> 　　nescit Amor priscis cedere imaginibus.

---

32. See Maltby 2002 *ad* 110 on the disease imagery.
33. Cf. also *Am.* II. 9 and Prop. 1.6.12: *a, pereat, si quis lentus amare potest.* The use of "*ah*" and other interjections by elegiac lovers has been seen as a key to their emotional state; see Tränkle 1960, 149–50 and Kershaw 1983.

quod si parva tuae dederis vestigia culpae,   25
     quam cito de tanto nomine rumor eris!
non ego tum potero solacia ferre roganti,
     cum mihi nulla mei sit medicina mali;
sed pariter miseri socio cogemur amore
     alter in alterius mutua flere sinu.   30

She will not let you sleep, she will not let you close your eyes.
She single-handedly straps down even fierce men with her anger.
Ah, how many times will you run scorned to my door,
when your brave words will dissolve into a sob,
and trembling, shaking and mournful weeping will overtake you.
Fear will trace ugly stains upon your face,
and whatever words you want to say will elude you.
You won't be able to know, poor wretch, who or where you are.
Then you will be forced to learn the harsh bondage of my girl
and what it's like to go home after being kicked out.
And then you won't marvel so many times at my pale face
and why I'm like a skeleton.
Nor will your nobility help you in love:
Love doesn't understand about yielding to ancestral portraits.
But if you leave any evidence of your crime,
how quickly will your great name become the stuff of scandal.
I won't be able to bring you any solace when you ask me,
since I have no medicine for my own troubles.
Yet equally miserable, we will bear this common love together,
and take turns weeping in each other's breast.

The lover anticipates that Gallus will experience a deterioration of health that will include insanity, burning, insomnia, trembling and shuddering, tears, fear, premature wrinkling, disorientation, aphasia, blanched complexion, and weight loss.[34] The range of symptoms surpasses those described by either Lucretius or Cicero and creates the impression of a truly debilitating emotional and physical condition.[35] One particularly pernicious outcome of love is disorientation or

34. See *TD* 3.7.14, where Cicero reports that the man subject to distress is prone to a range of emotions. In a stimulating article, Zetzel 1996 discusses Prop. 1.5 in terms of illness, cure, and poetry (91–100), but stresses the magical elements in the poem rather than the philosophical connections that are my concern here.

35. Toohey 1992 omits Prop. 1.5 (and other elegy) from his discussion of illness and melancholia (p. 271, n.30), viewing it as an example of love, not lovesickness, or at least too complex a presentation to be sure.

amnesia: the lover will know "neither who nor where he is." He no longer remembers what makes him who he is, a being capable of moral choice and dignity. This loss of identity is further hinted at by the manner in which his diminished weight is expressed: he is *nullus* in his whole body (22).[36]

Like the philosophers, then, the elegiac lover clearly sees love as an illness. But far from being blind to his condition, he is intimately attuned to it, as the wealth of detail attests. He is deeply aware of the significance of his condition: he recognizes its telltale symptoms and understands the prognosis. The metaphor does not function in exactly the same way, to be sure. Whereas the philosophers adopt the role of a surgical doctor, the narrators are more like therapists and advocates for the patient. More importantly, the lovers celebrate precisely what the philosophers are criticizing.[37] They relish the very same details the philosophers portray as evils; indeed, they do so while acknowledging love's detrimental effects. These elegiac lovers exploit their passion to a different rhetorical end. What the philosophers meant as a *reductio ad absurdum* is instead embraced and even given an enticing allure.

The Elegiac Cure

The use of the medical analogy indicates expertise and authority: both the philosophers and the elegiac narrators think of themselves as having skilled knowledge about love. Yet if their descriptions of love as illness have coincided for the most part until now, they diverge dramatically on the question of treatment. All three elegists speak of a cure, but it is not always the kind of "cure" the philosophers recommend. The best evidence that the elegists were trying to respond to philosophy's claims is provided by Ovid's *Remedia Amoris*.[38] This 800-line didactic poem teaches the unhappy lover how to be rid of his passion, incorporating much of Lucretius' and Cicero's advice, but also adding other, more ingenious ideas, often reversals of what he himself had preached in his treatise on how to

36. Cf. Neu 1980, 451–52 and Tov-Ruach 1980, 470–71 on fears of "annihilation" as part of the jealous experience. Kaster's remarks on *integritas* (2005, 145–48) as a kind of ethical wholeness are also relevant here. In addition to the elegiac examples (e.g., Prop. 1.4, 1.5, Tib. 1.5.30), see also Chaerea's sense of lost direction and identity in Ter. *Eun.* 305–6.

37. We find a response to philosophical views about control of the emotions elsewhere in Augustan literature as well: cf. e.g., Hor. *Sat.* 1.2 and 2.7; *Odes* 1.18 and 1.27; Virg. *Georg.* 3.209–83 and the destructive stories of Dido and Turnus in the *Aeneid*. On the role of the emotions in the *Aeneid*, see Dion 1993, Gill 1997, and now Polleichtner 2009.

38. See Henderson 1979, xii–xx on the literary background of the work, and Conte [1991] 1994, 43–44 on illness and cure in elegy. Ovid's exilic works can also be seen as a cure for the pain of isolation; cf. Nagle 1980 and Edwards 1996, 118–22 on parallels between the voice of the lovesick lover and that of the exiled poet.

attract a lover, the *Ars Amatoria*. Fundamentally, though, Ovid does not differ from the philosophers' approach, except, of course, insofar as he offers advice on the other side, too.

The Propertian and Tibullan lovers also explore possible cures for their misery. But although they try many remedies, at the end of the day there is only one source of relief, and it is not any one of the cures suggested by the philosophers.[39] They themselves provide a different sort of relief through the reading and writing of poetry.[40]

Some of the standard cures the elegiac narrators consider correspond to those recommended by the philosophers and Ovid in the *Remedia Amoris*: separation from the object of desire, change of scenery, and finding sexual satisfaction without romantic attachment.[41] Speed in applying the remedy is crucial in each case and is stressed by both philosophers and elegists. This is particularly so in the case of finding a new lover. Thus when the Propertian lover considers leaving Cynthia, he realizes that he must act fast: if the pain goes away, love will return (2.5.9–10, 14). The Propertian narrator often frames his position in the philosophers' own terms, only to invert the message. The advice about separation from the beloved and taking a new lover is a case in point. Lucretius himself is doubtful whether separation can work, since *simulacra* of the beloved will still be present to haunt the lover even when he or she is not physically there (*DRN* 4.1061–2). Both he and Ovid think trying a new lover more successful. To introduce the topic of choosing another lover, Lucretius uses the phrase *alio mentem convertere*, "to turn the mind elsewhere" (1064). The Propertian narrator picks up the phrase in his very first poem, but inverts its curative intention. He asks that those who possess magical powers turn his mistress' heart towards rather than away from love, so that she too can suffer and grow paler than he is himself (1.1.21–2): *en agedum dominae mentem convertite nostrae, /et facite illa meo palleat ore magis!*[42] This reversal is strengthened by means of allusion to other Lucretian usages in the poem, such as the opposition between *furor* and *ratio* or *consilium*.[43]

39. See Conte [1991] 1994, 62, where he briefly mentions the elegiac competition with philosophy: "The *autarkeia* of eros had presented itself as competitive with philosophical *autarkeia*." Maltby 2006 discusses the elegists' language of cure in connection with medicine rather than philosophy, stating that "Propertius had more than a passing interest in medical theory and practice" (154).

40. There are important precedents for the idea of writing poetry as a form of therapy: cf. Pind. *Nem.* 4 (and Machemer 1993), Call. *ep.* 46, Theocr. *Id.* 11, Verg. *Ecl.* 10, and the discussion of the latter in O'Hara 1993, 19–22. I discuss *Idyll* 11 further below.

41. On separation, cf. e.g., *TD* 4.35.75, Prop. 1.1.29–30, 3.24; on change of scenery, cf. e.g., Prop. 3.21; and on sexual satisfaction, cf. e.g., Tib. 1.5, Prop. 4.8.

42. See Ov. *AA* 1.729–31 on encouraging the lover's pallor, and on curses designed to induce love, Faraone 1999, ch. 2.

43. Cf. also Cicero's contrast between *ratio* and *mollis*, a key term for the lover in elegy, in *TD* 2.20.47.

Almost as if to spite him, Propertius uses Lucretius' language of cure for precisely the opposite end, namely increased desire.

One thing the poets do not advocate of course is the central cure that Lucretius and Cicero advocate, philosophical argument. And they suggest other cures that appear only in elegy and not in philosophy. Propertius and Tibullus look to magic, divine intervention, and wine, though most of these remedies fail the suffering lover in elegy: either they do not work at all or provide only temporary relief.[44] The lover in Tibullus is the one who generally resorts to drink, sorcery and the gods. He also tries new partners: unlike the other lovers, who are mostly devoted to a single love, the Tibullan lover has three relationships in only 16 poems (Delia, Marathus, and Nemesis). But besides these more conventional methods, he also finds solace for his misery in recalling the simpler, more blissful times that existed in the Golden Age, a time when one could engage in a healthy, uncorrupted sort of love. This sort of fantasy stands in contrast to the nature of Epicurean strategies of remembering that are based on actual past pleasures.[45]

We find the Tibullan lover experimenting with a sequence of remedies in a way that suggests that he undergoes a kind of development or even education. The culmination of these various attempts is his escapism into a fantasy of better times, as if love would no longer be an illness if only we could get back to this state. After something has gone awry, such as a fight with his mistress, the Tibullan lover slips into a eulogy of a Hesiodic Golden Age.[46] Everything was wonderful then: there was no travel, no trade, no war, and as a result no unanticipated death. No animals needed to be trained to plow or give milk, and the plants and trees gave forth their fruit without cultivation. More to the point, love needed no encouragement to grow, for "no house had doors; no stone was planted on the land to set fixed boundaries to men's estates" (1.3.43–4). The lover sees civilization as the cause of today's ills, much like Lucretius. But he then turns this picture to his own use by imagining his own love affair in a context free of society's corruptions. Girls would not be tempted by gifts or other men's advances. There would be no game-playing and keeping your lover outside the door all night. These are problems in the customs and institutions of the age, not simply the flaws of an individual. The narrator hopes to recreate a better world for love in his nostalgic poetry, both for himself and his readers.

---

44. On magic, cf. e.g., Tib. 1.2.41–64, Prop. 1.1.19–24; on divine intervention, e.g., Tib. 1.9.81–84; and on wine, e.g., Tib. 1.2.1, 1.5.37–38. On the question of the elegists' belief in the power of magic, cf. Ov. *RA* 249–90 for a rejection of magic as an aid in love, and Tupet 1976, 330–417.

45. Cf. e.g., Cic. *Fin.* 1.57 and *TD* 5.33.95.

46. On Tibullus' use of the Golden Age, cf. Musurillo 1967, *passim* (268), Bright 1978, 192–205, Kennedy 1993, 16–20, Fredrick 1997, 186–87, and Maltby 2002, 31, 52, 58, 61, 194–95. Fredrick argues for similarities between the descriptions of the mistress and the Golden Age. Cf. also the Golden Age passages in Lucretius (*DRN* 5.939–40, 944–52, 960–65).

The fifth poem of the first book provides a good example of how the country and the past provide an escape. The lover imagines himself and Delia living in the country where nothing can spoil the couple's happiness (19–34). This idyllic insert is placed between an angry scene where the lover realizes Delia is unfaithful on the one hand and a list of things he tried to help him forget her on the other (17–20, 35–40):

> omnia persolvi: fruitur nunc alter amore,
> > et precibus felix utitur ille meis.
> at mihi felicem vitam, si salua fuisses,
> > fingebam demens, et renuente deo.   20
>
> .
>
> .
>
> .
>
> haec mihi fingebam, quae nunc Eurusque Notusque   35
> > iactat odoratos vota per Armenios.
> saepe ego temptavi curas depellere vino:
> > at dolor in lacrimas verterat omne merum.
> saepe aliam tenui: sed iam cum gaudia adirem,
> > admonuit dominae deseruitque Venus.   40

I have paid everything, but another now enjoys my love.
He is the fortunate one and benefits from my prayers.
Foolishly I used to dream of a happy life for myself,
if you were well, but the god said no.

.

.

.

I was dreaming about these things, wishes that the East and South winds
now toss through perfumed Armenia.
Often I have tried to drive away my worries with undiluted wine,
but the pain turned all the wine into tears.
Often I have held another woman, but at the point of pleasure,
Venus reminded me of my mistress and deserted me.

The word *fingebam* is repeated before and after the description of the country retreat, emphasizing that it was only a fantasy.[47] Yet even if the dream of a country life with Delia is isolated by this framing device, it also pertains to the larger context. The escape into an idealized past is just one of the narrator's responses after admitting that he has lost Delia's love to another, like the use of wine or a new lover in lines 37–40.[48]

47. See Putnam 1973 *ad loc*. and Bright 1978, 153–66.
48. Cf. also Tib. 1.1, 1.3.35–50, 1.10.39–68, 2.1, 2.5.23–122.

To be sure, a more complex attitude towards the countryside is presented in Tibullus' second book. In the third poem, for example, the lover seems loath to meet Nemesis in the country, though he consents to put up with the sunburn and blisters.[49] He blames the countryside for drawing his mistress away from him and prays that the crops may suffer for this. Bright has explained this new, critical view of the country by focusing on the differences between Books 1 and 2 and between Delia and the greedier Nemesis.[50] The effectiveness of the lover's fantasy weakens precisely in those elegies addressed to Nemesis. With Delia, he could alleviate his troubles by picturing the two of them in the country, even if he knew it was just a dream. But with Nemesis the country is no longer the scene of perfect love. Because Nemesis is so avaricious, there is no difference between country or city: she will expect gifts in either place. Though the countryside may look exempt from the corruptions of the city, it cannot simply be identified with the Golden Age, for there must be internal as well as external difference. The Tibullan lover believes that happy love is possible, then, but not here and now. Romantic love is a sickness because of prevailing social conditions, an important factor in the spread of jealousy as well, as I discuss in Chapter 6.

If the Tibullan lover uses fantasy as an escape, the Propertian lover devises another sort of cure. For him, alleviation comes from writing about and recording the love affair. The lover can help his friends precisely because of his own distress. They benefit from his experience, as do those recently won over to love, whom he advises to pursue the subject of love and leave other studies behind. It is important for the success of this teaching that the Propertian lover himself be a victim of love, for it is the shared experiences that seem to help others cope with what they are now undergoing as a result of love. The Propertian *amator* puts himself forth as a guide, to other lovers who appear in the text and potentially an external reader as well. It is almost as if he is telling us that there is a better way to handle love, if only we listen to his advice. Though he is less direct about the benefits to himself, he also makes clear the benefit of writing to his own understanding of love.

In the poems framing his first three books, 1.1 and 3.24/5, the Propertian lover moves from declaring that he has no cure for love to announcing that he has at last discovered a remedy. These poems and the others that explore the possibility of a cure imply a comparison between poetry and philosophy. There are two questions for us here, then: what brought about his cure, and what is the nature of his response to philosophy?

49. Cf. the introductions to the poem by Murgatroyd 1994 and Lee 1982 and the interpretations by Gaisser 1977 and Whitaker 1979.
50. Bright 1978, 192–205.

In a typical poem, the Propertian lover seems to be at the end of his rope. He is desperate for a cure and claims to have tried almost everything.[51] At the end of the Gallus poem discussed above (1.5), he says he has no effective medicine for his malady. We meet a similar situation in the very first poem, even if in this case the lover claims he still has a few things left to try. After a dubious appeal to magic, he asks his friends to look for a cure, *auxilium*, and acknowledges his willingness to undergo "surgery" or take a trip far away (1.1.25–30):

> aut vos, qui sero lapsum revocatis, amici,   25
>   quaerite non sani pectoris auxilia.
> fortiter et ferrum saevos patiemur et ignes,
>   sit modo libertas quae velit ira loqui.
> ferte per extremas gentis et ferte per undas,
>   qua non ulla meum femina norit iter.   30

> But you, friends, who call me back too late from my fall,
> seek remedies for a heart that is unwell.
> I will endure the knife and savage fires bravely,
> if only I have the freedom to say what anger drives me to.
> Carry me through faraway lands and through distant waters,
> where no woman will know my path.

The passage recalls the philosophical texts we have been considering. Travel, of course, is a form of separation from the beloved. To undergo knife and cautery is reminiscent of the philosophical language for removing a harmful passion. The appeal to friends may also recall a familiar reference in philosophical texts. But from a philosopher's perspective, when the narrator says he will endure this "operation" so long as he can vent his anger (28), he is like an alcoholic asking for just one more drink before he enters the clinic. Is the narrator just missing or unwilling to accept the philosophers' point? Or is he making a different one? While the philosophical remedies are brutal and involve a change in person or wholesale change of values, the elegiac therapy is more accepting of our humanity.

There are other occasions in which the lover is no longer a victim of love but rather a healer of love. One poem that presents this surprising turnaround is 1.10, in which the narrator shamelessly admits to having watched Gallus in a

---

51. Cf. 2.4.7–16, where the Propertian lover lists the things that will not work (herbs, sorcery, soothsayer, dream-interpreters), and 2.1.57–58: *omnis humanos sanat medicina dolores: /solus amor morbi non amat artificem*. On the elegists' language of cure, cf. Tränkle 1960, 22–23, Knox 1986, 14–17, and O'Hara 1993.

night of love. Even when he grew tired, he says, he could not tear himself away.[52] After this confession, the confident narrator tells Gallus he has a cure with which can heal others' difficulties in love. The "medicine," he says, is in his words (14–20):

> est quiddam in nobis maius, amice, fide.
>> possum ego diversos iterum coniungere amantis,   15
> et dominae tardas possum aperire fores;
>> et possum alterius curas sanare recentis,
> nec levis in verbis est medicina meis.
>> Cynthia me docuit semper quaecumque petenda
> quaeque cavenda forent: non nihil egit Amor.   20

> I possess something greater than loyalty, friend.
> I am able to bring hostile lovers together again,
> and I am able to open the doors of an unyielding mistress.
> I am able to heal the recent love-pains of another:
> the medicine in my words is not insignificant.
> Cynthia taught me which things must be sought
> and which must be avoided. Love is good for something.

A change has taken place. The lover has a cure and can help others in exactly those areas where he previously could not help himself: bringing separated lovers together, opening stubborn doors, and healing love-wounds.[53] What are these things that Cynthia has taught him must be sought or avoided (19–20)?[54] Though not specified, they are presumably the examples of her behavior, both good and bad. These models, captured in his verse, function as the basis for the Propertian lover's teachings.[55]

His *medicina* acts through poetry, not philosophical argument. Elegy itself will cure sickness in love, and the narrator takes up the role of *praeceptor amoris* in a poem that is thoroughly didactic. From this new vantage point, he has the

---

52. Some scholars have suggested that he read about this night of love in Gallus' own poetry. I discuss this dimension and the poem itself at greater length in Chapter 5.

53. On the powers of song to open doors, see also Ov., *Am.* 2.1.21–28, 3.12.12.

54. For virtually the same expression, cf. Hor. *Sat.* 1.4.115–16, where Horace's father says, "*sapiens, vitatu quidque petitu /sit melius, causas reddet tibi . . .*," and Ter. *Ad.* 417–18. Richard Sorabji has suggested to me that these formulations recall the Stoic doctrine of selecting and rejecting indifferents: cf. Long and Sedley 1987, chs. 58–60, and also Cic. *TD* 5.24.68, Ps.-Plut., *The Education of Children* 7 DE, Mus. Ruf. Fr. 16, and Epict. *Discourses* 3.22.38–49.

55. Note, however, that Ovid recommends against reading love poetry when trying to be cured of love: *RA* 757–66.

opportunity to offer Gallus the benefit of his experience. But here in Book I, it seems to succeed only in curing others, not himself. When the narrator adopts the tone of teacher and expert, he can help his friends.[56] Otherwise, when he is depicted as the pathetic victim, he calls on the help of friends or tries other remedies.

But playing the victim is just a pose, one of many we shall see in the following pages and a useful one at the beginning of a collection that emphasizes the development of the relationship from book to book. If Cynthia has taught him what to avoid and what to pursue, this information must be useful for himself as well as others, something the narrator makes clear in later books. While the didactic nature of I.10 allows one particular stance to be highlighted (that of the expert in love, helping recent converts), other poems allow the narrator to comment on his experience more generally as well. In this way Propertius' corpus functions as a *medicina* for the narrator as well as for his readers, though he achieves this through writing rather than through reading.

Other references to the curative nature of writing support this, and tellingly they, too, occur in significantly placed poems in the collection. The poem concluding the second book opposes the study of philosophy and poetry as forms of help to the lover (23–8):

> sed numquam vitae fallet me ruga severae:
>> omnes iam norunt quam sit amare bonum.
> Lynceus ipse meus seros insanit amores!   25
>> solum te nostros laetor adire deos.
> quid tua Socraticis tibi nunc sapientia libris
>> proderit aut rerum dicere posse vias?

> But the wrinkles of a strict life will never deceive me:
> everyone knows already what a good thing love is.
> My friend Lynceus himself is madly in love, if rather late.
> I am overjoyed that you supplicate our gods.
> What help now is the wisdom in your Socratic books
> or the ability to recount the movements of the universe?

Here the lover makes a very pointed, and even competitive, remark about philosophy, most likely intending the Stoics as his target.[57] In this poem,

---

56. A didactic tone is common in Tibullus, Propertius, and of course Ovid. On Tibullus as a teacher of love, see Maltby 2002 on Tib. 1.4; for Propertius, see Wheeler 1910 and Keith 2008, 115–16. The philosophers describe the lover as one who takes advice only with difficulty: see Chrysippus on the lover's dislike for reasoned advice, recorded in Galen (*PHP* IV.6, 276.6–24 in de Lacy).

57. On the Stoics' desire to connect Zeno with Socrates and establish their school as his legacy, see Long [1974]1986, 1–13.

Lynceus has recently fallen in love.[58] By way of welcoming him to this state of affairs, the Propertian lover asks him what use his Socratic books will be now, or knowledge of the heavens.[59] Better, the narrator says, to write poetry in the manner of Callimachus and Philetas, his own sources of inspiration.[60] It is writing about love that will help the lover in the distress of an affair, not studying philosophical argument or the stars. What is important for the philosophers is of course not arguments *per se*, but understanding and appreciating them, thereby becoming convinced and altering one's own view about what is of value in the world. The recommendation in Propertius, by contrast, has to do with imagination and creativity and a working through of issues that brings to a higher level one's understanding and acceptance of oneself.

Yet another promotion of the elegiac cure over a philosophical one comes in 3.24, at the end of the third book (9–20):

> *quod mihi non patrii poterant avertere amici,*
> *   eluere aut vasto Thessala saga mari*[61],   10
> *hoc ego non*[62] *ferro, non igne coactus, et ipsa*
> *   naufragus Aegaea (vera fatebor) aqua:*
> *correptus saevo Veneris torrebar aeno;*
> *   vinctus eram versas in mea terga manus.*
> *ecce coronatae portum tetigere carinae,*   15
> *   traiectae Syrtes, ancora iacta mihi est.*
> *nunc demum vasto fessi resipiscimus aestu,*
> *   vulneraque ad sanum nunc coiere mea.*
> *Mens Bona, si qua dea es, tua me in sacraria dono!*
> *   exciderant surdo tot mea vota Iovi.*   20

What my friends at home were not able to divert me from,
or the Thessalian witches wash away in the enormous sea,
this I have done myself, not by the knife or fire,

---

58. There have been questions about the poem's unity (cf. e.g., the intro. note in Richardson 1977 and Stahl 1985, 172–88), but this issue is less relevant here than in Chapter 5, where I discuss the poem at greater length.

59. A reference to Virg. *Georg.* 2.475–92. See also Cic. *TD* 5.24.69 on the joys of studying nature and the universe, and on the popularity of Aratus' *Phaenomena*, see most recently Volk 2010.

60. See 3.1.1–2: *Callimachi Manes et Coi sacra Philitae, /in vestrum, quaeo, me sinite ire nemus!*

61. This couplet is moved to follow line 14 in Heyworth's text.

62. Heyworth 2007a prints *nunc* for *non* both times in this line, though this diminishes the emphasis on the shipwreck.

but by a shipwreck—I say this truly—in the Aegean sea.
I was seized and burned in Venus' savage cauldron;
I was bound up with my hands behind my back.
But now my garlanded ship has reached the harbor,
the sandbanks have been crossed, my anchor dropped.
Now at last, worn out from the rough sea, I have recovered my senses,
And my wounds have healed.
Mens Bona, if you are indeed a goddess, I give myself to your altar!
So many of my vows have been lost on Jupiter's deaf ears.

The narrator tells us that he has been cured, not through magic, not through the knife (*ferro*, 11), but by drowning in his own passion, a very Lucretian image.[63] But the elegiac narrator borrows the idea for opposite ends: in Lucretius, the drowning person is a victim, whereas in Propertius drowning is what brought him back to safe harbor. As we have already seen in Propertius 1.1 and 1.10, the lover describes his cure in terms that directly oppose his approach with that of the other authorities on the emotions.

There is further evidence of philosophical influence. Mention of the Aegean sea in line 12 recalls Propertius' claim in 3.21 that he was going to sail to Greece to study Plato and Epicurus rather than continue the affair with Cynthia (25–30):[64]

illic vel stadiis animum emendare Platonis　　　　25
　　incipiam aut hortis, docte Epicure, tuis;
persequar aut studium linguae, Demosthenis arma,
　　librorumque tuos, docte Menandre, sales;
aut certe tabulae capient mea lumina pictae,
　　sive ebore exactae, seu magis aere, manus.　　　30

There in Plato's Academy I will begin to improve my mind,
or in your gardens, learned Epicurus.
I will pursue the study of language, the weapons of Demosthenes,
and the wit of your books, learned Menander.
Or surely paintings will capture my interest,
or works of art crafted in ivory or, even more, in bronze.

63. Cf. *DRN* 3.853, 3.993, 6.1158, and on Epicurus' shipwreck, see Segal 1990, ch. 7 and Clay 1973. On sea and travel imagery in Propertius, cf. Khan 1968 and Leach 1966. Murgatroyd 1995 collects both Greek and Roman examples of the "sea of love" image, stressing the prominence of the *topos* at the time of the elegists. Cf. also Kennedy 1993, 49–51.
64. See Griffin 1989, 4 on traveling to Greece for a philosophical education.

Thus *Mens Bona* at 3.24.19 after may further intend to suggest the reasoning power of someone trained in argument. But the philosophical nuances of this terminology are intended to distinguish Propertius' approach to love, not assimilate it.[65]

At a fairly obvious level, then, Propertius' drowning in passion represents his infatuation with his mistress. But two literary themes contained in 3.24 also describe the activity of writing poetry and suggest that the poem is as much about his immersion in writing as about his immersion in the love affair. To begin with, we find many important precedents for writing or singing as a cure for pain caused either by love or death in both Greek and Roman literature.[66] While examples like Theocritus' *Idyll* 11 and Catullus' poems 65–68 raise similar problems to the ones we find in Propertius, they also highlight what is different about the elegist's cure. In *Idyll* 11, for example, Polyphemus' song about his love for Galatea, song is named both as a cure for love (lines 1–7, 17–18, 80–81) and, at the same time, a symptom of love (line 13).[67] The ambiguity is increased by the contrast between the clownish Cyclops and the doctor Nicias referred to at the poem's opening, whose medicine is said to be ineffective in comparison with the power of poetry. The irony of this claim, together with the uncertainty about song's role, makes it difficult to assume anything about poetry's curative role. In the Catullan examples, the narrator addresses in poem 65 his inability to write poetry after the death of his brother. Yet the very next poem is a translation from Callimachus, suggesting to what extent the poet is still struggling to recover his own voice and is obsessed with questions about lineage (of a poetic and familial kind). As in *Idyll* 11, writing about loss may provide some solace, but it can also seem to prolong rather than diminish a painful experience.

While the Propertian lover's claim to possess a cure through poetry ensures his place within this tradition, he gives a more positive answer to the doubts expressed in these examples. This depends in part on the development of the theme of therapy not just in a single poem, but through a sequence of poems stretching across several poetry books. The extended and recurring attempt to address his pain brings us to the second literary theme contained in the drowning image in Propertius 3.24: the use of sea imagery, a frequent metaphor for love and poetry in the ancient tradition and one that was especially popular among

---

65. Note that the activities Propertius will engage in once in Greece are all expressed in the future tense and not as "done deeds." Compare Prop. 3.5 on postponing the study of philosophical questions until old age, and the treatment of this in Burck 1981.

66. Cf. also Hom. *Il.* 9.186, Aesch. *Prom. Vinc.* 378, 698–99, Eur. *Med.* 143, 190ff. On Theocritus *Idyll* 11, perhaps the most important precedent, cf. Gow 1952 *ad loc.*, Cairns 1972, 147, Deuse 1990, Manuwald 1990, and especially Goldhill 1991, 246–61.

67. Goldhill 1991, 259 suggests that reading about desire has the effect of producing it, and that the poem in effect becomes a joke on the "sophisticated reader" rather than the unfortunate Cyclops.

the Augustan poets.[68] The lover's shipwreck implies the destruction both of his "ship of love" and the end of elegy, this coming, appropriately enough, at the end of a poetry book. Now, at the apparent end of their relationship, the narrator tells us of the therapeutic value of recording it in poetry. Book 3 also brings closure by alluding to the very first poem of Book 1, where the lover had no cure available for his suffering. At the opening of Book I, the lover was just beginning the account of his history with Cynthia. By the end of the Book 3, however, the benefits of chronicling the various events in their relationship had already taken place and the lover was able to declare himself cured.[69] More than just the catharsis or distraction in the Tibullan lover's cure, in Propertius, the lover claims to find illumination into the finer workings of love and to be able to share this with others as well.

Conclusions

We have seen that the philosophers and elegists agree in certain ways that love is an illness. Cicero and Lucretius emphasize the submission of the victim of love, using a devastating portrait of the failure to pursue more worthwhile goals in order to help the student overcome his or her affliction. The narrators in the elegiac poems also consider love an illness, replete with physical symptoms and loss of status and identity. Both the philosophers and poets also agree that love is something to be cured. But while Lucretius and Cicero turn to therapeutic arguments in order to change the beliefs that cause the illness, for elegiac narrators, writing poetry provides the antidote, whether they compose poems about an idealized time and place where love can flourish unimpeded or give a narrative account of the love affair that is both empathetic and critical.

The elegists agree with the philosophers to this extent, then. But their attitude towards a cure is less a form of therapy or argument and more a way of coping. The elegiac lover is not required to forsake his ideas about love, even though they entail much suffering. He cannot imagine his life without it. He does not, therefore, achieve the release from erotic passion the philosophers sought, nor does he ever come to regard it as something bad. The Tibullan lover will suffer with Nemesis rather than leave her, and even in his affair with Delia the picture of the Golden Age is but a fantasy. Still, composing the

---

68. See n. 63 above. For further examples and bibliography, cf. Fantham 1972 and Jacobson 1974, 42–43, 19–26.

69. On the ending of Book III, cf. Jacobson 1974, Barsby 1974, 135–37, and Conte [1991] 1994, 43.

pastoral descriptions of the countryside and times of peace and harmony does allow him to dream of a better time and to forget his current difficulties. Although he continues to be prone to lovesickness, the Tibullan lover has found his own treatment for the negative side of an emotion that is essential to him. If escaping into the past via his poetry does not cut out the problem at the root, it does assuage the lover's pain and offers him a means of imagining a world in which he could successfully capture his desire. The Propertian lover, too, gains relief from his pain and on two occasions at least confidently claims that he is over Cynthia and presumably unhealthy love relationships more generally. Yet despite his assurances that he is cured, he betrays his inability to rid himself of his feelings for Cynthia by his continuing fascination and passion for his mistress. Neither patient is wholly successful in overcoming his pain and weakness.

In Propertius' case, though, his suffering is still advantageous to others. The lover can help his friends precisely because of his own distress. They benefit from his experience, as do those recently won over to love, whom he advises to pursue the subject of love and leave other studies behind. It is important for the success of this teaching that the Propertian lover himself be a victim of love, for it is the shared experiences that seem to help others cope with what they are now undergoing as a result of love. The Propertian *amator* puts himself forth as a guide, to other lovers who appear in the text and potentially an external reader as well.

The Propertian lover claims the power to cure lovesickness, and does so as a writer of verse rather than someone who understands and accepts arguments and so changes his beliefs. He expresses the elegiac cure in terms that recall philosophy, only to reject the latter as of no avail. Philosophical analysis is clinical and, it is implied, drawn to predictable movements like those of the stars and planets.[70] The poetic experience of love, by contrast, is empathetic in depicting the experience of the lover from a first-person perspective. Love is seen as a general and human experience, something undergone by characters in myth, by the gods, by the narrators' friends. The narrative of the love affair in Propertius includes all the unexpected ups and downs, thus coming closer to the actual course of a relationship.

Not only do these fluctuations create a certain realism, but the sequence of poems within and across the poetry books also simulates the passage of time in which the lovers' experiences have occurred. As we have seen with the end of Book 3, the lover marks the end of the affair with shipwreck and drowning, images of the death of his affair but also the end of the narration. Death itself

---

70. Cf. Tib. 1.4.19–20, 1.9.35–36, 2.4.17–20, Ov., *Am*. I.13.27–28.

provides a way out from the suffering, a final resolution of the story, though not an actual cure.[71]

The chronological realism effected by the sequence of poems has in the past been mistaken as evidence of biographical veracity, but we need not take things so literally. The elegiac poet has, of course, created a fiction, and the personal experience is embedded in a literary context. The narration of scenes from the erotic relationship across the poetry books means that the lover, too, has a distance from the passion he portrays that allows him to examine it from every angle.[72] Thus the lover, and his readership, can better comprehend its power over him. The elegiac attitude towards a cure can offer greater healing than philosophy, because it identifies with and shows compassion for those suffering from a destructive passion, at the same time that it presents this empathy from a critical distance.

71. This was suggested to me by one of the anonymous readers on an earlier version of this chapter (Caston 2006).

72. See the collection on narrative and elegy by Lively and Salzman-Mitchell 2008; some articles stress continuity, others the episodic in elegiac narrative.

2

The Nature of Jealousy

In the representation of love as an illness, we saw the elegiac narrator clinging to his affair despite its debilitating effects and insisting that both the experience of love and writing about it gave him a superior perspective on managing his own and others' emotions. With that background in mind, I turn now to jealousy itself, another negative element of erotic love and something that is used even more emphatically to establish the narrator's authority with beloved, rival, and reader. In this chapter, I address some of the general questions surrounding the topic of elegiac jealousy. What, for example, arouses jealous feelings in elegy? Is the provocation real or imagined? What kind of character is susceptible to jealousy? Is anything effective at stopping a fit of jealousy, or is it always obsessive? How do others react in the face of another person's jealousy? What kind of advice do jealous characters offer to others who might find themselves in the same position? Rather than deal with such questions individually, I consider them as they emerge from an analysis of a number of rich and detailed cases of elegiac jealousy. These are by no means the only instances of jealousy in the genre (we shall see others in the remaining chapters), but they are ones in which jealousy is central and that exemplify what I take to be the central features of the emotion's representation in elegy. Because my aim here is to establish a body of evidence, the discussions below will focus on features of the poems that bear directly on romantic jealousy. More detailed discussions of other themes will come in subsequent chapters, where I address poetic and sociopolitical dimensions to the elegists' representation of jealousy not discussed here.

The first set of examples reveals the feelings and expressions of jealousy, poems in which a character is in the throes of the emotion. But the elegiac conception of elegy is not limited to such cases: the elegiac narrators also comment on where another character should feel jealousy, even though he does not, or when it is advisable not to express jealousy, even though one may be justified in feeling it. Such criticism has much to say about the parameters of jealousy and about the underlying conditions that make it appropriate or not. Elegiac lovers not only provide evidence of jealous persons acting jealous, then, they also comment on the dispositions and circumstances in which jealousy is fitting and when it should be shown.[1]

The Symptoms of Jealousy

In dealing with cases that illustrate the manifestation of jealous feelings, I have chosen three elegies for discussion: Propertius 1.3, Propertius 3.15, and Ovid *Amores* 2.7. Propertius 1.3 provides a useful starting point for introducing the central features of elegiac jealousy. The elegy is infused with jealousy and explores it from a number of different dimensions. Although the focus of many studies, the poem has never been examined from this perspective.

To begin with, 1.3 includes most of the central features of jealousy outlined in the Introduction, as well as some I will explore in greater detail in Chapters 3 and 4. We find, for example, the various layers of seeing and visualization that jealousy typically entails: darting glances at a lover's appearance as well as prolonged gaze at the beloved, and allusions to well-known examples of Roman art as well as creative fantasies of the beloved's infidelity, themselves described as if works of art.[2] The elegy also describes both male and female jealousy. Even if the male poet is obviously responsible for constructing both depictions, it is significant that the two are differently portrayed. This gender difference emerges most clearly in the response to jealousy. In 1.3, Cynthia manifests her jealousy with anger, while the male lover displays an increase in physical desire, though the depiction of gender is complicated by several layers of role-playing, as we shall see.

The location and context of the elegy is also significant. The representation of jealousy in 1.3 does not appear in isolation, but the theme is in fact programmatic in the opening sequence of Book 1.[3] In 1.2, the narrator pleads with Cynthia not to covet the gifts of rich rivals, which would naturally provoke the lover's jealousy, even if he does not say so explicitly. In 1.4, Bassus' offer to introduce the narrator to other women inflames Cynthia's jealousy. In 1.5, the narrator is jealous because Gallus is interfering in his relationship with Cynthia. Finally, in 1.6, the narrator rejects the life pursued by the kind of rival implicit in 1.2, someone whose greed and rapacity extend from land and money to other

---

1. See Kaster 2005, whose study of emotions addresses both when they should and should not be expressed.

2. On the role of the imagination and fantasy in jealousy, see Lloyd 1995, *passim* and Goldie 2000, 225.

3. We find a similar sequence in Propertius' second book with elegies 16–23. We might also think here of Catullus cc. 50 and 51, though not everyone agrees that jealousy is at issue: see, for example, the discussion in Konstan 2006, 240–41.

men's girlfriends. The prominence of jealousy right at the start of Propertius' first book of elegies reveals its centrality to the portrait of the lover and the role that deception and trust are going to play throughout the corpus. Nor is this pattern exclusive to Propertius: many of the same features of jealousy, and the persistent interest in it, are represented in the genre as a whole.

Turning now to 1.3 itself, we find a poem that includes two perspectives on a single event: the male lover's failure to show up on time for his date with Cynthia. Both members of the couple express jealousy as a result. As we shall see, Cynthia has good grounds. Her lover arrives late, drunk, and disheveled, all this after Cynthia had waited up for him until falling into a teary slumber. The basis for the male lover's jealousy is more complicated. He has suspicions of what happened during his absence but relies on less tangible evidence. I begin with the more straightforward case of Cynthia's jealousy, even though it comes later in the poem.

Expectations of Fidelity (Propertius 1.3)

Cynthia is asleep when her lover arrives in her room. He watches her sleep and then kneels close to her, making advances that she resists even in her sleep (21–6). Finally the light of the moon shining through the window awakens her (31–3). Cynthia relies on visual clues for an instant determination of what her lover has been up to during his absence. She notes the moonlight and thus the late hour, her lover's intoxicated state, and presumably the apples he had put on her lap (24–6). She takes these as proof not simply that he has been out carousing, but more specifically that he has been with another woman (35–8):[4]

> '*tandem te nostro referens iniuria*[5] *lecto*
> *alterius clausis expulit e foribus?*
> *namque ubi longa meae consumpsti tempora noctis,*
> *languidus exactis, ei mihi, sideribus?*

4. Camps 1961 *ad loc.* notes that her outburst is the inverse of the door's speech in Propertius 1.16.17–44. Harrison 1994 23 thinks her anger might be a sign of guilt at her own infidelity, noting that her wool is purple (implying fancy clothes and hence rich lovers) and that lyre-playing implies she is a "disreputable professional party-entertainer." Whether she is innocent or guilty need not affect the question of her jealousy.

5. Commentators differ on the sense of *iniuria* here. Richardson 1977 thinks it is a wrong Propertius has committed against someone else, while Butler and Barber 1933 see it as a rejection by another woman. The latter explanation makes better sense of *clausis foribus*, though Cynthia must see the rejection as coming after lovemaking (*consumpsti* and *languidus* clearly have sexual connotations). On lines 37–38 and the importance of imagery of the *convivium* (sex and drinking), see Kaufhold 1997, 89–90.

Has some wrong finally driven you out of the shut doors of another
and brought you back to my bed?
For where have you spent the long hours of the night that was
supposed to be mine,
you who return exhausted when the stars, alas, have run their course?

Cynthia spins these and other visual clues into a story. By using words like *con-sumpsti* (37) and *languidus* (38) of his presumed encounter, she reveals that she envisions this illicit night to have been both passionate and exhausting. While a scene involving abandoned lovers may seem a familiar one in Latin poetry, it is important to stress how this one fits the parameters of jealousy. Cynthia's belief in the threat fits our definition exactly. Cynthia feels entitled to an exclusive romantic relationship, suspects trust has been broken, and responds with anger and self-pity (39–46).[6] Her reaction implies a lack of trust in the relationship, and this sits ill with her expectations. Her use of visual clues and story-telling are typical of a jealous figure, as we shall see in this and subsequent chapters.

It is common for the jealous figure to assume different roles as an attempt to understand or assert control in a difficult relationship. When Cynthia takes up the position of loyal but betrayed lover, she adopts a role usually reserved for the male lover in Roman love elegy. And her portrayal in this poem is designed to resemble the male lover's in certain other crucial respects, as others have noted.[7] Her response is angry and verbally abusive, like many of his responses on other occasions upon the discovery of her infidelity. She whiled away the time waiting for him by spinning and playing the lyre, her creative equivalent to telling a story or writing a poem.[8] The complaint about his disloyal behavior is phrased using a term the narrator employs for his own laments about infidelity: *querebar* (43).[9] The narrator thus assigns her a role much like his own.[10] Poetry and creativity

6. For Richardson 1977, *externo amore* in 44 shows that Cynthia views Propertius as "virtually her husband." For a sociological treatment of the assumptions of possession underlying feelings of betrayal, indignation, and love, see White and Mullen 1989, 179. Kaufhold 1997 challenges the emphasis that has been placed on Cynthia's anger in her speech, arguing that insofar as her speech resembles that of the male lover, her "anger" expresses her love (96–97). But it is better understood as an expression of her jealousy, which rests on a certain understanding of this love and the expectations she is entitled to. Anger marks a strong difference between male and female reactions to jealousy, as we shall see in Chapter 4.

7. Cf. esp. Kaufhold 1997, 94–96.

8. Cynthia's connection with wool-working also suggests a comparison with the model wife Penelope (see Fedeli 1980 *ad loc.*). I discuss this characterization below.

9. See Pichon 1966, s.v., Saylor 1967, and more recently James 2003a, ch. 4.

10. Gender inversion is a well-established feature of elegy: for an especially clear discussion, see Greene 2000. On the changing roles Propertius assigns to Cynthia, see Gold 1993, 445.

are the recourse of those who have lost love, and in this case, she has both a speaking part and creative output.

But the role-playing goes beyond just gender inversion. As the reference to her spinning in line 41 makes clear, Cynthia also assumes a traditionally feminine role, that of Penelope waiting for Odysseus. The narrator is thus comparable to Odysseus, delayed in his homecoming and the entire scenario an allusion to the end of the *Odyssey* and the threat of the suitors.[11] Cynthia's epic guise helps explain the narrator's anxiety about the risk of a rival. Yet for Cynthia, adopting Penelope's role is also a way to establish her innocence and high moral ground in contrast to the damaging way she feels she has been treated by her Odysseus.

Propertius 1.3 is unusual in allowing female jealousy to stand without a critique. More commonly the narrator treats a female mistress' harangues with derision, the situation we find in the next two examples. Here, however, Cynthia's position occupies a prominent and unchallenged position in the elegy because it has been carefully manipulated to resemble two impeccable roles: those of Penelope at the end of the *Odyssey* and of the narrator himself. It is one of the few times Cynthia seems to be above criticism, and thus reveals an important connection between the adoption of different roles and winning sympathy.

Unrestrained Suspicions (Propertius 1.3)

Let us return now to the male lover, whose perspective the poem describes first. He slips in late and watches Cynthia in bed. Her sleep is far from peaceful: she stirs and sighs, signs of a restlessness that stem, we may suspect, from her anger at being stood up and slighted. Yet to the lover, her tossing and turning prompt suspicions that she herself has been unfaithful (27–30):

> *et quotiens raro duxti suspiria motu,*
> > *obstupui vano credulus auspicio,*
> *ne qua tibi insolitos portarent visa timores,*
> > *neve quis invitam cogeret esse suam:*

> And as often as you sighed and gave an occasional shudder,
> I froze, trusting readily in an empty sign,
> lest some dream be bringing you unfamiliar fears,
> or someone be forcing you to be his against your will.

The emotion expressed here again fits all three parts of our definition. The lover expects exclusive attentions from Cynthia: hence his shock (*obstupui*, 28)

---

11. Stanford 1963 dismisses the significance of Odysseus in elegy: "The references to Ulysses in Propertius, Tibullus, and Martial are conventional" (p. 138, n. 2). See now Perutelli 2006, who devotes a chapter, albeit a short one, to the role of this hero in Propertius' poetry.

and anxiety at the thought that someone else might try to possess her, even though he himself is responsible for constructing this rival. For him, the loss he fears seems tangible and real.[12] The loss seems so real, in fact, that he tries right then to reclaim what he has imagined another man is trying to steal from him and leans over her body in an attempt to take Cynthia for himself.

The lover's jealousy may strike us as unjustified. As far as the reader can ascertain, the narrator could have invented the prospect of a rival and Cynthia's infidelity to him. There is little evidence of a rival desiring her, except insofar as the narrator invokes such a figure through his description of her dream. And some of the details of the dream seemed designed to make the situation more bearable for the narrator, even if he is responsible for it in the first place. It may be easier for him to imagine Cynthia as passive victim, the object of male desire rather than someone actively pursuing male attention. Cynthia's vulnerability is emphasized not only in the interpretation of her "dream," but also in her comparison with Io (19–20). Like Argus, appointed guard for Io against Jupiter's adulterous advances, the narrator stations himself over Cynthia because of his fear that a suitor might snatch her away, a fear he projects onto her as well, as *invitam* (30) suggests.[13] The mythological allusion domesticates his fear but also highlights his sense of entitlement: like Argus, he is guaranteeing something comparable to conjugal rights, ones he apparently considers to be his own. In this reconstruction of Cynthia's dream, the lover paradoxically creates both a rival and a marriage, symbols of his own tendency for fantasy and role-playing.

The fantasy as to what Cynthia's dream is about highlights two especially complex features of jealousy in this poem. One has to do with the speculative substance of the lover's interpretation of the signs. We should emphasize from the outset that the lack of justification for jealousy is no impediment to its arousal. Just because a jealous person believes there is a threat does not mean there really is one, or any good grounds for thinking there is. The fact that his beliefs and fears may be groundless, though, is no obstacle to jealousy. What matters is that he *believes* them to have a basis. As the doctor and author Gonzalez-Crussi puts it:

12. Compare Tanner's description of Pozdnyshev's jealous state in Tolstoy's *Kreutzer Sonata*: "The second notable trait is his habit of projection. He notes every word, gesture, glance and 'attributed them with importance.' He fancies, surmises, and interprets. He is in fact creating the situation he considers to be evolving . . . He is indeed half aware of this, but when he does come home and see them together, he is sure that reality and imagination have at last coincided. Or as we say, for him the imaginary has become the real. And this is how he wishes things to be" (Tanner 1979, 76).

13. See Curran 1966, 203 on the Argus exemplum and what he takes as a switch from the lover's more aggressive approach to that of mere observer. He also points out a connection between the Argus story and the lover's jealousy concerning Cynthia's supposed dream (204). All of the myths alluded to in 1.3 refer to well-known subjects of painting: on this see Breed 2003 and Valladares 2005.

The true jealous man is always jealous *a priori* . . . the jealous man drinks his cup of sorrows not because he has a rival but has a rival because he is jealous. He needs a rival so badly that if he did not have one he would invent him. This is why extreme jealousy sees a rival in *every* man.[14]

Ovid explicitly addresses the invention of a rival in *Amores* 1.8.95–6: *ne securus amet nullo rivale caveto:/non bene, si tollas proelia, durat amor.* Whether or not he has a rival, what matters is that he needs one.

A second striking feature of the narrator's jealousy in Propertius 1.3 has to do with the parallels drawn between the narrator and his rival. When we compare what we learn the narrator-lover does upon his arrival in Cynthia's bedroom with what he suspects is going on in her dream, we discover a striking resemblance between the two.[15] Just as he imagines a rival making love to Cynthia against her will, so the male lover himself leans over the body of the defenseless Cynthia.[16] His attempts to possess her are just as unwelcome as the ones he attributes to a rival: the garlands and apples he places on her body in lines 21–4, attempts to touch her and offer himself sexually, roll off as she tosses and turns (25–6). The lover sees himself and his rival as in some sense alike, almost as if he *were* the rival.[17] By drawing this connection between the two, the lover turns his late arrival into an illicit entry, an attempt at seduction that functions as a form of displaced passion. The idea of stealing Cynthia from himself, however paradoxical, encourages his dominance and accentuates his aggression. It corresponds directly to the third part of my definition, the lover's desire to reclaim what he believes he has lost to another. Her resistance only heightens his desire in the process, making it even more imperative for him to re-establish his claims.[18]

---

14. Gonzalez-Crussi 1988, 37. See also Descartes *PA* III.167: "[Jealousy] does not result so much from the strength of the reasons which make us believe we may lose the good, as from the high esteem in which we hold it. This causes us to examine the slightest grounds for doubt, and to regard them as very considerable reasons."

15. As noted by, e.g., Kaufhold 1997, 92.

16. Cf. Curran 1966, 198–99 and Harrison 1994 on the lover's intentions: Harrison, following Veyne, finds the poem comic, calling it "one of stormy passion but described in a manner calculated more to amuse than to move the reader" (24).

17. I discuss homosocial interest in the rival later in this chapter and again in Chapter 5. For other examples of the conflation of lover and rival, see *Her.* 15.1–2 and *Her.* 16.233–46. There are telling modern examples as well: cf. e.g., Shakespeare sonnet 42 and the similarities between Kings Leontes and Polixenes in *The Winter's Tale*. In the novel *Enduring Love*, Ian McEwan writes of a scene in which a man, reunited with his wife, imagines himself as the rival: "Or, I imagined, I was another man, my own sexual competitor, come to steal her from me" (p. 5).

18. Jealousy and increased sexual desire are discussed prominently in the psychological literature: cf. e.g. White and Mullen 1989, 36 on sexual arousal as an initial response to jealousy.

We find this same correlation between lover and rival in the mythological tableaux in the opening section, a passage that highlights particularly clearly the fluid identity of both male and female lovers.[19] In these highly artistic scenes, the lover compares the sleeping Cynthia to three mythical figures. All three women are abandoned, alerting the reader right at the start of the poem to Cynthia's treatment by her lover. The similes may seem quite distinct from the Penelope allusion. Cynthia is compared to Ariadne swooning as Theseus' ship sails away, to Andromeda just released from the rugged cliff, and to an exhausted Thracian bacchant. We also know from details in other versions of these same stories that at least two of the three women will be rescued by other males. Ariadne and Andromeda, though first abandoned by Theseus and Cepheus respectively, were later rescued by Dionysus and Perseus and subsequently became their lovers.[20] At the moment the narrator describes them, in other words, they are on a threshold of sorts, abandoned by one man and about to be rescued by another. Cynthia, too, occupies this pivotal position. But in her case, though the narrator-lover may think he is only her rescuer, Cynthia points out he was also the one to abandon her (36–7). Just as for Penelope, the man who abandons her and the man who arrives are one and the same.

Right from the start of his first poetry book, Propertius highlights the narrator's many poses. The speaker is a lover who takes up the part of Odysseus, himself a master of disguise. He is a lover, but at the same time adopts other perspectives, including that of his own rival. He allows Cynthia's charges about his infidelity to stand in 1.3, yet will go on, in the majority of elegies that follow, to assert his own undying fidelity. The instability of the narrator's *persona* has a lot to do with the experience of jealousy itself. The self-doubts that jealousy produces encourage us to see a situation from another person's angle. What does the rival see in my beloved? What does she see in him? What is the difference between me and the rival, in my eyes but also from the perspective of outsiders?[21] The jealous lover is driven to look at Cynthia through the eyes of a suitor rather than those of her established lover, whether out of guilt and a desire to escape responsibility for his own behavior or out of drunken desire. He

19. See the insightful remarks about the lover's different roles in Valladares 2005. Maleuvre 1998 focuses on "le caractère 'protéen'" of the elegiac narrator as well, though he suggests that the opposition between different voices is a means of displaying, from a safe distance, the elegists' hostility to Augustan rule.

20. On these mythological comparisons, cf. Curran 1966, Dunn 1985, and Harrison 1994. Dunn's interpretation is the most relevant here: he gives a persuasive demonstration of the way in which the three female comparisons reveal the narrator's own emotions as he views his mistress (241–2).

21. Davis's article is one of the few general studies of jealousy to stress the crucial role of outsiders on the expression of jealousy (Davis 1935/6). See Kaster 2005 on the effect of the public and community in Rome on the expression of other emotions. Nagle 1988, 95 discusses the shifting perspectives within triangular relationships in selected episodes of Ovid's *Metamorphoses*.

wants to test how she would respond to him if she thought he were someone else. And he wants to know what it feels like to be in the position of the rival, who by definition steals away what belongs to another. A rival must be someone like him and possibly capable of edging him out. The identification raises questions about whether there is someone else who is as suitable, someone who may have an even better claim to her attentions. Desire for a beloved is superseded by the desire to have what another possesses, a dynamic well explored by René Girard.[22] The lover's passion for his mistress, however much it is destined to bring disappointment, also offers an opportunity to imagine and fantasize what it feels like to be someone else.

Vehement Reactions (Propertius 3.15)

In Propertius 3.15, a poem that has received much less attention than 1.3, we find another example of female jealousy, though the presentation is more critical this time. Cynthia has become jealous over her lover's former girlfriend.[23] He assures her that the relationship is over and done with, but she believes otherwise. It is also possible that she is jealous of a past relationship even though it has been terminated, a phenomenon recorded in several modern treatments of jealousy.[24] As for the male lover, instead of finding in her jealousy a proof of Cynthia's love for him, he considers it an irritation. He assures her that he does not love anyone else but her. Yet as we shall see, this reassurance is coupled with a not-so-veiled threat to stop meddling.

The poem, and Cynthia's jealousy, begin with a rumor informing Cynthia of her lover's previous relationship with a woman named Lycinna. As in 1.3, fears about broken fidelity are immediate, and Cynthia makes no attempt to understand the behavior as anything other than a betrayal. She expects exclusive attentions, and her jealousy is piqued by her anxiety that she might not in fact be the only one. The narrator reassures Cynthia about her importance to him, telling her that in the three years since the affair with Lycinna ended, Cynthia has completely taken Lycinna's place in his life (7–10).

Yet despite this attempt to mollify Cynthia, the rest of the elegy develops into a harsh warning. The narrator recounts the mythical story about Dirce and

---

22. Girard 1961, discussed again in Chapter 5.

23. Though see Richardson 1977, 380, who does not take 3.15 to be describing the relationship with Cynthia.

24. See La Rochefoucauld Maxim #361: "La jalousie naît toujours avec l'amour, mais elle ne meurt pas toujours avec lui" (*Jealousy is always born with love, but it does not always die with it*). We find fictional examples of jealousy over past relationships in James Joyce's short story *The Dead*, Julian Barnes' novel *Before She Met Me*, and in Graham Greene's *The End of the Affair* (see e.g., p. 54 or 137). Parrott 1991, 22–3 discusses the psychology of jealousy over past, present, and even future relationships.

Antiope to caution Cynthia against the danger of letting jealousy go uncontrolled.[25] In this section I examine a new element in the portrayal of elegiac jealousy having to do with the inappropriateness of an action prompted by jealousy. Jealous feelings may be justified in the circumstances, but not if carried too far.

In this version of the myth, Dirce grew crazy (*saeva*, 11) with jealousy at the charge that the *famula* Antiope had slept with her husband Lycus and punished the girl by overworking and starving her (15–19).[26] Antiope's sons punish Dirce by binding her to a bull and plowing the fields bloody with her body (37–41). The sons' action is not directly connected with the issue of jealousy, except insofar as Dirce's jealousy leads her to overreact: that is the mistake that causes her to suffer the consequences. In the analogous situation, the message to Cynthia is clear: stop harassing Lycinna or pay the cost.[27] The myth draws a line between the suspiciousness involved in jealousy and the proper judgment about the grounds for jealousy. But it also indicates the risk of taking things beyond due measure, a concern in the poems I discuss in Chapter 4 as well.

In contrast with Propertius 1.3, the rival in this poem has a name and a history, and her social rank may play an important role in provoking the jealousy experienced here as well. Lycinna occupies the same position as Antiope, a *famula* whose servile status is highlighted in this version of the myth. Some scholars have thought that Lycinna might have been a slave because of Ovid's treatment of a similar conflict.[28] Yet even within the Propertian corpus, rivals of inferior status are particularly galling to Cynthia. In two elegies from Book 4, we see that if the rival is not a near equal, then one has to suffer the indignity of being beaten out by one who is regarded as a social inferior, thus lowering one's own status even further. In 4.7, for example, the poet imagines that the deceased Cynthia, charred from the pyre, comes back to haunt her lover for recovering so quickly from her death and for taking up with someone who is basically a prostitute (39–40). Reference to this woman's low status adds another layer of

25. The version of Dirce's story presented here is based on Hyginus *Fab.* 7 and 8 (Apollodorus 3.5.5). In the former, Antiope was an earlier wife of Lycus, making the story of Dirce's jealousy parallel to that of Cynthia over Lycinna (as pointed out by Butrica 1994, 141). By contrast, Fedeli finds Propertius' version closer to *Fab.* 8. (Fedeli 1985, 477–8).

26. There are textual problems with the adjective defining *crimen* in line 11. The mss. have *vero*, but *sero* (Phillimore) and *vano* (Franz) have also been proposed. Choice of reading is complicated by the different versions of the myth. Butrica 1994 argues that the ambiguity is part of the poet's "deceptive strategy" in the poem (138, n. 11). Yet the narrator does not deny that he had an affair with Lycinna, he argues only that it is over now and so Cynthia's anger is groundless. There is also a problem with the sequence of lines: cf. Macleod 1974, 93, Butrica 1994, 140–41, and now Heyworth 2007b, pp. 363–5.

27. See Macleod 1974, 93.

28. It is also possible that Lycinna was the maidservant of Cynthia. This identification finds support in Ovid *Amores* 2.7 and 2.8 (discussed below), which seem to be modeled on Propertius 3.15 and where the affair is with a slave-girl.

injury.[29] The rival's long *cyclas*, a long cloak worn by rich women, is just a superficial attempt to make herself appear noble.[30] And in this case the jealousy is reciprocal: Cynthia's replacement is herself unhappy with the formidable reputation of her predecessor, mistreating any servant who pays tribute to Cynthia or asks a favor in her name (41–6). In 4.8, too, a poem I discuss further in Chapter 4, the deserted lover takes up with two women who appear to be Cynthia's social inferiors. It is worth asking if the violence of Cynthia's response in that poem has something to do with her outrage at being deserted in favor of women she considers beneath her.[31]

As for the narrator in 3.15, his response shows his intolerance of female jealousy. Cynthia's feelings may complicate two relationships, not only the one with Cynthia but also the one with Lycinna, if in fact we are meant to believe that they have an ongoing relationship. The narrator's initial denials of harboring feelings for Lycinna show his awareness of Cynthia's claims, in particular her expectation of special attentions and attempt to regain them. But despite his reassurance towards her at the poem's opening, he is more concerned about his own interests. The poem seems at first to focus on Cynthia's perception of Lycinna as a rival. Yet it quickly shifts to the lover's perspective, a view in which Cynthia becomes a rival or intruder. The narrator warns Cynthia away using a mythological story that is more sympathetic towards Antiope's suffering than to Dirce's. He is manipulative, wanting both to placate Cynthia and to keep Lycinna happy. And he uses the myth to have it both ways. Perhaps the jealousy even reawakens his interest in Lycinna as a suitable, and thus attractive, rival. In any case, Cynthia's attention to Lycinna ends up magnifying Lycinna, presumably the last thing Cynthia would have wanted. By reorienting the poem's sympathy away from Cynthia, the narrator allows that the jealous person is aggrieved, but also claims that he, unfairly suspected, has been mistreated as well.

Jealousy Out in the Open (Ovid *Amores* 2.7)

In Ovid *Amores* 2.7, jealousy arises in the theater, not surprisingly: any reader familiar with Ovid's poetry knows the potential of this arena for flirtation and

29. According to Parrott (1991, 12), envy begins with social comparison. We might say the same for jealousy. See for example [Tib.] 3.16, where Sulpicia is upset that Cerinthus has left her for an inferior rival, *ignoto toro* (6). She calls this other woman a *scortum* (4) or prostitute, while she describes herself as *Servi filia* (4), with the pun on her name only emphasizing the issue of status (the pun is noted by Hinds 1987, 45). Cf. as well *Amores* 2.8.9–14 on choosing servants as lovers and the discussion of this in James 1997, 64–74.

30. On replacing Cynthia with lower-class women, cf. also Propertius 3.6.1–2 and 4.8.29–32. See also Cairns 2003, 239 on *pthonos* as a "top-down as well as bottom-up emotion."

31. The violence may stem in part from the elegy's manipulation of the end of the *Odyssey* and the killing of the suitors. On the relationship between 4.8 and the Homeric passage, see Evans 1971. I discuss this elegy at greater length in Chapter 4.

amorous encounters. For Corinna, the people who make up the audience constitute a breeding ground for rivals, while for the Ovidian lover, they become a jury who will judge his loyalty to Corinna. Though jealousy may seem a personal and private affair, this elegy reminds us of the opportunities for and constraints of managing intimate relations in a public setting. The subsequent elegy, *Amores* 2.8, forms a pair with 2.7, moving away from the public setting to a more private one, a secluded place in the house where the lover will harangue Corinna's maid. The juxtaposition between public and private, appearances and reality, deception and trust, is at the heart of the two poems.[32] In the end, jealousy casts everything into doubt, as even contradictory evidence would seem to point in the same direction.[33] The jealous person becomes paranoid and as she does, her jealousy paints every detail.

No matter what the male lover does or says in 2.7, Corinna suspects he is communicating with another woman, and right there in front of her. As in Propertius 3.15, we hear about the mistress' jealousy exclusively from his perspective:

> *Ergo sufficiam reus in nova crimina semper?*
>   *ut vincam, totiens dimicuisse piget.*
> *sive ego marmorei respexi summa theatri,*
>   *eligis e multis unde dolere velis;*
> *candida seu tacito vidit me femina vultu,*   5
>   *in vultu tacitas arguis esse notas.*
> *si quam laudavi, miseros petis ungue capillos,*
>   *si culpo, crimen dissimulare putas;*
> *sive bonus color est, in te quoque frigidus esse,*
>   *seu malus, alterius dicor amore mori.*[34]   10

Will I continually stand as a defendant on some new charge?
Though I win, I'm worn out from having to stand trial so many times.
If I scan the upper rows of the marble theater,
you pick one girl out of the many whom you decide is a rival.
If a beautiful girl looks at me with silent face,
you detect unspoken signs on her face.

32. See Sharrock 2002b, 155 for stimulating remarks about the almost non-existence of the private in Ovid's poetry, where both the regular intrusion of third parties into the love affair and allusions to earlier love poetry undermine the notion of anything private or exclusive.

33. Compare Crommelynck's play *The Magnificent Cuckold* in which the jealous husband always misinterprets the evidence. When his wife is loyal, he accuses her of adultery. When his accusations finally drive her to become unfaithful, he thinks she must be loyal (for why would she sin out in the open?).

34. All quotations of Ovid's *Amores* are from Kenney's Oxford edition (1961).

> If I praise someone, you pull out my hair with your nails.
> If I criticize someone, you think I'm hiding a crime.
> If my color is good, you think I am cold towards you;
> if it's bad, I'm dying with love for another.

Not only does she fear she has lost him to another, she fears that everyone is a potential rival. According to his account, she reacts, without logic, to every change in his appearance, no matter how contradictory the evidence (e.g., good color or bad). The narrator describes Corinna as obsessive, inconsistent, and precipitous. By contrast, he uses Corinna's fears to magnify himself. They inevitably suggest he is highly alluring and capable of attracting the desire of every woman around.

But despite the ways she arrived at her conclusions, Corinna will turn out to be right when her suspicions are vindicated in 2.8. Just because someone is paranoid does not mean the fear is always ungrounded. In the follow-up to the scene at the theater, the narrator accuses the maid Cypassis of telling Corinna about their affair. In this case, the lover's anger is directed at the rival, unlike the focus of anger in the previous example, Propertius 3.15, where the narrator turned on the mistress herself.[35] All of Corinna's fears are confirmed, if not for her, then for us. Even though the description of Corinna's behavior is among the most hyperbolic in elegy, her suspicions are at the same time some of the most clearly defensible.

The narrator here also indicates his intolerance for female jealousy, which becomes an annoyance and worse, an impediment to pursuing his pleasures. Ovid portrays the lover as concerned only with getting what he wants and Corinna as a suspicious and interfering mistress. The narrator-lover's guilt, which was more covert or slyly revealed in Propertius, is in Ovid overtly presented, with the latter poet characteristically taking things to an extreme.[36] More often, however, the claims made by different elegiac characters pull in different directions, and there is no clear assignation of guilt or innocence. The reader is often left in a state of *aporia* about whom to believe and when. As I will suggest in Chapter 5, this inability to believe or trust puts a reader in a similar position to that of jealous figures, who hope for fidelity yet cannot bring themselves to trust the beloved's account.

Gender and Showing One's Feelings

At this point we have seen several recurring elements in the elegiac portrayal of jealousy: a reliance on visual clues, angry reprimands, the status of one's rival,

35. See Fitzgerald 2000, 63–68 for a sophisticated treatment of the pair of poems. His central interest is in the relationship between slave and free, but his discussion of the role of the reader and his/her shifting allegiances will be relevant to issues that come up in Chapter 5.

36. On this view of Ovid, see James 2003a, 157. By contrast, Gibson 2006 argues for Ovid's more moderate voice, at least in the *Ars Amatoria*, taking Propertius as the poet of extreme views (135).

and issues about infidelity that pertain to the jealous character, not just the beloved. Yet even though the poems I have considered so far present a mostly uniform picture, there are tensions in the evidence, especially concerning differences between the representation of the narrator's experience and that of the female mistress. While the narrator looks upon his own jealousy in an uncritical way, he is impatient and almost disgusted at his mistress' jealousy. This leads to a further problem with the critique of female jealousy: the narrator-lovers both insist on the expression of jealousy in elegy as proof of love and then complain about its outpouring in their very own mistresses, one of many examples of their own imperfections.

I suggest two ways to resolve this conflict, one having to do with the difference in perspective between a first- and second-person experience and another with the issue of the narrator's own trustworthiness. First, there is often a gap between the tolerance we feel for our own weaknesses and the irritation of having to witness someone else behave badly. Jealousy is often irrational and persistent. As we have seen in the three elegiac examples so far, it can be hard to shake off a jealous person's fears and paranoia, no matter what kind of reassurances you give. Jealousy is severely disruptive, creating complications in the lives of two, and possibly more, people. The narrator's impatience with his mistress' jealousy thus lends a certain psychological realism to the representation of a love affair in which disappointments, fights, and frustration are endemic.

The complaint about female jealousy may also be a way for the narrator to aggrandize himself, but obliquely and without being obviously boastful. Under the surface of the narrator's critique comes the sigh of "how hard it is to be popular!" Female jealousy may be disagreeable to him, but it does reveal the extent to which women are fighting over the narrator. He highlights himself as a successful lover and uses the mistress' loss of control as a form of self-advertisement. Complaining about female jealousy is thus not so much aimed at the mistress as an indirect reference to the narrator's popularity and expertise, at least according to the narcissistic portrait of himself that he would like to promote.

Yet there are cracks in this façade, in particular the indications, even revelations in the case of *Amores* 2.7, of the narrator's own infidelity. In Propertius 3.15, we are left unsure whether Cynthia is "right" about Lycinna's continuing role. In both Propertius 3.15 and Ovid *Amores* 2.7, it is unclear why the narrator would undermine himself by introducing questions about his loyalty in the first place. This exposure of the lover's guilt affects the relationship between narrator and reader. The inconsistencies in the report, either within a single elegy or across a sequence of poems, force readers to participate in a more direct way with evaluating claims and suspicions than they might have otherwise wanted. As suggested in the Introduction, other features of elegy, such as the confessional first-person voice, have the same effect. We cannot stand back as casual observers, but become engaged in the problem of whether or not to believe what we are being told and how sympathetic, or not, to feel.

When Jealousy Is Appropriate (or Not)

I turn now to those cases where elegiac lovers note behavior that is inappropriate, given their understanding of jealousy. In these examples, the circumstances are right for jealousy to appear, but either it is expressed but should not be (because it may cause more harm than good) or it should be but is not (a failure of certain men to love in the way that they should). In both types of situation, we learn when jealousy ought to show up and how, its appropriateness (or not) on various occasions, and the effects of jealousy on a relationship.

Superficially, these two sets of cases may seem to represent conflicting positions, recalling the tension we saw in the beginning of the chapter between cases where male lovers both want and do not want displays of female jealousy. Here the lovers recommend the repression of jealousy as a successful strategy for maintaining an erotic relationship but elsewhere chastise people for not showing any jealousy at all, even when the situation clearly calls for it. Yet we will see in what follows that there is in fact no real conflict, for the first case concerns merely the expression of jealousy, while the second emphasizes the absence of any feelings of jealousy at all. We will also see how, in marking the absence of jealousy in some elegiac characters' behavior, the attitudes expressed in these poems intersect with a number of contemporary Roman attitudes towards the emotions, marriage, and adultery. Thus I address here some of the themes I am concerned with in other chapters about the ways in which the elegiac narrator promotes his own views about love in language that explicitly evokes a contrast with discussions by other "authorities."

When Jealousy Is Counterproductive

In two passages from Propertius and Ovid's *Ars Amatoria*, the narrator adopts the role of *praeceptor amoris* and gives advice to others about how to handle the discovery of a beloved's infidelity. Both narrators advise *not* showing any jealousy, since no one, they argue, wants to be the object of adultery charges. This advice to keep quiet is rather surprising given what we learn about their own behavior in similar situations. Yet the elegiac narrators obviously recognize the ways in which expressing jealousy (as distinct from feeling it) can be counterproductive to their own erotic aims. Their awareness of this harmful dimension may not be able to stop them from revealing their own jealousy, but they do represent for the benefit of others what it feels like to be on the receiving end of a jealous outburst. Cynthia's meddling into her lover's affairs in Propertius 3.15, and Corinna's insistent questions in *Amores* 2.7, are proof of the point. A mistress gains nothing by interrogating a lover with questions about his feelings for her.

The advice from Propertius comes in 2.18A and runs as follows (1–4):[37]

> *Assiduae multis odium peperere querelae:*
>   *frangitur in tacito femina saepe viro.*
> *si quid vidisti, semper vidisse negato!*
>   *aut si quid doluit forte, dolere nega!*

> Continual accusations have made many unpopular.
> Often a woman is overcome by a man's silence.
> If you have seen something, always deny you have seen it!
> Or if perhaps something has hurt you, deny you are hurt!

The behavior that needs to be suppressed is consistent with what we find in the familiar features of jealousy. We find an emphasis on seeing (*vidisti . . . vidisse*, 3), where visual evidence is often taken to provide the first sign of infidelity, as we have noted already in Propertius 1.3 and Ovid *Amores* 2.7. The reference to *dolor* emphasizes the pain caused by jealousy and the thought that affection that is owed to oneself is now being given to another. And *querelae*, which are usually understood to mean the lovesick complaints so frequent in elegy, here more specifically describe the expression of jealous feelings and an attempt to establish one's own claims.[38] To be sure, the point in this excerpt is the futility of *querelae* in securing sympathy.[39] The view that jealous retaliations are harmful to the relationship is confirmed by the repeated disappointments both members of the couple experience in the elegiac relationship. Yet though these narrators may seem like poor advisors, their failures are in fact what give them credibility.[40]

The advice of the Ovidian lover/teacher is essentially the same, consisting in the recommendation that the love relationship will be more successful if the lover keeps his suffering to himself. The argument begins at *AA* II.539–40:[41]

---

37. Commentators diverge on how to handle this fragment, either defending its unity (Enk 1962) or suggesting it forms the conclusion to 2.17 (Butler and Barber 1933 and Richardson 1977). For arguments in favor of taking all four fragments as part of a unified poem, see Williams 1980, Nethercut 1980, Hubbard 1986. Contrast Heyworth 2007b, 184–85 who takes the fragments to be separate.

38. On *querelae* and *queror* as terms describing elegiac poetry itself, see Pichon 1902, s.v.

39. *Doleo* and related forms in elegy usually refer specifically to pain from adultery or loss of love.

40. See Sharrock 2005 for some similar ideas about authority in didactic poetry.

41. Cf. also *AA* 2.151–60.

rivalem patienter habe: victoria tecum
  stabit, eris magni victor in Arce Iovis.

Endure a rival with patience. You will attain victory,
  and will be a victor on the citadel of great Jupiter.

The lover, he continues, should ignore it if the mistress writes to another lover (543) and should let her come and go as she likes (544). This narrator is more open than the Propertian *magister* about the gap between the advice and his own practice. He confesses that he does not in fact do any of these things he recommends himself, but admits he has suffered as a result (547–54). He then goes on to explain in more detail the benefits of enduring the disloyalty in silence. If the unfaithful couple is caught, this may only encourage their illicit love (*crescit amor prensis*, 559), a point that he elaborates with the story of Vulcan's entrapment of Venus and Mars, a notorious example of divine adultery.[42] Once the affair is out in the open, all obstacles are removed. Instead of ending the adultery, the trap cleared the way for it to continue. This warning is emphasized again at the conclusion of the passage with another reminder to the lover not to devise any snares for the mistress. He points out that catching a woman in the act is the job of husbands, not lovers (595–600). The responsibility of husbands is the topic of the next set of examples I discuss. In the context of these didactic examples, however, this theme signals another piece of advice, that lovers need to resign themselves to infidelity. As with the earlier recommendation to keep one's jealousy to oneself, the narrators derive their knowledge not from theory, but from their own negative experiences.

In Propertius and Ovid, the recommendation of denial and tolerance in the face of infidelity is a lover's strategy for preserving an erotic relationship. Harping on infidelity will only encourage it all the more. Far better to say nothing if you want the woman to remain yours. The emphasis in both excerpts is directed only against the expression of jealousy, and it is an open question whether, in their role as teachers, the narrators believe that lovers should not even *feel* jealousy. As we shall see below, this is a point they take up directly in the case of negligent husbands.

When Jealousy Is Demanded

Despite the advice we have just seen about keeping one's jealousy to oneself, we also find the lovers criticizing those who ought to feel jealousy, but do not. The problem here is not simply with the expression of jealousy, but rather that

---

42. *Od.* 8.266–332.

the characters in question do not seem even to feel jealousy, however much the situation demands it. I focus on a set of cases not previously studied as a group, so far as I know: Catullus 17, Tibullus 1.6 and 1.9, and Ovid *Amores* 2.19. In these examples, the lovers take a stand against lax husbands, angrily attacking them for ignoring the signs of infidelity.[43] They are furious at the husbands' failure to demand loyalty and sexual exclusivity, things that are fundamental to their own understanding of love.[44] The love poets use this complaint to define their values, despite the fact that their attack on indifferent husbands goes against their own interests in the case at hand. In stressing jealousy's absence, these examples again help clarify who is susceptible to jealousy, in which situations, and for what reasons, in ways that support the three parts of my characterization of jealousy (see Introduction, p. 10).

In the first example, Catullus 17, the narrator scorns a fellow townsman for his blindness towards his young wife's behavior:

> *cui cum sit viridissimo nupta flore puella*
> *et puella tenellulo delicatior haedo,*   15
> *adservanda nigerrimis diligentius uvis,*
> *ludere hanc sinit ut lubet, nec pili facit uni,*
> *nec se sublevat ex sua parte, sed velut alnus*
> *in fossa Liguri iacet suppernata securi,*
> *tantundem omnia sentiens quam si nulla sit usquam;*   20
> *talis iste merus*[45] *stupor nil videt, nihil audit,*
> *ipse qui sit, utrum sit an non sit, id quoque nescit.*

Though he married a girl in the freshest flower of youth,
a girl more pleasing than a very tender kid,
who ought to be watched over more carefully than the ripest grapes,
this girl he lets play as she will and values her not a hair,
nor does he trouble himself on his own account,
but like an alder in a ditch cut down by a Ligurian axe,
perceives everything just as much as if it weren't there at all.
Such is his stupidity, that he sees nothing, hears nothing,
and does not even know what he himself is, whether he is or not.

---

43. Cf. Ovid, *AA* III.613–14 and tolerant husbands in other genres: e.g., Horace, *Odes* 3.6.17–32, *Sat.* 2.5.81–83; Juv. 1.55–57; Tac. *Ann.* 2.85, Suet. *Tib.* 35.2; Plin. *Epist.* 6.31.5, *Pan.* 83.4; *Dig.* 48.5.30. I am grateful to Robert Kaster for mentioning these passages to me in correspondence.

44. Compare what looks like willful ignorance on the part of husband/narrator John Dowell in Ford Madox Ford's *The Good Soldier*.

45. *Merus* is Passerat's excellent emendation for *meus* (cf. Cat. c. 13.9 for the paleographical error). See also Thomson 1997 *ad loc.* in support of the change.

The description of her playfulness, bloom, and fertility emphasize her sexuality, and *ludere ut lubet* in line 17 her unfaithfulness.[46] The fact that her husband allows her (*hanc sinit*, 17) to do this is what angers the narrator.[47] His response is a desire to throw the man in the mud.[48] This expression of violent desire belongs to a tradition of invective and shaming ritual that one scholar has explored in terms of a "Mediterranean poetics of aggression."[49] What is significant for us, though, is not so much the aggression or who exactly is under attack[50] as the distinction posed between husbands and lovers. Those who ought to assert their claim do nothing, while the fiercely possessive lovers, who worry incessantly about threats to the love affair, do not have a legitimate or recognized claim on these women. Jealousy would be justified, yet husbands are unmoved. They have justified claims that are in fact threatened, and they may well recognize both of these facts. But they do not desire to re-establish their rightful claims and thus fail to meet the third condition in my definition. It is this failure that the narrators find maddening and incomprehensible.

In Tibullus 1.6, the narrator derides a husband for not watching his wife carefully. As it turns out, the husband in question is the spouse of the narrator's own mistress. But Delia deceives both her husband *and* her lover with someone new (9–14). The lover rebukes the husband for his willful ignorance:

> *at tu, fallacis coniunx incaute puellae,*   15
>   *me quoque servato, peccet ut illa nihil,*
> *neu iuvenes celebret multo sermone caveto*
>   *neve cubet laxo pectus aperta sinu,*
> *neu te decipiat nutu, digitoque liquorem*
>   *ne trahat et mensae ducat in orbe notas.*[51]   20
> *exibit quam saepe, time, seu visere dicet*
>   *sacra Bonae maribus non adeunda Deae.*

46. On the woman's flirtatiousness, see Quinn 1973 *ad* 15 and 17 and Rudd 1959, 241. Cf. also Khan 1969, 94 on *delicatior haedo* in line 15.

47. Note that the narrator in this poem does not seem to be the woman's lover, as he will be in the other examples below.

48. There has been little consensus on how to interpret this poem: compare Khan 1969, Rudd 1959, Rankin 1968, and more recently the illuminating study by Wray 2001, 135–8.

49. Wray 2001, ch. 4. On Cat. 17 itself, he comments: "The 'Priapic' poem 17, for example, with no other editing than the necessary geographic and cultic alterations, would be perfectly suitable for performance at an Andalusian carnival" (134–5).

50. This is a concern in Chapter 4, where I examine physical attacks in the context of responses to jealousy.

51. Maltby suggests this may be an allusion to Propertius 1.5.16: *et timor informem ducet in ore notam* (Maltby 2002, *ad* 19–20). The parallel is relevant to my discussion of 1.5 in Chapter 5, where I discuss a lover's ability to "read" the evidence of infidelity and jealousy.

> But you, incautious husband of a deceitful wife,
> watch out for me, too, that she commit no sin,
> and take care that she doesn't hang out and chat with young men,
> or recline with her garment loosened and her breast exposed,
> or deceive you with a nod, and dip her finger in the wine
> and trace signs on the round table top.
> Fear how often she goes out, or if she says she wants to visit
> the rites of the Bona Dea which are forbidden to men.

The lover is torn in two. On the one hand, he thinks the husband should be a better watchdog so as to keep out rival lovers. On the other hand, he wants to re-insert himself as the rival, the very kind of person the husband ought to watch out for.[52] He is tortured by the fact that the tricks he has taught Delia to use on her husband have now been used against him, always the adulterer's worry.[53] He is angry at himself but even more so at the husband, who evidently needs advice on how to supervise his wife. The complaint obviously puts the narrator in an awkward position. By teaching the husband how to guard his own wife, he may succeed at warding off current and future rivals, yet at the same time he jeopardizes his own affair. But the key point is the same as before: a real lover would keep a jealous eye on his woman. He would care whether his claims to her attention were honored. This is not selfless or altruistic. It is an affirmation of the lover's credo, and his devotion to the importance of *amor*.

Even more dense is the man who does not even suspect anything in his wife's careful appearance and new skills in lovemaking (Tibullus 1.9.65–74):[54]

> at tua perdidicit: nec tu, stultissime, sentis,   65
>> cum tibi non solita corpus ab arte movet.
> tune putas illam pro te disponere crines
>> aut tenues denso pectere dente comas?
> istane persuadet facies, auroque lacertos
>> vinciat et Tyrio prodeat apta sinu?   70
> non tibi sed iuveni cuidam vult bella videri,
>> devoveat pro quo remque domumque tuam.

52. See Lee-Stecum 1998, 190 on the power play in this poem between the poet and the *vir/coniunx* as well as other rivals.

53. Cf. also Tib. 1.2.53–64 and 1.5.69–70. See also the adulterer/narrator's acknowledgement of this problem in Graham Greene's *The End of the Affair*: "Henry's blinkers were firmly tied. I had hated his blinkers even when I had benefited from them, knowing that others could benefit too" (9).

54. This elegy forms a close pair with 1.8, though here I am interested in its relation to 1.6 and the other poems about negligent spouses. On the pair, cf. Booth 1996 and James 2003a, 10. James also points to the jealousy in *Am.* 1.9.

> *nec facit hoc vitio, sed corpora foeda podagra*
> *et senis amplexus culta puella fugit.*

> But your wife has become an expert, and yet you, idiot,
> sense nothing when she moves her body with new skill.
> Do you think that it is for you that she styles her hair
> or combs her fine locks with a close-toothed comb?
> Is it your lovely appearance that persuades her to fasten gold to
> her arms and go forth adorned in Tyrian garments?
> She wants to look beautiful not for you, but for a certain youth
> for whom she curses your property and home.
> Nor does she do this from moral failing, but the elegant girl
> flees a body repellent with gout and the embrace of an old man.

The repetition of "s" in *sentis* and especially *stultissime* in line 65 draws attention to the man's obtuseness. The lover condemns the fool for his complete lack of suspicion: how can he not notice any of the changes in his wife or manage to consider himself desirable, old and ugly as he is? Here again the lover has personal reasons to wish the man would feel a little jealousy and take some action, for the wife has become involved with the lover's male lover, Marathus. The complaint makes more sense this time, since it seems designed to punish a wayward lover or to preserve a relationship rather than to do something that directly threatens it.[55] Nevertheless, this poem fits the self-undermining pattern of the others in which a lover whose lifestyle depends upon the deception of husbands condemns a husband for letting himself be deceived.[56]

Finally, in a twist on the theme of the ignorant husband, Ovid *Amores* 2.19 complains about a husband who is too lax with his wife, because the lack of an obstacle dulls his own passion:

> *Si tibi non opus est servata, stulte, puella,*   1
>   *at mihi fac serves, quo magis ipse velim.*
> *quod licet, ingratum est; quod non licet, acrius urit:*
>   *ferreus est, si quis, quod sinit alter, amat.*
> .
> .
> .

---

55. See Booth 1996, who emphasizes that Tibullus is not being "benevolent" here but is rather trying to win Marathus back, however unsuccessfully.

56. See also Lee-Stecum 1998 on the use of *foedera* in this poem, esp. p. 263: "the processes, pacts, and exchanges (*foedera*) which function in other spheres of society, which bring stability and which the poet seems to desire, are seen in this poem to break down entirely." This point will be relevant to my discussion of *fides* in Chapter 6 as well.

> ... *speravi saepe futurum,*   49
>   *cum bene servasses, ut bene verba darem.*
> *lentus es et pateris nulli patienda marito;*[57]
>   *at mihi concessi finis amoris erit.*

> If, fool, you have no need of guarding your wife for yourself,
>   see that you watch her for me, so that I might want her all the more.
> What is allowed is unwelcome, what is not, burns more sharply.
> He is iron-hearted, who loves what another concedes.
>
>   .
>
>   .
>
>   .
>
> ... I have often hoped the time would come
>   when you would guard her well, so that I might deceive you well.
> You are slow and endure what should be endured by no husband.
> But your agreeableness will be the end of my love.

Ovid is explicit to the point of parody. Love that is easy is less desirable. The lover warns the husband that unless he begins to pay a bit more attention to the evening visitors, the lover's relationship with his wife is over. What this man endures is not normal; a husband in his position *ought* to feel jealous at knocks at the door, dogs barking in the night, slave-girls bringing and taking away tablets, and his wife choosing to sleep apart (37–42). In a playful reversal of the *topos* in which lovers are unwillingly kept away from their mistresses, the lover actually begs to have the usual obstacles back.[58] While Ovid humorously exaggerates a tradition in the other elegists, he also defines as standard the desire to fight for one's claims to another's attention and to protect the integrity of these claims.

By attacking these husbands, the narrators have chosen a very surprising target of criticism. Elegiac poetry is predicated on an illicit and unfulfilled relationship, one that often centers on the narrator's affair with a married woman.[59] This association depends entirely on deceiving the woman's husband and keeping other would-be intruders at bay. Any effort to keep husbands and wives together is directly counterproductive to the narrators' own relationships, which depend

---

57. See McKeown 1998, *ad loc.* on *patientia* ("a condition recognized by law"). McKeown 1998 and Maltby 2002 (*ad* Tib.1.6.15–6) also note similarities between *Am.* 19 and Tib. 1.6, discussed above (e.g., *opus est*, 1.6.33; *fac serves*, 1.6.33-4).

58. McKeown 1989, 408 discusses the lover's desire for obstacles here and suggests there may be a connection with the *renuntiatio amoris* theme, though with a twist. Instead of a farewell to the mistress (as at the end of Propertius' third book), here Ovid wants the husband to say farewell to his wife.

59. Cf. Konstan 1994, 150–9 on the misconception that the relationships in elegy are all adulterous. James 2003a also emphasizes that the mistress is not always or necessarily someone else's wife, but frequently an unattached woman like a comedic courtesan in need of a financial sponsor.

on the ignorance or tolerance of such husbands. Many poems teach precisely how to avoid the notice of the beloved's spouse.

These reprimands are useful to the narrators for justifying their own claims and sense of entitlement. The similarities among them suggest that they might derive from a scene-type of the sort that would have been familiar from comedy or mime, one in which a cuckolded husband is the butt of jokes and mockery.[60] Yet the focus of the elegiac examples is very different. The narrators address the husband directly, but they emphasize not shame or humiliation so much as indignation and self-justification, contrasting the husbands' apathy with their own more deserving love. The principal emphasis is not on any sexual inadequacy, but rather an inadequate understanding of what love requires. They represent the lovers' recognition that they have no legal claim to the women in their lives, despite the seriousness of their own affections. They use this difference as a way to illustrate their own claim. The husbands' lack of jealousy is taken as telltale evidence of everything that is missing in them, but abundant in the lover. In the end, they believe, this is what makes the husbands undeserving of their wives' love, while they show themselves to be far more deserving, a superior stance familiar from Chapter 1. Paradoxically, jealousy would not exist without the marriage bond in the first place: elegiac love depends on marriage at the same time that it despises it. It is perhaps to justify such feelings of hatred that lovers attempt to project their own jealousy onto the husbands.

Husbands who fail to exhibit jealousy in such circumstances taint the name of marriage and love. Elsewhere in Roman love poetry, the imagery of weddings and marriage is co-opted by the narrators to describe the poets' own relationships, as if to reclaim the symbolism of the everlasting bond for their own romantic arrangements.[61] If these husbands cannot be roused to feel indignation or concern at spousal infidelity, then they do not deserve the wives as much as the narrators do.[62] Lovers feel all the possessiveness and jealousy over the beloved, yet they must endure the fact that their claim of possession is unsupportable. They are outraged about the husbands' lack of feeling: without jealousy, there can be no real love.[63] To their minds, jealousy per se is not a sign of vulnerability, nor

60. On *Amores* 2.19, see McKeown 1998, 406–33. On mime, cf. Reynolds 1946, McKeown 1979, and Fantham 1989, with further bibliography in Fantham.

61. Cf. e.g., Catullus c. 68.70–2 and 131ff., where the narrator compares his relationship with Lesbia to the marriage of Protesilaus and Laodamia (see Macleod 1974). In Catullus and Propertius, marital vocabulary and the expectation of fidelity are also applied to the non-marital relationship: cf. e.g, Propertius 2.6.41–2 and 3.20. On this, see James 2003a, 42ff.

62. Perhaps the most blatant case of a husband's stupidity is Menelaus, who went off leaving his wife, just the most beautiful woman in Greece, alone with another man (see Ovid, *AA* 2.359ff). In the love letter Ovid has him write to Helen (*Her.* 16.299–316), Paris concludes that Menelaus must not have appreciated what he had (309–10): *nec, si bona magna putaret/quae tenet, externo crederet illa viro.*

63. See Alcestis' aria to Jealousy in Act 2 of Handel's *Admeto*, where she is identified with the fury Alecto: "Gelosia, spietata Aletto . . . chi non prova il tuo veleno, nò, non sa, che cosa è amor."

is it anything to feel guilty about. It is evidence that they care about being entitled to certain special attentions and seeing that those claims are protected. If
this attack on indifferent husbands resonates with other claims about elegiac
love and its lifestyle, it is also important to observe to what extent it intersects
with other cultural attitudes that we find in philosophy and Augustan legislation
about marriage and adultery. I begin with the allusions to philosophy.

In these examples about lackadaisical husbands, we find another inversion of
the philosophical argumentation that we saw in the attitudes towards love as a
disease in Chapter 1. In two of the examples above (Tib. 1.9, *Amores* 2.19), the
lovers refer to husbands using forms of *stultus*.[64] Perhaps this label fits the husband in Catullus 17 as well even though the term is not applied here, since he is
described as someone who is as dense and unperceiving as a log.[65] The Stoics
use *stultus* or its equivalents to refer to the person who has not achieved true
wisdom—in other words, someone who makes poor choices that conflict with
the way things truly are and ought to be, and someone who experiences emotions that should instead be excised and removed.[66] In the case of elegy, by contrast, lovers apply the term *stultus* to the person who feels *no* emotion, implying
that the person who responds emotionally is the *sapiens*. In their view, jealousy
is called for when a loved one has been unfaithful.[67] The adoption of Stoic terminology for precisely opposite ends amounts to a strong denunciation. The elegiac narrators respond to the philosophers' antagonism towards love, and the
emotions generally, by using and undermining the latter's very own arguments,
something we have seen with the metaphor of love as illness.[68] Their own involvement in love, as lovers, teachers, and readers, puts them in a stronger position than someone who claims to understand it from a distant and theoretical
position.

64. There are actually three examples in all, since *stultus* appears twice in *Amores* 2.19 (the second
time at line 46).

65. Putnam 1973 well compares Tib. 1.9.66, noting the use of *stultus* there for "duped lover." Cf.
also the oblivious husband (*fatuus*) in Catullus 83.2.

66. The Greek terms are *ho sophos* and *ho phaulos* or *aphron*; in Latin we find *sapiens* and *stultus*,
ineptus or *insipiens*. For Ciceronian usage, cf. *De Fin.* 1.57, 1.61, 3.60, and *Tusc. Disp.* 4.6.12, 14, 5.18.54.
In Seneca, cf. the index in Inwood 2005 s.v. "sage" and "non-sage." *Stultus* does not seem to be used in
this technical sense elsewhere in elegy, though we find it and related forms, together with *sapiens*, used
frequently in Horace's *Satires* (cf. e.g., I.3.24, 124, 127, 128, 132, 140; I.4.115; II.1.17; II.7.83).

67. The use of *stultus* in Propertius 2.34 is somewhat more complicated, for there the term is
applied not to the one who feels no emotion, but to the lover himself for his obsessive jealousy:
stultus, quod stulto saepe timore tremo (20). But this example, too, may involve a crucial inversion, as
I discuss in Chapter 5.

68. The love poets may not have in mind a specific philosophical school here. Cairns 2004 thinks
that Propertius may have Epicurean morality in mind in 2.34, but the opposition between the *stultus*
and the *sapiens* is most pronounced, notoriously, in Stoicism, where nearly all of humanity is held to
be in the condition of the *stultus*. For our purposes, the most important point is the general contrast
with a philosophically rigorous moral ideal.

A second inversion emerges in the ways in which certain features of these poems concur with elements of the Augustan legislation on marriage and adultery. Even though both laws are subsequent to the publication of elegiac poetry, the ideas contained in them were probably in the air at the time the elegists were writing.[69] The adultery law, the *lex Julia de adulteriis coercendis* (18–16 BCE) aimed to control both male and female sexual behavior, though there was greater emphasis on female adultery, the issue in the examples at hand. Both a wife and her lover, when caught, were subject to punishment.[70] But it was also possible for a husband to be liable, if, that is, he knowingly kept silent about his wife's illicit behavior.[71] According to the law, a husband who knew about his wife's infidelity needed to respond within sixty days, or else he himself could be punished, perhaps including being charged with *lenocinium*, or pimping.[72]

Superficially, the narrators' criticism of the husbands resembles the legislation, for both the poems we have been looking at and the laws encourage men to keep a better watch over their wives. The goal of each critique, however, is quite different. There is little consensus on whether the aims of the legislation were primarily moralistic or political (to boost the number of upper-class). But whatever motives inspired them, the laws directly attempt to curb adulterous relationships, and the marriage law, issued at the same time, had a similar aim, even if more positively expressed. The *lex Julia de maritandis ordinibus*, later supplemented by the *lex Papia Poppaea* in 9 CE, encouraged legitimate marriage and children by means of economic benefits, with corresponding penalties for anyone who failed to make the appropriate marriage. The elegiac narrators, however, reprimand spouses because they fail to act as loving husbands should, that is to devote themselves to passion rather than complacency.[73] It is a complaint about erotic commitment rather than an attempt to rebuild the noble Roman family or dissolute morals. Thus the narrators argue in a way reminiscent of the marriage and adultery legislation only to turn the argument in favor of the

69. Cf. e.g., Cic. *Pro Marcello* 23: . . . *comprimendae libidines, propaganda suboles*, Dio 43.25.2, and Hor. *Odes* 3.6 and 3.24. Livy also proposes the need for reform in his preface, and Sulla had earlier enacted laws on marriage (Plut., *Comp. Lys. Et Sullae*). On the existence of such laws earlier than 18 BCE, see Treggiari 1991, 277 and Raditsa 1980, 295–6. For a recent treatments of the legislation, see McGinn 2003, esp. chs. 5 and 6, and Milnor 2007, 150–54.

70. See the thorough treatment by Treggiari 1991, 277–98, with further bibliography cited in her n. 84.

71. Edwards 1993 suggests that the upper classes wanted to avoid "violent revenge," which they would have regarded as "uncivilized and inappropriate" (56).

72. Cf. Richlin 1981, 386–7, Cohen 1991, and now Langlands 2006, esp. 20–1. On the use of legal terminology more generally in the elegists, see Keith 2008, 40–3 and Gebhardt 2009.

73. Both McKeown and Booth suggest that in Ovid's case there is also mockery of the laws: cf. McKeown 1998, 407 and 433 on 2.19.60 and 3.14, and Booth 1991, 39, where she suggests that the Ovidian narrator in *Amores* 2.5 poses as a married man giving evidence about his wife's infidelity.

priorities of sentiment and attachment. No matter how we understand the intentions of the legislation, it straightforwardly prioritized marriage and punished adultery. Yet for the elegiac narrators, husbands who fail to protect their
wives' fidelity are proof that true feeling should stand *above* marital love.

Conclusions

Jealousy in elegy demands a belief in one's expectations of special attentions, a
belief that these claims are threatened, and a desire to reassert them. The third
part of the definition is what makes the elegiac lovers worthy of the claims in the
first part. Husbands who do not bother to draw on their claims as lawful spouses
undermine their rights. The examples we have examined in this chapter illustrate the ways in which jealousy is not a sign of vulnerability or shame—though
this dimension will surface in subsequent chapters—but rather an essential feature of the lovers' principles, as we saw in the case of lovesickness as well. The
narrators may recommend suppressing such feelings for the purposes of maintaining a relationship, but this advice seems to concern only the expression of
jealousy, not the feeling itself. In other respects, the manifestation of jealousy
highlights the ways in which elegiac love surpasses any legal or nominal claims
to possession, including a philosophical understanding of the emotions.

We have also seen the ways in which jealous figures identify and compete
with other roles as a way of exploring and adopting other points of view. This is
true not only of other characters within elegy but also with other authorities
who purport to set rules concerning the practice of love. The elegiac narrators
claim to possess something that others who talk about love cannot: vast experience. They are *experts*, competing with other apparent experts on the subject of
love.[74] And their method of repudiation is to pick up and invert their opponents'
claims. This strategy has a parallel in Lucretius' technique in the *De Rerum Natura*
where, as we saw in Chapter 1, Lucretius uses the tropes of erotic poetry to show
up the foolishness of lovers, incorporating lines reminiscent of Catullus into his
own argument so as to disprove misconceptions about love.

Like Lucretius, the elegiac narrator adopts his opponent's language for the
purposes of refutation. The incorporation of specific terminology both identifies
the substance of the debate and gives the dismissal greater force. The linguistic
inversion is both direct and simple, requiring no skills in argumentation to
understand the point. In her book on Propertius' fourth book of poetry, Jeri

---

74. See Sharrock 2005, 261 on Ovid's didactic presentation by way of a contrast with Horace:
"Horace is generally willing to admit to faults, for various rhetorical purposes . . . But even Horace
does not make explicit claims of experience of past failure which authorise his present (understated)
instruction." See also the excellent discussion by Brunelle 2005 on Ovid as satirist.

DeBrohun suggests that the poet "favors dramatization over exposition as his method of presentation"—that is, allusion to what would have been familiar language, imagery, and *topoi* of a given source, instead of naming it outright.[75] This method of allusion is not limited to poetic sources: it is the same phenomenon we find with the terminology of disease and health, and of the wise man and the fool, as well as contemporary attitudes towards controlling love and marriage. In these cases, however, the elegiac narrators refer to philosophical arguments and aspects of moral legislation not to signal their allegiances, but with the goal of making opposing claims. Elegiac narrators may not assign names to their adversaries, yet the vocabulary and imagery they adopt in the poems discussed here point to specific sources and rivals of love, though this time of a professional rather than erotic sort.

75. See DeBrohun 2003, 2 on Propertius' discreet allusion to his sources.

3

The Triggers of Jealousy

Suspicions and Evidence

From the general cases we have just examined, I turn now to take a more detailed look at the experience of elegiac jealousy, examining first what sparks it and then how lovers respond to it once it has been aroused. A temporal study of these two main stages of jealousy, not unlike the categories of "primary and secondary appraisal" used by Lazarus and Folkman, has the advantage of highlighting the importance of the senses and the role of violence.[1] In this chapter, I focus on the first stage and the triggers of jealousy, in particular the role of seeing and hearing. Like the white handkerchief that Othello takes as a sign of the loss of Desdemona's fidelity or the passionate performances of the Kreutzer Sonata in Tolstoy's story of the same name, elegiac lovers often take a visual or aural detail as evidence of a rival, and this provokes their first sensations of jealousy.[2]

Several recent studies have explored the role of visualization and the gaze in Roman literature, for example Salzman-Mitchell's book on Ovid's *Metamorphoses* and a number of articles in the volume of Ancona and Greene on love elegy.[3] It is not suprising that the focus in these works is love poetry, where we often read about the intense scrutiny of a beloved. This new work is important in reversing some of the assumptions about the male gaze, showing the extent to which poets represent the female beloved as maintaining some control over the gaze as well. Yet this approach still concentrates on seeing as a form of desire and possession. I will be emphasizing a different element

1. Lazarus and Folkman 1984, where "primary appraisals" are judgments that one has suffered some kind of harm or threat, and "secondary appraisals" involve judgments about what can be done about it.

2. For modern examples of the role of the visual in stimulating jealousy, see e.g., Shakespeare's sonnets 61 and 139, the role of a photograph in Maupassant's *Pierre and Jean* and Machado da Assis' *Dom Casmurro*, or the swimming clothes in David Grossman's *Her Body Knows*.

3. Salzman-Mitchell 2005, Ancona and Greene 2005, Part II: The Gaze. On the eroticization of the gaze, see most recently Bartsch 2006, esp. 67–83. For other recent works on the role of the gaze, see Fredrick 2002 and Morales 2005.

here, for in cases of elegiac jealousy, watching or fantasizing about a beloved is not so much a reflection of desire as an indication of suspicions and fear. Whether we speak about hearing a rumor, seeing a beloved in new clothes, looking at the beloved talking to a rival, or following the path of the lover's gaze, hearing and seeing in elegy do not so much point to erotic desire— though they are often taken this way—as convey unsettling realizations that lead to jealousy.

The interpretation of sensory evidence is not the same for both male and female characters, however. When the male narrator is not reporting her point of view (as was the case in the examples in Chapter 2), the female lover tends to view the evidence provided by the senses with hesitation and disbe-lief. She is skeptical about the lover's infidelity and does not immediately draw conclusions based on what she has seen or heard. In the end, her jealousy will emerge, but only when there has been such an accumulation of evidence that she can no longer ignore it. By contrast, the male lover needs no confirmation of what he sees or hears: he takes it to be the truth without a moment's doubt.[4] Though sight is usually prized as the most reliable of the senses, for the male lover there is no better or worse perceptive power: everything confirms what he already knows.[5] The following description by Mele, though written about contemporary jealousy, captures something essential about the elegiac lover's attitude:

> . . . can our insecure man's jealousy regarding his wife render his ap-parent evidence that she is having an affair significantly more vivid than it would otherwise be, and render his competing evidence pallid by comparison? Can his jealousy lead him to focus his attention on rare memories of a seemingly flirtatious or secretive wife at the expense of attention to competing memories that an impartial spec-tator would regard as much more telling? Might he entertain the hy-pothesis that his wife is having an affair largely because he is jealous, thus unintentionally setting the stage for an operation of the confir-mation bias that increases the probability of his believing her to be unfaithful?[6]

---

4. I contrast male and female behavior in the next chapter as well. Sociological research on jealousy often addresses gender difference: cf. Harris and Christenfeld 1996 and Buunk et al. 1996.

5. On the superiority of sight over hearing, see Most 2005, ch. 1 on "Seeing and Believing," and Bartsch 2006, 45.

6. Mele 2001, 98–99. See also de Sousa 1987: "For a variable but always limited time, an emotion limits the range of information that the organism will take into account, the inferences actually drawn from a potential infinity, and the set of live options among which it will choose" (195).

The male lover does not derive conclusions from what he sees; he seeks the evidence he needs to substantiate his conclusions. There is no room for questions or doubt: his effort is not to understand but to confirm.[7]

This hasty rush to judgment on the part of the male lover marks a substantial change from the position of mastery and control we saw in Chapters 1 and 2. There the narrator presented himself as an authority on love and jealousy, on when and how to display them, even claiming to be able to help others cope with these difficult emotions. The evidence in this and subsequent chapters offers a different picture, however, one in which that authoritative figure has been replaced by someone who is impulsive, paranoid, and desperate for attention.

Female Skepticism

I begin with three poems presented as if from a woman's own voice, Ovid *Heroides* 5 and 6 and Propertius 4.3, cases in which a female lover sees or hears something that is compromising about her male lover. We have far fewer examples of the mistress' response to jealous triggers, as elegiac poetry centers mainly on the male lover's own experience, and with the exception of Ovid's *Heroides*, the poets seem less interested in exploring the female perspective. Yet perhaps because of the length and form of these examples, they do nonetheless provide informative descriptions of both jealous triggers and the process of registering their significance. As we shall see, elegiac women resist the implication of the evidence, coming up instead with alternative explanations or demands for further proof, even though in the end they finally give way to jealous feelings.

In the first example, *Heroides* 5, Oenone writes to Paris just after his return to Troy with Helen.[8] She gives a lengthy description of what she saw as his ship drew into the shore. Her difficulty in taking in the sight of him all at once stems in part from the distance of his ship, of course, but also from a psychological unwillingness to accept what she sees. Oenone relates only one piece of information at a time, a gradual unveiling of a truth that she would have preferred not to see or understand.[9]

---

7 . It is worth comparing the male lover's confidence about his perceptions with what the Stoics called the "cataleptic condition"; see Nussbaum 1990, 265. The connection between sight and understanding and knowledge is also important for Lucretius and Plato (on the latter, see Gosling 1973, ch. 8 on "Knowledge as Vision").

8 . All quotations of the *Heroides* are taken from Knox 1995.

9 . Of course this method of gradual revelation also slows down the pace of the narrative and increases the suspense. Knox 1995, 141 points out that Ovid does not depict Oenone as possessing the gift of prophecy which she has elsewhere, so that she (like Paris) is ignorant of the future. But see also Medea's hesitancy in putting together what a chant of Hymen and the sight of blazing torches mean about Jason (*Her.* 12.137–59).

She describes her initial glimpse of this ship from her vantage point on a mountain overlooking the sea (63–8):

> hinc ego vela tuae cognovi prima carinae,
>> et mihi per fluctus impetus ire fuit.
> dum moror, in summa fulsit mihi purpura prora.   65
>> pertimui: cultus non erat ille tuus.
> fit proprior terrasque cita ratis attigit aura;
>> femineas vidi corde tremente genas.

From here I first recognized the sails of your ship,
and my inclination was to jump into the waves.
While I hesitated, purple gleamed at me from the front of the boat.
I was terrified: this was not your usual dress.
The boat came closer and touched shore because of the swift wind.
I saw with trembling heart a woman's face.

After detecting the ship, she notes his purple clothing. However much their bright color is responsible for attracting her attention, the garments also catch her eye because of the change they mark from his usual shepherd's clothing: *cultus non erat ille tuus*, 66.[10] In returning with Helen from Sparta, Paris has changed: his pastoral identity now gone, he has become urbanized, a lover of foreign, glamorous women, the same fate that will befall his fellow Trojan Aeneas under the influence of Dido (cf. e.g. *Aeneid* 4.261–4). For Oenone, Paris' colorful clothes symbolize his transferred allegiances. More than a sign of identity, they are a manifestation of his recent behavior.

But the next details cause fear and a rapid heartbeat: she catches a glimpse of Helen's face, a sight that leaves her little room for hope.[11] Oenone has the jealous lover's watchfulness and attention to visual clues. But she takes a while to put it all together: she does not immediately articulate the significance of seeing Helen, as she seems unable to admit to herself what the evidence amounts to. But when Oenone perceives that Helen is not just standing near Paris but actually in his embrace, she can no longer ignore the evidence of her desertion. Her jealousy flares up in full force (69–74):

> non satis id fuerat? quid enim furiosa morabar?
>> haerebat gremio turpis amica tuo!   70

---

10 . See Knox 1995 *ad* 66.

11 . Note also how she harps on the difference in status between Paris and Helen, on which see Jacobson 1974, 180–82. Status is always a sensitive issue for the jealous figure. Paris makes use of his status in a more positive way to argue that Helen should not be ashamed to marry him (*Her.* 16.51–2, 173–88).

tunc vero rupique sinus et pectora planxi
  et secui madidas ungue rigente genas,
implevique sacram querulis ululatibus Iden.
  illuc has lacrimas in mea saxa tuli.

Wasn't that enough? Why was I so mad as to hang around?
Your shameful girlfriend was clinging to your embrace!
Then truly I tore my breast and beat my chest
and cut my damp cheeks with sharpened nail.
I filled sacred Ida with my mournful cries.
I have brought these tears to my familiar rocks.

Oenone rages and mourns as she must finally admit the loss of Paris' affections to another. These suspicions may seem more securely founded than those of Arethusa, whose case I address next, but in effect the anxiety of both women feeds off altered appearances and the fear that this means altered affections as well. Unlike the cases of male jealousy we will see shortly, Oenone does not give in to isolated signs of infidelity, however much she suspects what they imply. The unpleasantness of the truth makes her hold on for as long as she can to the belief that her lover has been faithful to her.

We find the next example of female jealousy in Propertius 4.3, where Arethusa's jealous fears are revealed in the letter she writes to her soldier husband, Lycotas.[12] An elegiac-style lament is transferred to a warlike context as Lycotas, probably a mercenary soldier, is imagined in a variety of places defending Rome from the enemy and insurgents.[13] And imagination is the operative word, as the visual evidence that leads to jealous fears is supplied in this case entirely by fantasy and imagination. Yet even though Arethusa herself is responsible for creating the suspicious data, she hesitates over each element as if she cannot accept its implications.

Arethusa begins by pointing to their separation as the cause for her unhappiness (cf. 2, 11–2, and *passim*) and dwells on Lycotas' physical condition. The first image is triggered by her attempt to picture him in military dress, ready to face the enemy on the battlefield.[14] She worries first that his armor could be causing him discomfort (23–8):

12 . On the relative dating of this poem and the *Heroides*, cf. Hutchinson 2006 on Prop. 4.3.

13 . Lycotas is supposedly in central Asia, Thrace, and India. Hutchinson 2006, 101 suggests that "Lycotas is most likely to be envisaged as an equestrian officer, who goes off on a series of separate campaigns, each on a kind of short-term contract."

14 . Note that she refers to her own clothing as well (51–2), fancy clothes that she says she now has no reason to wear. But perhaps we should see this as her attempt to frighten him into thinking he may have a rival, too.

dic mihi, num teneros urit lorica lacertos?
  num gravis imbellis atterit hasta manus?
haec noceant potius, quam dentibus ulla puella   25
  det mihi plorandas per tua colla notas!
diceris et macie vultum tenuasse: sed opto
  e desiderio sit color iste meo.

Tell me, doesn't the breastplate burn your tender arms?
Doesn't the heavy sword tear the skin on your unwarlike hands?
I'd rather these things hurt you than that a girl make love bites on your
neck, marks for me to weep over!
They say your face has grown thinner, but I hope
this paleness of yours stems from desire for me.

Rather than viewing his sword and breastplate as elements of protection, Arethusa sees them as signs of vulnerability.[15] A more natural fear on her part, concern over the danger Lycotas endures in wartime, is subordinated to the thought of his torn skin, maybe from the clothes, or maybe from the love marks of a rival.[16] One thought leads to another: from his armor, to marks on his skin, to sexual contact. Pain and distress consume her as she hesitates over whether or not to succumb to the possibility that he has been unfaithful to her (cf. *plorandos* in 26 and her insistent questions in 23–4).

    Their separation creates the need to generate images of him. But rather than supplying a presence or any kind of reassurance, the pictures she creates only emphasize his absence and change. So Arethusa's attempt to see him in military dress leads her to a fantasy of him in a new relationship. Her efforts to imagine his location on a map (35–40) reveals how little she now knows about his whereabouts. Imagining Lycotas in unfamiliar dress leads to fantasies about his infidelity, in much the same way as transforming a sleeping Cynthia into various mythological figures in 1.3 led to fears of a rival. The loss of familiarity brought on by a changed appearance leads unavoidably to one conclusion. Yet Arethusa, like Oenone, relates the steps leading towards her "realization" of his infidelity individually and slowly, as if she were unable grasp or accept the news all at once.

    When we turn to evidence supplied by another sense, hearing, we find that women show the same skepticism we have seen in the case of visual evidence.

15 . The significance of clothing is especially emphasized in this poem: cf. 18, 23, 33–4, 51–2, 64. On dressing and cross-dressing in Book 4, cf. Lindheim 1988 and DeBrohun 2003. For a discussion of the role of clothing in Roman society more generally, see Sebesta and Bonfante 1994 and Edmonson and Keith 2008, and on women's dress and its relevance to moral issues, see Olson 2008, esp. ch. 3.
16 . Note that when she does mention the dangers he undergoes, she describes the anxiety of the nurse rather than her own (41–2). Her real worry is not about the threat of war, but the possibility of another woman.

Ovid's *Heroides* 6 illustrates the difficulty in accepting news of infidelity via rumor, though it, too, is a rare example of female response to jealous triggers. Typically when rumors circulate about the male lover, the mistress barely has an opportunity to respond to them before the narrator rushes to defend himself or divert attention from the damaging report. In Propertius 3.15, for example, the entire poem is a defense of the narrator's behavior after a rumor about him has reached Cynthia's ears. Likewise in Propertius 2.21, the narrator was the subject of a nasty report by Panthus in which Cynthia presumably learned some unsavory details about infidelity. But the topic quickly turns away from the male lover's behavior to the way in which Cynthia herself has become the subject of gossip (*tu sermo es*, 7).[17] Male narrators give just enough information to arouse the reader's suspicions about their behavior, then move on without answering the doubts they have raised. I suggest below that these intimations are not actual clues about the male lover's infidelity but rather part of a deliberate strategy to provoke the mistress' jealousy. Since rumors are so effective at arousing his own jealousy, he tries the same thing on her, often in the very same poem in which he admits he has heard rumors about her faithlessness.

Even if it is not a typical example, *Heroides* 6 nonetheless offers an extended glimpse of one woman's reaction to a rumor about her lover. In this letter, sent by Hypsipyle to Jason, the information that Jason has a new woman is first conveyed through rumor and later confirmed by a messenger.[18] It bothers Hypsipyle that the news comes via a rumor rather than a letter from Jason (*cur mihi fama prior quam littera nuntia venit*, 9). The report might have been bad either way, but at least she could be sure that it was true if it came from Jason's own hand. Hypsipyle implies by her reaction that a rumor is so untrustworthy that she does not know whether to believe it or not.

The rumor tells of the *aristeia* of the bulls and worse, the fact that Jason is now involved with a "barbarian witch" (19–20). Hypsipyle has definite expectations about the attentions she should receive and believes that only one woman can have Jason's affection. Her first inclination is to hope that she has made a mistake by believing this story (*credula res amor est*, 21). To this effect, she couches all the language referring to Medea as second-hand information, distancing the report and leaving the truth of it still undetermined in her mind. Hypsipyle's disinclination to believe what she has heard recalls the unwillingness of Oenone to accept what is present before her eyes.

But what Hypsipyle has first learned by rumor is later repeated by a Thessalian visitor, and with his arrival at her gates (23–4), the truth is harder to

17 . I return to this elegy later in the chapter.

18 . See Jacobson 1974, 104 and Verducci 1985, 66. Jacobson points out the emphasis on rumor throughout the letter: *fama*, 9; *narratur*, 19; *narrat*, 32, 39; *diceris*, 132 (p. 99).

ignore.[19] At the mere mention of Medea, for whom she is now supposed to relinquish her place, physical symptoms of jealousy arise: *cor dolet, atque ira mixtus abundat amor*, 76. Yet though Hypsipyle must have known the bad news was coming, she cannot help herself from doggedly questioning the messenger, so great is her need to delay full acceptance of the rumor's significance. She completes her letter by wishing upon Medea the same woes that she now suffers from, and worse, predicting the part of the myth told in Euripides' *Medea* (lines 155–64). This vengeful wish is in keeping with the pattern I explore in the next chapter, where female jealousy often leads to anger and revenge.

Female characters are represented as sensitive to visual and aural evidence, scrutinizing it for accuracy and meaning. They are susceptible to jealousy, then, but they are not predisposed to it. A case like Arethusa's may seem to suggest otherwise, given the way in which she herself creates the evidence that furnishes her suspicions. Yet as in the other cases we have seen, not one but many pieces of evidence are necessary to convince her that she has been betrayed. These examples of women who believe in their men may reflect a kind of wishful thinking we see elsewhere in love elegy: male lovers want to convince themselves and others that their mistresses love them, that they are not to blame for any trouble in the relationship. Thus the portrait of a mistress who refrains from jealousy may be just as self-serving as that of a mistress who is wild with jealousy, as we saw in Chapter 2.[20] In the examples I consider both here and in Chapter 4, the depiction of jealous women is consistently antithetical to that of jealous men. While women are represented as suspicious and wary of sensory evidence, men are painted as rash and paranoid. In the next chapter on violent responses, however, it is the other way around: men are depicted as hesitant and restrained, with women lashing out at the slightest provocation. The narrator offers an asymmetric picture of male and female experiences of jealousy with the goal of demonstrating his deeper understanding of love and strength of will. Yet the convenience of this representation is not difficult to detect.

Male Credulity

Female characters are not the only ones whose jealousy is triggered by visual and auditory evidence. For male lovers, new clothes and rumors again prove to be frequent provocations to jealousy, but there are some new causes as well, such as

19 . See a similar confirmation by a visit in *Her*. 9. At the opening of her letter to Hercules, Deianira says that a rumor has spread to all the Pelasgian cities that Hercules has been made captive by Iole (3–6). Later (119–24) she admits she could have disregarded what she heard with her ears, but not what she saw with her eyes: Hercules' actual return with Iole.

20 . Indeed, the point of stories like of Procris and Cephalus in *Ars Amatoria* 3, discussed in Chapter 5, is to teach other women not to be suspicious.

cosmetics and even the actual sighting of rivals. As already mentioned, male lovers seem to have no difficulty in believing the signs of infidelity: they never assume that an effort to look nice was done for the lover himself, they never doubt the source of funds for a new dress. In the examples that follow, then, we find little of the more skeptical process that was apparent in the previous section. However painful jealous thoughts are, the male lover accepts the evidence for them without the slightest hesitation and never questions whether what he sees or hears is actually true.

Ovid *Amores* 2.5 provides one of the most vivid examples of the male lover's inclination to believe that he is being deceived. This elegy describes a dinner party at which the narrator finds himself in a position to observe his girlfriend and a rival flirt and kiss while they thought he was sleeping. As the narrator sneaks glances through supposedly closed eyes, he sees them exchange signs that he believes can only mean one thing. To begin with, the narrator's girlfriend and rival "spoke" meaningfully to each other with their brows, nods of the head, looks in their eyes, and letters traced in wine on the table (lines 15–20). Actual speech, too, contained hidden messages of love. Finally, the narrator witnessed their not-so-innocent kisses (25–6):

> *qualia non fratri tulerit germana severo,*
> *sed tulerit cupido mollis amica viro.*

> Not the kind (of kisses) a sister might give to her strict brother,
> but the kind an encouraging girlfriend would offer her eager lover.

The male lover takes every visual clue as corroborating what he already suspects. He includes a possible objection—could the two be related?—but dismisses it at once in order to conclude that the kisses are passionate. There is never any real doubt about what the *puella* is up to, at least insofar as the male lover is our interpreter. Whether he sees a raised eyebrow, a blush, or a kiss, the narrator is already convinced of her guilt.[21] His elaboration of the evidence thus becomes superfluous. He is an interpreter of signs where no interpretation is necessary. The point is rather to establish his own view as definitive: no one could argue with such a conclusive case.

The situation in *Amores* 2.5 bears some resemblance to Catullus c. 51, where the lover also watches his girlfriend delight in another's company. Both poems portray the view of an insider cast into the role of outsider, the precise predicament of

---

21 . On the blush, see Boyd 1997, 110–6, and note also mention of her improved kissing style at very end (55–61). Booth's discussion of the poem emphasizes the legal metaphors and suggests that Ovid comes across as a married man giving evidence under the adultery laws that he has witnessed his wife's infidelity (Booth 1991, 39).

jealousy. It is much too easy to find oneself occupying another point on the love triangle: the favored one may at any time become despised. Yet unlike Catullus' poem, the lover here does not focus on his own physical and emotional symptoms of this displacement, but instead dwells only on the visual clues. It is not the difficulty of the experience so much as the corroborative power of the evidence that interests the Ovidian narrator.

Other examples show a similar interest in establishing authority through the interpretation of signs, even if the narrators are not usually so indifferent to the pain of jealousy. In the cases that follow, we find that visual provocations to jealousy result in better-articulated feelings of exclusion. The mistress' new clothes are a worry for the male lover, and her use of cosmetics adds to the feelings of distress. Though the emphasis may differ from poem to poem—sometimes it is on the deceptive quality of fancy dress, other times on its artificiality or foreignness—all of the elegiac poets depict clothing as clear evidence of intent. Either the mistress hopes to attract a new man, or worse yet, she already has, the expensive clothes representing gifts from the rival.[22]

For example, Propertius 1.15 links Cynthia's new clothes with proof of her betrayal without revealing any need for investigation. The narrator is upset at what he seems to believe might be the end of the relationship, though he does not specify what has happened.[23] Eventually (*lenta*, 4) Cynthia does come to see her devastated lover, but once there she acts totally unconcerned for his feelings:

> *et potes hesternos manibus componere crinis*   5
> *   et longa faciem quaerere desidia,*
> *nec minus Eois pectus variare lapillis,*
> *   ut formosa novo quae parat ire viro.*

> And you are able to arrange your hair, untouched since yesterday,
> with your hands,
> and stare at your face at long leisure.
> You decorate your throat with Eastern gems
> just like a woman who is preparing to look beautiful for a new lover.

The sight of her fussing with her hair and face reveals her callousness towards her wounded lover, while the care she has spent on choosing her jewelry suggests she has someone else on her mind.[24] The lover's anxiety about a rival

---

22 . On the mistress' greed, see James 2003a, 71–107.

23 . Note that the mythological exempla that follow all concern a woman's abandonment by her lover.

24 . Fedeli 1980 *ad* 8 takes the expression *novus vir*, like *novus maritus*, to indicate a husband, not a lover, but this is more likely a sign of the transfer of marital imagery to adulterous relationships, as noted in Chapter 2. Cf. also Tibullus 1.8.9–16, and Maltby's introductory note to the poem, which emphasizes the triangular structure and traces it to New Comedy and mime (Maltby 2002, 302).

emerges again at line 32: *sis quodcumque voles, non aliena tamen*. Cynthia's cool behavior towards him and apparent interest in another man provoke the narrator's fears for his own position (cf. *periclo*, 3 and *timore*, 4). Yet unlike the parallel cases we have seen among female lovers, the inferences made on the basis of a gesture and a necklace are conclusive. He presents it as so obvious that she has betrayed him that he believes his experience can serve as a warning to other lovers: *o nullis tutum credere blanditiis*, 42.

We find the same leap to judgment in a second example from Propertius, 2.18B, with clothing and makeup to blame this time.[25] In particular, Cynthia has adopted a style of dress from abroad: *imitare Britannos* (23), *externo tincto* (24), *Belgicus color* (26). Not only has she chosen artificial over natural beauty, the complaint in Propertius 1.2, but the imported goods suggest a rival who is a soldier and thus someone completely unlike the narrator. One look is enough to clinch the association between the new clothes, their foreign nature, and the rival who must have given them to her as a gift. The narrator's paranoia is so great that even rouge can signal an opponent.

Visual clues are just one cause of jealous feelings in the male lover. Rumors, too, circulate throughout the city of Rome, as the mistress is apparently the subject of gossip that makes its way to the lover's ears.[26] In Propertius 2.32, when the narrator warns his mistress about the negative press concerning her conduct, he does so in terms that have little trace of bitterness or sorrow. Instead we hear a vengeful threat, as he warns Cynthia of the humiliation she faces now that the entire city has been made witness to her loss of reputation (21–4):

> *sed de me minus est: famae iactura pudicae*
> *   tanta tibi miserae, quanta meretur, erit.*
> *nuper enim de te nostras me laedit ad auris*
> *   rumor, et in tota non bonus urbe fuit.*

> But this is less about me: the loss of your chaste reputation
> will be as great a source of pain as you deserve.
> For recently a rumor about you wounded my ears,
> and the news was bad throughout the city.

Cynthia's common behavior and the involvement of Rome in the couple's life go against everything that is supposed to distinguish the elegiac relationship: the

---

25 . I discuss fragment 2.18B below; 2.18A (the lines about keeping silent when you suspect the beloved of infidelity) was mentioned in Chapter 1. Though Heyworth 2007b, 184–5 suggests they are discrete fragments, there have been several articles arguing for the unity of these various fragments (see Williams 1980, Nethercut 1980, and Hubbard 1986). The interest in jealousy may be further grounds for taking these fragments as belonging to a single elegy.

26 . See Fear 2000, 228–9 and Keith 2008, 109–10.

pledge of loyalty to one another, the exclusivity of the relationship, the mistress' refinement and uniqueness. Cynthia risks losing her standing as a result of these actions—deservedly, the narrator adds.[27] She is said in another elegy to pay these worries no heed: *quamvis contemnas murmura famae*, 2.5.29. By contrast, the rumor feels like an attack to the lover: note the use of *laedit* at 2.32.23, a term that appears frequently in the examples of jealous rage in the next chapter.

Rumors can even transcend Rome's city limits, as Propertius 2.18B shows.[28] In what is supposed to look like an attempt to discipline Cynthia, the narrator claims vehemently that he will believe any gossip about her, gossip that will reach him wherever he might be (37–8):

> *credam ego narranti, noli committere, famae:*
> *et terram rumor transilit et maria.*

> I will believe what rumor reports, so don't do anything wrong.
> Rumor jumps across land and sea.

Here we see the remarkable credulity on the part of the male lover: the mistress has not yet done anything, and he already knows she is guilty. What is worse, he will not be the only one to know it: word will spread quickly not only within Rome but also outside the city. Like new clothes, rumors offer conclusive proof of infidelity that is available to the lover and others as well. The lover takes the rumors at face value and suffers a total loss of faith in the mistress.

One way to interpret the male lover's capitulation to rumor is to see the mistress as a symbol of elegiac poetry and her infidelity a sign of the poetry's success.[29] Elegiac women are not portrayed as actual women, or not just: their beauty and desirability on a physical level speak to the high craftsmanship of the poetry as well. They are learned (*docta puella*), like the Callimachean-inspired poetry in which they appear, and many of the words used to portray them play on the ambiguity between body and poetry (e.g., *forma*, *pes*). Other features of the woman's depiction suggest her symbolic function, too. For example, when the Propertian lover mentions a rival who threatens to take Cynthia abroad with him, as in 1.8A and B, he argues not only for his superiority over the rival but also his choice of love poetry over epic.

---

27 . Note that he contradicts the charge immediately afterwards and tells Cynthia that her good name has not in fact been destroyed (25–8). The next chapter examines other erratic shifts in behavior as part of a jealous reaction.

28 . The migratory nature of rumor is memorably captured in Ovid's description of *Fama* in *Metamorphoses* 12.39–63. Cf. Virgil, *Aen.* 4.173–97 and Pease 1935 *ad loc.* for more parallels.

29 . Cf. Wyke 1987 and Wyke 1989, Keith 1994, Fredrick 1997, and James 2003a.

If the mistress represents elegiac poetry, then her infidelity marks the spread of the lover's poetry and the growth of his audience.[30] In Propertius 2.24A, for example, someone has ribbed the lover for talking (presumably boasting) about the success he has achieved with his "Cynthia," his first book of elegy: *tu loqueris, cum sis iam noto fabula libro/et tua sit toto Cynthia lecta foro*?(1–2). Here there is little camouflaging the collapse of Cynthia as mistress and Cynthia as poetry collection. The evidence of rivals and circulation of rumors, while apparently painful for the lover's self-esteem, are at the same time a welcome sign that others are reading about the love affair. Paradoxically, then, the betrayals the lover worries about actually signal an advantage in terms of his reputation.

While this dimension of the mistress' infidelity is undoubtedly present, we should not ignore the more straightforward representation of the lover's jealousy in favor of a positive reading. Both levels may of course be operative at the same time, something I suggest in Chapter 5 as well in another context. Elegy is vitally concerned with the representation of lovers' fears and suspicions, and rumors have the potential to reveal not only confidence about literary success but also the vulnerability and paranoia of the lover whose life is open to view. Although the narrator and other characters' reactions may sometimes seem extreme or exaggerated for effect, their behavior reflects the telltale signs of their jealousy.

Several dimensions of rumor's effect on male lovers show the importance of understanding them against the backdrop of jealous suspicions. To begin with, the narrator uses rumor as a way of punishing Cynthia and provoking her jealousy: if gossip triggers his jealousy, then why not try to produce the same effect on her? For example, in Propertius 2.21, the opening two lines refer only in passing to a rumor about the narrator that a certain Panthus has delivered to Cynthia. The remainder of the poem then turns to Cynthia's own infidelities and the fact that she herself is the subject of gossip (1–8):

> A quantum de me Panthi tibi pagina[31] finxit,   1
>   tantum illi Pantho ne sit amica Venus!
> sed tibi iam videor Dodona verior augur.
>   uxorem ille tuus pulcher amator habet!
> tot noctes periere: nihil pudet? aspice, cantat   5
>   liber: tu, nimium credula, sola iaces.
> et nunc inter eos tu sermo es, te ille superbus
>   dicit se invito saepe fuisse domi.

30 . On the characterization of poet and mistress as "pimp" and "prostitute," cf., e.g., Myers 1996, Fear 2000, James 2003a, and now Keith 2008, 109–10. Compare Hor. *Ep.* I.20 and Harrison 1988.

31 . Commentators are divided whether to read *pagina* as a letter (Camps 1966b, Butler and Barber 1933) or poem (Richardson 1977), but both meanings are relevant to the representation of gossip in elegy, which pertains to both the affair and poetic reputation.

May Venus be as unfriendly to Panthus
as he was to me by fabricating that note.
But to you may I seem a truer augur than Dodona.
Your pretty lover has a wife!
So many nights have been lost: aren't you ashamed? Look, he sings,
a free man, while, you, overly confident, lie alone.
And now you are the talk among them, and he says haughtily
that you were often at his house against his will.

The tone is harsh and mocking, especially lines 4 and 6–8. In deceiving the narrator, Cynthia has herself been tricked.[32] The vague and unspecific charge directed at the narrator pales in comparison with the detailed evidence he has about Cynthia. Even now that Cynthia has been forced to realize that she was deceived by her lover, she spends her time looking for another lover (17–8). Despite Cynthia's cruel treatment of him, the narrator concludes the poem with a declaration of his own constancy (19–20):

> nos quocumque loco, nos omni tempore tecum
> sive aegra pariter sive valente sumus.

> I am yours, no matter the place or time,
> whether in sickness or in health.

The pledge of loyalty at the end of the poem conflicts with the rumor about the male lover posed at the opening. It reads not as a sincere pronouncement but rather a defensive move designed to cover up what is in fact a vengeful poem. The narrator relishes the fact that Cynthia is now in the position she has put him in all too often: she is now the excluded one and the victim of others' mockery. The narrator goads Cynthia by forcing her to confront the humiliation of others' contempt. The mythological analogies in the center of the poem are also intended to sting. Cynthia's lover never truly cared about her, the narrator says: this other man's only glory was to overcome her, as Jason did with Medea and Ulysses with Calypso (lines 11 and 13, respectively).

Additional hints about the male lover's roving attention occur in the neighboring poems and suggest again that he is trying to stir up Cynthia's jealousy. In 2.19, for example, the narrator voices suspicions about Cynthia even though he himself plans to go on a hunting expedition that raises the specter of his own amorous pursuits. In 2.20, he acknowledges openly that Cynthia has complained about his infidelity—perhaps a sign that his trick is working—and mounts a

---

32 . This recalls the *tu quoque* argument we saw in Chapter 1, where the point was that everyone falls in love, even those who mock others for doing so.

passionate defense. Finally, in the poem immediately following 2.21 and the dismissal of Panthus' rumor about him, the narrator in 2.22 openly confesses that he enjoys having many women: *sic etiam nobis una puella parum est* (36). When taken together, this sequence of poems undermines the claims of loyalty that the Propertian narrator makes elsewhere. Yet these revelations about the lover are closely tied to the mention of the scandal circulating about the mistress in 2.21. While Panthus' rumor could be an indication of the narrator's infidelity, then, more likely it is a resentful and desperate measure created by the narrator as a way of scaring Cynthia. What is relevant for us here is that this maneuver would not work unless the lover believed that rumors were an effective way to trigger jealousy and something more than a reference to literary success.

Even cases that clearly point to the question of poetic reputation emphasize the narrator's vulnerability more than his confidence. Allusions to intruders into the lovers' relationship may point to interest in the narrator and his poetry, for example, but they often reveal anxiety over having attracted the wrong kind of notice as well. So when the Tibullan narrator describes shadowy figures following him on a nighttime visit to his mistress, the context of fear and suspicion suggests these may include people who are inferior readers or who are hoping to bring him down.[33] In [Tibullus] 3.19, too, the narrator worries that he may unwittingly have attracted unwelcome attention to his mistress, since the reference to *invidia* and *gloria vulgi* (7) hardly points to the kind of select or favorable audience the poet desires.[34] Elegiac narrators also admit to anxiety over ridicule. The narrator in Tibullus 1.4 has learned the teachings of Priapus, yet fears at the conclusion of the elegy that his teachings will be rendered laughable because of his failures with Marathus. He asks the latter to spare him so that he does not become a laughingstock: *ne turpis fabula fiam*, 83. And in a final example, Ovid *Amores* 3.1, a reference to gossip throughout the city is put in the mouth of *Tragoedia*, who mocks the poet for his notorious love affairs. She tells him, again using the word *fabula*, that he is on the lips of everyone in the city (*fabula, nec sentis, tota iactaris in urbe*, 21). While *iactaris* could mean "displayed" and "boasted about" in this context, it can also mean "tormented" or "tortured," pointing again to the vulnerability and bad press that the lover risks when his affair is made public.[35]

33 . Cf. Tibullus 1.2.33–40, 1.6.41–42, 2.1.75–78, and also Ovid, *Am.* 3.1.19–20.

34 . Tränkle 1960 *ad* 7 deliberates between two possible meanings of *gloria vulgi*: does the poet want to distinguish himself from ordinary people who babble on about how wonderful their mistresses are, or does he want to avoid the praise of the uninitiated? As Hor. *Ep.* 1.20 shows, unease and confidence may occur simultaneously in poets anticipating the reception of their work, but in elegy there is more apprehension than assurance. On *turba* and an appropriate audience for elegy, see Fear 2000, 219.

35 . *OLD* s.v. 12 and 8b, respectively.

Conclusions

If it seems all too easy for the male lover to believe the news conveyed by rumor, this acquiescence stems from his deep-seated suspicions about the mistress. The male lover's rush to judgment reveals his propensity for mistrust and his need to find the evidence to confirm the mistress' infidelity. By contrast, female lovers take their time and assess the value of evidence against their lovers, giving greater credence to certain forms of information over others. The narrator seems to think that his self-representation in the poems discussed here lends him great authority in the spheres of love and jealousy. He knows how to read the signs of infidelity, while the mistress is slow to put things together. He is wounded by the cruelty of the mistress, while she does not even realize the extent of her humiliation. Yet any appearance of superiority that the lover believes he has conveyed is undone by his desperate need for retaliation and attention. The emphasis on the spread of rumors in Rome and beyond is a case of point. However much it serves to advertise the narrator's growing audience, it also underscores the lover's fears and vulnerability, as well as a narcissistic desire to magnify them.

4

Responses to Jealousy

Violence and Restraint

In addition to describing the onset of jealousy, the poets also give attention to the later stages and reactions to the emotion. As stated in the definition given in the Introduction, jealous lovers are not merely disappointed when their expectations of fidelity are unmet. They also take definite steps either to restore their love or, more commonly, to punish the rival and/or beloved. In the latter case, the direction of the response is far from predictable: who is more to blame, beloved or rival (or both)?[1] Yet what *is* reliable, at least in elegy, is the difference in how the poets represent the reactions of male and female lovers. Female lovers consistently use blows and physical attacks to retaliate against their lovers, while for their part, male lovers disavow the use of violence and aggression, though they cannot always maintain this resolve.[2] If they seem repulsed by physical punishment, however, they are not above retaliating with words, whether in cruel remarks or even entire poems that serve to denigrate and humiliate the mistress.[3] Yet their point in the poems I discuss here is to define themselves precisely in terms of violence and control.[4]

---

1. The target of jealous rage is unpredictable in real-life cases as well. In one study, Mathes and Verstraete 1993 found that aggression tends to focus on the partner more often than on the rival. Since their data came from college students, though, the evidence may not be representative of people in long-term relationships.

2. James 2003b looks at the evidence for female tears in elegy and argues that the Ovidian narrator acts in a way that is "particularly unscrupulous and exploitative" (120), and further that this abuse is latent in Propertius and Tibullus as well; see also n. 32 below. More recently, Fögen 2009 has examined evidence of male and female weeping and takes the more light-hearted view that both are intended for show and humor. My own focus is not on violence or its repercussions *per se*, but on the question of restraint versus control, which elegiac narrators clearly see as something positive.

3. Cf. e.g., Prop. 1.15 or 2.5.27–30.

4. James 2003b focuses more on differences between Ovid and the other two elegists. For an interesting study of gender differences and violence in another genre, see Scourfield 2003 on Chariton's *Chaereas and Callirhoe*.

While the narrators' representation of female behavior need not correspond
to any historical reality, it does seem to reflect ancient stereotypes of women as
hysterical and uncontrolled (and men as capable of restraint and reason).[5] This
view of male and female behavior derives in part from traditional misogynistic
attitudes and a widespread concern with moderation in Greco-Roman culture.
But the elegiac narrators' jealous response also engages with the concern about
anger control in antiquity, something that has not been recognized in previous
studies of elegy.[6] The deliberation over whether to respond or not, and how, is of
central interest in the examples I discuss, revealing the narrators' awareness of
the issue. We have only to compare the male lovers' struggle with Aeneas'
revenge at the end of the *Aeneid* to see the ways in which elegy once again engages with contemporary debates about the emotions.[7]

Yet however much the narrators seem aware of the debate and take the side of
restraint, the situation in elegy does not advocate this position in every respect. To
begin with, his expectations for himself do not extend to the mistress. The male
lover does not criticize, but in fact welcomes the wildness of female behavior,
despite the intolerance for her complaints that we saw in Chapter 2. Nor does he
describe himself as entirely devoid of violent impulses: he has the desire to strike,
but also the strength to hold back. As in the case of lovesickness, he understands
and acknowledges a problem about the emotions in a way that resonates with
philosophical advice, but portrays himself as less than perfect in this regard.

In this chapter, we will see that the reason is not only his commitment to love
but his masochism. The male lover welcomes his mistress' blows, for the scratches
and wounds he accumulates as a result stand as advertisements to the rest of the
community of his love and allegiances.[8] But while he is proud of these wounds,
they are at the same time marks of shame and humiliation, much like the scars on
a slave. While the blows confirm the narrator's prowess as lover and poet, pro-
moting his image and desire for fame, they also emphasize his passive and servile
status. The scars he bears are "badges of honor,"[9] showing his commitment to
love, no matter what the cost or embarrassment. The shame and humiliation are,
in fact, a welcome part of the experience.

5. See Harris 2001, Kaster 2005, and Konstan 2006, 56–65, esp. p. 58.

6. On anger control, see Harris 2001, esp. ch. 9 on the Roman material. Studies of anger and
violence in love elegy have understood them in terms of *militia amoris* or evidence of physical abuse
of women. As I show, however, the male lovers describe an inclination towards physical violence but,
more importantly, a very self-conscious effort to control that impulse.

7. On anger and the end of the *Aeneid*, see the bibliography cited in the Introduction, n. 1.
Aeneas' victim Turnus is not a beloved, of course, but the moment is eroticized: on this, see Putnam
1998.

8. Compare Fredrick 1997, who reads these blows instead as epic marks upon elegy and "the
violation of its own poetic values" (188–9). I return to this interpretation below.

9. See Fitzgerald 2000, 40.

Female Aggression

As mentioned above, the depiction of female emotional responses in Latin love elegy fits the stereotypical view of women as wild and unpredictable. In Catullus and the elegists, women are represented as dominant and merciless, unlike their male counterparts, who wish to represent themselves as passive and defenseless. According to this prejudiced presentation, we find the adjective *dura* applied to women, while *mollis* describes the male lover.[10] In one of the more striking portraits of female aggression towards the male lover, the concluding lines of Catullus c. 11, the narrator describes his love as a flower that has been crushed by a passing plow. The male lover resembles an innocent and vulnerable part of the natural world (cf. *flos* and *prati*, 22–3), while the aggressive and destructive female effectively rapes and destroys him (cf. *tacta aratro est*, 24 and *ilia rumpens*, 20). Women are violent, out of control, and ineffective, too. Violence seems to be the frustrated expression of their impotence, at least in the view of the male narrator who provides our main perspective.

In what follows, I have chosen four examples that illustrate female violence committed out of jealous rage: Tibullus 1.6, Propertius 3.8 and 4.8, and Ovid *Ars Amatoria* II.451–62. Several features recur in all of these examples. To begin with, the mistress' attack is never a calculated affair, but instead a reckless, desperate, and ineffective attack. Second, however wild and frenzied they may be, her blows invariably take aim at the lover's eyes. Because his wandering eye lies at the root of the cause of the jealousy, it seems natural that the mistress seeks revenge by damaging the cause of her pain. Finally, despite the secrecy and privacy that typically surround the elegiac affair,[11] all of the examples describe a noisy scene that emphasizes instead the public nature of the lover's humiliation and the interest of others in the love relationship, a dimension of elegiac jealousy that we saw in the previous chapter as well.

These features, in particular the mistress' lack of control and desire to strike her lover's eyes, emerge clearly in my first example, Tibullus 1.6. This elegy will in fact provide evidence for both parts of this chapter, since it treats both male and female responses to jealousy. The poem centers on Delia's infidelity, first towards her husband because of her involvement with the narrator, and now with another man, thanks to what the narrator has taught her. The narrator devotes most of the elegy to the question of an appropriate response to Delia's behavior. But then near the end, he speculates about what would be the right punishment for him were he to betray Delia in the way that she has deceived

---

10. These terms also refer to genre, with *mollis* descriptive of elegy and *durus* of epic, on which see Kennedy 1993, 30–4.

11. Cf. e.g. Tib. 1.6.41–42 and 2.1.75–78.

him. The elegy contrasts male and female reactions to the same kind of event in a way that doubly flatters the male lover.

For now I focus on the attack that the lover imagines he would receive for his own infidelity. He wants the full punishment:

> et mihi sint durae leges, laudare nec ullam
>> possim ego quin oculos appetat illa meos;   70
> et si quid peccasse putet, ducarque capillis
>> immerito pronas proripiarque vias.

> And let the laws be harsh for me: let me never praise any girl
> without that one [Delia] attacking my eyes.
> And if she thinks I have sinned, let me be led by my hair
> and undeservedly thrown head-first onto the street.

The focus here is on the punishment rather than any actual wrongdoing, which is hypothetical in any case. Even though he may allow for the possibility of his own infidelity (something he usually denies), the male lover clearly holds himself to a strict standard. If he *were* to deceive Delia, he would want her to hurt his roving eyes and drag him into the street by his hair.[12] The narrator also intends this picture of punishment for infidelity as a balance to Delia's behavior in the poem's opening. He is prepared to take responsibility for his errors, and she should too. The attack on his eyes suggests the appropriateness of the punishment he desires as well.

The lover assumes that his mistress would rage and want revenge, though he admits other scenarios are of course possible. His confidence in her reaction is a way of assuring himself (and his readers) how much she cares. He welcomes the attack not because he believes he deserves it (see *inmerito* in line 72);[13] he wants to be punished simply because she thinks he should be.[14] When he asks to be dragged out into the street, though, he wants an even more public humiliation. The desire to have an audience for his punishment suggests that he wants others to corroborate his mistress' preference for him over his rivals. It also reinforces the connection between jealousy and seeing, both from within and outside of the love affair, and by those who are desirous as well as those who are envious.

---

12. Putnam 1973 *ad loc.* points out that such punishments typify the sacking of a city and are deliberately exaggerated in the context. Cf. also Smith 1913 *ad* 70 on the phrase *oculos appetat*, a conventional symptom of female jealousy and of female anger generally. Murgatroyd 1994 *ad* 69–72 points to Ter. *Eun.* 648 and 740 as examples from comedy of women attacking their lovers' eyes; he also gives examples of attacks on hair in both comedy and elegy.

13. Murgatroyd 2001 *ad loc.* notes the word's emphatic position.

14. See also more violence in the poem in lines 43–56, which describe the prophecy of Bellona's priestess.

What might seem shameful or humiliating is in addition a point of pride and justification for his love, though one with a strong masochistic streak.

In Propertius 3.8, the mistress' loss of control is even greater and the attack even more public than in the previous example. But the elegy raises similar issues about the contrast between female lack of control and male restraint, between anger and pleasure, and between private and public. The poem begins with a lover admitting pleasure in the attack: he tells Cynthia how much he enjoyed the fight and encourages more of the same. The repetition of vocabulary denoting her rage and insanity makes clear Cynthia's loss of control: *insanae, furibunda, audax, minitare* (lines 2, 3, 5, 7). The contrast with his own perception of the fight, summed up as *dulcis*, could not be more dramatic:

> Dulcis *ad hesternas fuerat mihi rixa lucernas,*
> > *vocis et insanae tot maledicta tuae,*
> *cum furibunda mero mensam propellis et in me*
> > *proicis insana cymbia plena manu.*[15]
> *tu vero nostros audax invade capillos*   5
> > *et mea formosis unguibus ora nota,*
> *tu minitare oculos subiecta exurere flamma,*
> > *fac mea rescisso pectora nuda sinu!*
> *nimirum veri dantur mihi signa caloris:*
> > *nam sine amore gravi femina nulla dolet.*   10

> The fight we had last night was delightful to me,
> and so, too, the many curses made by your crazed voice,
> when, raging from drink, you hurled the table
> and threw the full cups against me with a furious hand.
> Attack my hair and tear my face with your pretty nails.
> Threaten to burn out my eyes with a flame,
> and cut my toga and bare my chest!
> Then surely you give me signs of true passion,
> for no woman suffers without a profound love.

The entire poem up until the final two couplets continues in this vein, extolling the wonders of sleepless nights, combat in bed, and other forms of amatory warfare. The attack symbolizes the vehemence of the mistress' feelings, providing certain proof that he, and not one of his rivals, is the one she cares about. The opposite kind of girl, someone cold and unresponsive, would be just right for his enemies: *hostibus eveniat lenta puella meis* (20).

---

15. Heyworth 2007a moves lines 3–4 to follow line 8.

In contrast with her fears, the male narrator maintains his own control throughout. The use of military vocabulary is a case in point. The poets regularly transfer the imagery of warlike battles to the love relationship as a way of distinguishing their material from epic and bringing out the turbulent nature of the elegiac affair.[16] Yet as these examples about jealous responses show, the parallel is not exact. In battle, both sides engage in the fight; in love, the engagement is one-sided and asymmetric. The male lover refuses to fight and feels superior as a result. He does not fear the wounds she might inflict or the public embarrassment they might cause. He exhibits restraint and control, whereas the mistress' attacks reveal how insecure and desperate she feels.

Yet even if the approximation of love and war is imperfect, the suggestion of a battlefield magnifies the attack and heightens our awareness of the clamor and din. Lovers typically make a fuss about privacy, arranging rendezvous late at night out of a concern that others might see them and know their business. But in the present case, the lover expresses no anxiety that the noise may have traveled and revealed the fight to others. As in the example from Tibullus, the narrators seem to welcome not just the blows, but the public dimension of the fight as well. Lines 21–2 give a possible reason, when the lover vaunts his bruises: *in morso aequales videant mea vulnera collo:/me doceat livor mecum habuisse meam* (21–2).[17] Still, heavy repetition of the first-person pronoun and possessive adjective (*mea, me, mecum, meam*) suggests the lover's need to convince not just others but even himself. The fight is proof of the mistress' affection, and this proof is just as necessary for the lover as for the lover's rivals.

An even noisier exchange occurs in Propertius 4.8, a poem carefully designed as an elegiacized counterpart to the *Odyssey*.[18] In this case, the fight is not only a means of proving the lover's place with Cynthia, but vying, however playfully, with Homeric models, in particular expanding features that were dormant there. The lovers have switched the roles they adopted in Propertius 1.3, a poem discussed in Chapter 2. Here it is Cynthia who takes on the role of Odysseus: she leaves home for what seems like a good cause (a religious festival), yet this is in fact a cover for her meeting with another man (23–6). The Propertian lover plays

16. See i.e. Propertius 2.1.13–14, where the description of the battles between the lover and Cynthia are compared to private *Iliads*. For a study of this feature of elegy, see Murgatroyd 1975 and Cahoon 1988.

17. Note the term *livor* here, which makes an etymological connection between jealousy and violence. Forms of *livor* and *laedo* appear in almost all the other poems I discuss in this chapter as well, thus marking a link between jealousy and the bruises caused by jealous rage (see also *quo numine laeso* describing Juno in Virg. *Aen.* 1.8). These terms are thus the Latin equivalent for *zēlotupia*, discussed in the Introduction. As for the sequence of thought in the poem, it makes better sense to see the brawl as a justification to the rival than to view the brawl as the fight that led to Cynthia's involvement with another man.

18. Cf. Evans 1971 on parallels between the Propertian elegy and the ending of the *Odyssey*.

Penelope, left home alone. Or not quite: angry about his desertion by Cynthia, he entertains two "suitors" who are present at his own invitation. Disloyalty arises on both sides of the relationship, even though the male lover does so as a form of revenge, a "tit for tat" in response to what he views as Cynthia's disloyalty.

Both lovers actually lay eyes on their rivals, and so it is a short step from the sighting of intruders to a jealous reaction. The narrator knows his rival from seeing Cynthia's departure (23–6). Cynthia sees her rivals when she returns home earlier than expected and surprises her lover and the two girls (49–50). Unlike Odysseus, who directs his revenge on the suitors alone, Cynthia attacks both her rivals and her lover. Cynthia first makes her move against the women, in particular their faces, hair, and clothes (57–62). Not satisfied with this, she also strikes the male lover himself.

> *Cynthia gaudet in exuviis victrixque recurrit*
>   *et mea perversa sauciat ora manu,*
> *imponitque notam collo morsuque cruentat,*   65
>   *praecipueque oculos, qui meruere, ferit.*

> Cynthia rejoices in her spoils and returns as a conqueror.
> She wounds my face with the back of her hand
> and marks my neck, bloodying it with bites,
> and strikes especially my eyes, which deserve it.

She is, as we have now seen several times already, particularly vindictive towards her lover's eyes, poking them (line 66) and ordering him never again to look around in the theater or peer into an open litter. Her focus on his eyes, the source of his deceit, destroys his capacity for the gazing at other women. And the male lover accepts the attack willingly, as if knowing that he deserves it (*meruere*, 66).[19] There is, at least, no denial or pretense about guilt here.

The male lover is a veteran of love's wars, and he has the scars to prove it. And he wants to prove it. The elegy as a whole unfolds noisily and with the neighborhood on alert.[20] The combination of overturned furniture and an attempted escape from a raging Cynthia must have created pandemonium: line 60 makes clear that the scene awakens the entire street: *omnis et insane semita voce sonat*. The fight announces Cynthia's possessiveness not just to a rival, but the entire community.

The marks she makes on the lover's body (*notam*, line 65) are just further evidence of who matters most to her. It cannot be a coincidence that these signs are called

---

19. Contrast *immerito* in Tibullus 1.6.72.

20. Cynthia's flamboyant departure is described as a *spectaclum* (21), while the noise caused by her return is said to have reached the Esquiline and an out-of-the-way tavern (1–2, 19–20).

notae, a word that points to both bruises and writing.[21] Marks on the body reveal physical humiliation like a master's blows upon a slave, imagery that fits easily with the motif of *servitium amoris* operative in the elegiac context.[22] And while *nota* can refer to writing generally, it may also indicate critical writing in particular, for example corrections added to a passage or the *nota censoria*, the mark recorded by the censor next to a citizen's name as a rebuke for some offense or immoral act.[23] The mistress' critical and demeaning attack thus fits with her evaluation of the male lover's behavior towards her. However much the lover wants to interpret the scratches and scars as proof of his prowess, they are at the same time signs of his abjectness and humiliation. They symbolize the cost of jealousy to his identity and self-esteem. And his authority is undermined not only in the relationship with the mistress, but in the larger community, who has witnessed or heard about his defeat.

As often, an example from Ovid modifies the attitude taken in the other elegists. While the narrator in a passage from *Ars Amatoria* II shares in the sentiment that the male lover deserves and needs female attacks, he also alludes to the need to set limits on the offensive, which can easily get out of hand. A mistress' blows are a good thing, but only in moderate doses, it would seem (451–62):

> *ille ego sim, cuius laniet furiosa capillos;*
> > *ille ego sim, teneras cui petat ungue genas,*
> *quem videat lacrimans, quem torvis spectet ocellis,*[24]
> > *quo sine non possit vivere, posse velit.*
> *si spatium quaeras, breve sit, quo laesa*[25] *queratur,*   455
> > *ne lenta vires colligat ira mora.*
> *candida iamdudum cingantur colla lacertis,*
> > *inque tuos flens est accipienda sinus;*
> *oscula da flenti, Veneris da gaudia flenti:*
> > *pax erit; hoc uno solvitur ira modo.*   460
> *cum bene saevierit, cum certa videbitur hostis,*
> > *tum pete concubitus foedera: mitis erit.*

May I be he whose hair she pulls in her fury.
May I be the one whose tender cheeks she seeks with her nails,
whom she looks at while crying, whom she considers with savage eyes,
without whom she is not able to live, though she wishes she could.

---

21. See *OLD* s.v. 6 and 9.
22. See Fitzgerald 2000, 33 on the slave's scars.
23. *OLD* s.v. 3 and 4.
24. This time we hear of the mistress' eyes, their "savage" nature indicating her loss of control.
25. Note another instance of a form of *laedere* in the context of jealousy.

If you ask how long she should complain about her wounds,
let it be short, lest her sluggish anger gather strength with delay.
Wrap your arms around her white neck immediately
and take her as she weeps into your embrace.
Give kisses to her as she weeps, give her then the joys of Venus.
There will be peace, this is the one way anger will dissolve.
When she has raged well, when she seems a certain enemy,
then seek treaties in bed. She will be gentle.

Here the advice has to do with capitalizing on the excesses and exposure of the emotional person in order to gain affection (an ancient example of makeup sex). The narrator desires to be a victim of his mistress' physical assault, but her loss of control seems designed to highlight his own composure and the advantages of a clear head in this situation. The advice about making the mistress worry (*fac timeat de te*, 445) reveals to what extent the lover views himself as in control of the situation, both in regulating his own actions and those of the mistress.[26] This is either wishful thinking or a desire to contrast himself with the other elegiac narrators.

Male lovers in elegy welcome physical blows from their mistresses and depict the attack on eyes, clothing, and hair in details that are consistent across the examples. Female lovers have lost their bearings, and this is welcome news to the male lovers. There is something to be proud of in getting struck, unlike the otherwise related situation we find in Roman comedy. Violence abounds in comedy, with fights and brawls regularly erupting between masters and slaves, lovers and pimps, usually over questions of love and often scenes of grave humiliation.[27] But the situation in elegy is different, where the aggression comes from women, not other men. And while being the object of attack is humiliating, there is a flip side: the blows are also testament to the lovers' powerful effect on their mistresses and the fact that the women care. The mistress' loud and violent attacks always leave traces: rivals and others, too, can see the results, and know that these lovers are the victors in the struggle for the mistress' love.

These poems underline the narrator's manipulation of the presentation for self-serving reasons, whether in proving his successes in love or in poetry. The *notae*, bruises and scratches, serve as visible markers to everyone of the mistress' passion, an embedded text that reinforces other forms of verbal communication in elegy. In a dramatic reversal from the other instances of female jealousy, there is no critique, but rather a masochistic celebration of a loss of control that the lover accepts and relishes. The distinction in the representation of male and

26. Propertius 4.8 corroborates this advice, for in deciding to repay Cynthia in kind for her infidelity, he gives her a taste of her own medicine and means to scare her into complicity.

27. See Plautus, *Bacch.* 859f., *Cist.* 523ff., *Truc.* 926f.; Ter., *Ad.* 120f., *Eun.* 646, and n. 9 above.

female responses becomes even more apparent in the following examples, which address the male lover's restraint despite a temptation to strike the mistress with blows.

Male Attempts at Self-Control

In contrast to the mistress' readiness to attack, male lovers claim that they want to avoid the use of violence themselves. Hitting a woman, they say, is the act of a *rusticus*, not a poet, whose greater sophistication keeps him from resorting to physical abuse. This position allows lovers to promote their innocence and toler- ance yet at the same time brandish their wounds as a sign of victory and suf- fering. I turn now to examine three examples illustrating this different standard of behavior: Tibullus 1.6 and 1.10 and Propertius 2.5. But in these cases, the pattern is not, importantly, without exceptions, and we also find cases where the narrators either allude to or even openly admit their use of violence against mis- tress or rival as a result of jealous feelings.[28] I address these exceptions at the end of the chapter, after examining the more common cases where the male lover resists violent impulses.

Although lovers depict their decision not to strike the beloved as a moral or ethical one, their actual words suggest not so much outright aversion as deliber- ation followed by rejection. For example, in Tibullus 1.6, examined earlier in the section on female responses, the narrator comes close to admitting he could hit her, only to recoil from that idea in the next breath:

> non ego te pulsare velim, sed, venerit iste
> 　　si furor, optarim non habuisse manus.
> nec saevo sis casta metu, sed mente fideli:　　　　　75
> 　　mutuus absenti te mihi servet amor.

> I hope I don't strike you, but if that fury comes,
> I would hope not to have hands.
> Don't be chaste through fear of my savagery, but from a loyal heart.
> Let mutual love keep you safe even when I am absent.

The narrator has *furor*, too (line 74): he openly acknowledges his proneness to anger and its potential vehemence. But the difference is that he will not give in to the temptation to use it in a violent act. The ostensible reason is that he wants his mistress to give affection spontaneously and willingly: he hopes she will be

---

28. See also *AA* II.373–86, and the discussion in Tennenhouse 1989 on violence actually carried out against women in Renaissance drama.

chaste from a loyal heart (*mente fideli*, 75) and not from fear of his anger. The lovers want fidelity that is unprompted and genuine.[29] But the contrast between male and female responses in a single poem suggests that more is at issue.

Renunciation of physical abuse occurs in Tibullus 1.10 as well.[30] Violence is an option, but ultimately the use of force does not sit easily with the lover's vision of himself. In this elegy, the narrator bewails the toll of war and violence. Yet even when he turns to the topic of peace, he dwells on the ways in which fighting and violence infiltrate even quiet times:

> *sed veneris tunc bella calent, scissosque capillos*
> > *femina, perfractas conqueriturque fores;*
> *flet teneras subtusa genas: sed victor et ipse*   55
> > *flet sibi dementes tam valuisse manus.*
> *at lascivus Amor rixae mala verba ministrat,*
> > *inter et iratum lentus utrumque sedet.*
> *a lapis est ferrumque, suam quicumque puellam*
> > *verberat: e caelo deripit ille deos.*   60
> *sit satis e membris tenuem rescindere vestem,*
> > *sit satis ornatus dissoluisse comae,*
> *sit lacrimas movisse satis: quarter ille beatus*
> > *quo tenera irato flere puella potest.*

Then the wars of love get heated,
and the woman complains of her torn hair and broken doors.
She weeps with bruised cheeks, but the victor himself weeps
that his wild hands had so much strength.
Mischievous Love encourages their hostile words
and sits calmly between the two of them in their anger.
Whoever strikes his own girl is made of rock and iron:
he snatches the gods down from the sky.
Let it be enough to tear her thin dress from her limbs,
or take down her hair or provoke her tears. He is four-time blessed
whose gentle girl can weep when he is angry.

The narrator criticizes those who seriously harm or injure their loved ones, especially if he is so aggressive that even the perpetrator feels regret. He does seem

---

29. Compare the similar sentiment expressed by Micio about his son's love for him (Ter. *Adelphoe* 57–58: *pudore et liberalitate liberos/retinere satius esse credo quam metu*). The way in which father–son love is described in this play closely resembles the portrayal of romantic love in Catullus and the elegists.

30. In his introduction to the poem, Murgatroyd 2001 discusses extensive similarities between this poem and 1.1. See also the discussion in James 2003b, 107–8.

willing to tolerate a certain amount of lighter hitting, if it occurs in the context of love and establishing loyalty (lines 61–4). The weeping of the *puella* demonstrates her feelings for the man, and if anger provokes that, then he believes there is some justification for it. Yet because he commits himself to the belief that it is wrong for a man to strike a woman out of real anger, this stance corresponds to the position voiced elsewhere that violence is not the method by which male lovers should respond to jealousy.

In a final example of restrained male behavior, Propertius 2.5, the lover is furious at the latest news of Cynthia's treachery, rumors of which are circulating throughout the city (lines 1–2). The lover threatens her with the end of their relationship: *nunc est ira recens, nunc est discedere tempus* (9). She rages back so, that he has to tell her to control herself: *parce tuis animis* (18). And thus, as we might expect, he backs off, promising that he will control his anger:

> nec tibi periuro scindam de corpore vestis,
> > nec mea praeclusas fregerit ira fores,
> nec tibi conexos iratus carpere crinis,
> > nec duris ausim laedere pollicibus.
> rusticus haec aliquis tam turpia proelia quaerat,   25
> > cuius non hederae circuiere caput.

> And I won't tear your clothes from your perjured body,
> nor will my anger break down your closed doors.
> I won't tear your braided hair in my anger,
> nor dare to bruise you with strong thumbs.
> Let some bumpkin whose head is not encircled by ivy
> seek such rough battles.

The lover wants Cynthia, and us, to believe that he possesses the self-control missing in the mistress. The list of violent acts that he will avoid closely resembles the ones described in Tibullus 1.10: torn clothes, broken doors, pulled hair, and beaten faces.[31] He allows himself to enact verbally what he is unwilling to enact physically. It is not only a veiled threat, but a kind of subliminal enactment. The characterization of the one who commits the violence, the *rusticus*, also occurs in both elegies (Tibullus 1.10.51; Propertius 2.5.25). Both narrators raise themselves above a crude and rough treatment of the mistress, though it is significant that their mistresses perceived the male lovers to be on the verge of

---

31. On common elements in Tib. 1.10 and Prop. 2.5, see Solmsen 1961, 273–77 and Lyne 1998. The latter explores Propertius and Tibullus' humorous attempts to outdo each other in poems, including Prop. 2.5 and Tib. 1.10.

doing this very thing. Instead of admitting such a proclivity, the narrators contrast themselves, poets crowned with ivy, with the rough farmer.

We might read this literally as drawing familiar distinctions between country and city, simple and urbane, narratives that foreground violence and those that do not. In highlighting their own non-aggressive stand, the male narrators indicate how far they stand from the raw feeling and generally unreflecting behavior of characters in other genres. But this is not only a literary question, but also one of a broader intellectual question about moderation and anger-control. The narrator is someone who is aware of the debate about self-restraint, and the way in which he dwells precisely on the point of making a decision suggests that he is framing his response to jealousy in just those terms. Yet the lover is able to control his emotion not because he has eradicated the impulse altogether, but because he represents himself as conscious of the costs. He enjoys the wild attacks of the mistress but considers himself morally superior to her. He will fantasize about himself as a more violent man in the examples below, but ultimately will allow himself only to be on the receiving end of the blows.

Loss of Self-Control

There are some exceptions to the pattern I have just traced. In particular, the Ovidian narrator does not live up to the standards set by his predecessors in Propertius and Tibullus.[32] The narrator in *Amores* 1.7 and *Ars Amatoria* II.169–176 (the latter passage recalling the scene described in the earlier poem[33]) does not succeed in holding himself back and strikes his mistress on account of jealousy. Both times the issue of his physical abuse comes up, the Ovidian narrator expresses something resembling remorse. Yet the reasons for this are not the ones offered by the lovers in the other poets, and he does not come across as genuinely ashamed or repentant.[34]

In *Amores* 1.7, the narrator undercuts an apology offered for hitting the mistress. He reports how he struck her and tore her clothing.[35] He demands to be restrained on account of this crime:

32. Contrast James 2003b who finds in Ovid a key to what is only more discreet in the other elegists: "Ovid, however, particularly in the *Ars Amatoria*, provides a key to elegiac weeping: though Ovidian lament typically seems much less real than the expressions of grief in Propertius and Tibullus, it turns out to be the exception that proves the rule, for by appearing to deviate from the norm, Ovid reveals that norm as a fraud" (100).

33. See Hinds 1998, 3–4 on the use of *memini* at *AA* II.169 as a "reflexive trope" of allusion.

34. Note that he fails to meet the requirements of true remorse, at least according to the definition offered in Kaster 2005, 80.

35. In lines 61–8 of the same elegy, the lover invites the female mistress to attack him in return, as if this were the proper punishment. See the discussion of this in Greene 1999, 416–7.

Adde manus in vincla meas (meruere catenas),   1
dum furor omnis abit, si quis amicus ades:
nam furor in dominam temeraria bracchia movit;
flet mea vesana laesa[36] *puella manu.*
tunc ego vel caros potui violare parentes   5
saeva vel in sanctos verbera ferre deos.

If any friend is present, put my hands in chains (they deserve them)
until all my anger is gone.
For anger spurred my rash arms against my mistress;
my girl wept, wounded by my own fierce hand.
Then it was possible that I would injure even my dear parents
or bring savage blows even against the holy gods.

We do not learn the cause of the attack, only the effects on the mistress and the narrator's apparent guilt about it. He describes how he tore her gown, pulled her hair, and rent her cheeks (47–50), all in disbelief at his loss of control.[37] The narrator expresses contrition, asking to be handcuffed until he becomes calm again. Even so, what has stunned him most of all is that he could not control himself, and that he needs help to do so. Once this pent-up rage has been let out, moreover, there is no guarantee if and where it will stop, no matter if it is his parents or even the gods whom he faces.

The narrator may have lost his cool, but he did not actually deliver a blow. In many ways, the poem reads as more of an exercise or parody of earlier poems describing the same scenario.[38] The comparisons to Ajax and Orestes (7–11), for example, and the mock triumph he imagines for himself as victor over a girl (35–8) are exaggerated and self-deprecating more than penitent.[39] Similarly, he admits that his victim looks somewhat attractive with her hair disordered (12), an attempt to turn his aggression into a form of flattery. When he asks her at the very end of the poem to straighten her hair and remove evidence of his crime (67–8), he suggests either that she is not as beat up as he had indicated or that the entire event can be erased by the simple act of combing her hair.[40]

36. Note another example of *laedere* in the context of jealous violence.

37. See McKeown 1989 *ad loc.* Greene 1999 takes a different view that emphasizes instead the male lover's pleasure in subjugating his mistress.

38. The poem resembles a declamation piece, as McKeown 1989 points out (164). On the poem as parody, see Boyd 1997, 123–9 and 157–9, who admits the irony and argues on behalf of the poem's sophisticated style. Greene 1999 offers an important feminist reading of the poem.

39. See Galinsky 1969 for a survey of the elegists' use of the triumph theme.

40. Cf. Barsby 1973, 83, 91; McKeown 1989, 164; Boyd 1997, 123 and 159; and Fredrick 1997, 189.

A passage in *Ars Amatoria* II addresses the very episode recounted in *Amores* 1.7, when the *praeceptor* describes the importance of being gentle with a mistress and mentions a failing in this regard. Once, he tells his readers, he hit his mistress in anger, although he later attempts to diminish the assault by describing it only as "messing up her hair" (*dominae turbasse capillos*, 169). The results, he suggests, should be a lesson to all of those who find themselves in a similar position:

> me memini iratum dominae turbasse capillos;
> haec mihi quam multos abstulit ira dies!   170
> nec puto nec sensi tunicam laniasse, sed ipsa
> dixerat, et pretio est illa redempta meo.
> at vos, si sapitis, vestri peccata magistri
> effugite et culpae damna timete meae;

> I remember how once when I was angry, I messed up my
>   girlfriend's hair.
> How many days did that anger deprive me of!
> I don't think I tore her dress, nor was I aware of it,
> but she said I did and took it out at my expense.
> But you, if you are wise, avoid the mistakes of your teacher
> and fear the penalties of my crime.

Some new features emerge in this version of the story. In contrast with the mistress' anger, the lover's anger does not constitute a proof of his love, but rather mistreatment. And he informs us that he pays for it: his misstep costs him a few days of intimacy and a financial loss as well. Far from feeling regret for hurting her, the lover advises others to avoid striking a mistress for prudential reasons. The point is an entirely self-serving one, even if it is included as a tip to help other lovers. Yet the passage also puts both parties in a bad light, especially the remarks about messing up her hair (169) or the torn dress (171). Either he is blind to the true nature of the offense he has committed and so callous that he does not even notice what he has done, or he wants to diminish his crime to highlight the imbalanced response: these mistresses are so greedy that they make up false charges in order to take more of your money.[41] If we connect this with passages in which women attack their men with relish, we find that the Ovidian lover also seems to attribute to her a double standard: she can dish it out, but she sure can't take it.[42]

Some have argued that these descriptions of male violence are not an anomaly, but rather a more overt reference to what was in fact implicit in the other elegists'

---

41. On the greed of the mistress and her status as courtesan, see esp. James 2003a, esp. pp. 35–68.

42. See Barsby 1973, 91.

narratives as well: physical abuse of the mistress.[43] Others have pointed to a poetic reading that equates violence on the body with a tension between "scopophilia and voyeurism," or epic elements in an otherwise unblemished elegiac surface.[44] But I take a different view of these passages and the callousness they bring out in the lover's *persona*. These are not epic moments in an elegiac setting, nor are they exaggerations of the abusiveness latent in Propertian and Tibullan elegy. Rather, they fit the pattern established in the other generic examples and center on the issue of self-restraint. The narrator in both the *Ars Amatoria* and *Amores* 1.7 touches on all same elements brought up earlier: that violence is harmful and belongs to the sphere of war, not peace; that female attacks bring something positive whereas blows by a male lover are only ugly; and that this kind of attack invariably brings something private out into the open, which may spread into other areas (loss of respect for parents and gods, in the case of *Amores* 1.7). The central difference is that in this case, such concerns are not enough to make the lover control himself. He recognizes the costs and yet cannot help himself.

We can explain the representation of the Ovidian lover in these instances as due to a less engaged relationship with the mistress and a greater interest in manipulating the *topoi* of elegy, with the result that he has less to lose. He can represent himself as participating in anger and violent behavior because the contrast between himself and the beloved is not as central to his self-portrayal as his role as a poet. Thus while the narrator recognizes that he should refrain from hitting the beloved, he either does it anyway and barely cares, or goes completely overboard to the point that he needs to be restrained. In both cases, he outdoes the other poets by expressing what they did not, either the lack of concern or the truly violent act. This is a case of *variatio* rather than an exposure of an elegiac tendency towards violence.

Crimes of Passion

Perhaps the most extreme case of violence resulting from jealousy is the so-called crime of passion.[45] Though a frequent concomitant of operatic and novelistic treatments of jealousy, there is little representation of these crimes in ancient literature.[46] Lysias I, *On the Murder of Eratosthenes*, details the murder of

---

43. On this point, see James 2000b and also James 1997 on slave rape in Ovid.

44. See Fredrick 1997.

45. On crimes of passion in general, cf. e.g., Mowat 1966, Guillais 1991, Weir 1992, Mullen 1993 and Mullen 1996, Stearns 1989, 28–30, Kahan and Nussbaum 1996, Caulfield 2000, and Baron 2004.

46. For studies of crimes of passion in antiquity, see Cantarella 1991. Perhaps if we had more extensive examples of mime or Republican drama, we would find more literary references to such crimes.

an adulterer and gives ample detail about how the intruder met the man's wife, arranged visits, and duped the husband. In Konstan's view, we cannot describe this case as a crime of passion, since there is little to suggest the husband killed the adulterer out of love for his wife rather than a sense of property and anxiety over the legitimacy of his son.[47] At the very least it is over-determined. Similarly, Plato discusses homicides committed in anger at the beginning of *Laws* IX, yet gives no mention to crimes of passion or erotic anger specifically.[48] Perhaps such matters were handled privately, within the family, and not by appealing to a legal system or outside arbitrator. As for the Roman period, although important legal changes took place during the Augustan period and beyond, in particular as to the punishment available to a husband who caught his wife "in the act," we find none of these changes in legislation reflected in the literature of the time.[49]

In Roman love poetry, I have found only a single allusion to a crime of passion.[50] In Propertius 2.8, the narrator confronts certain knowledge of Cynthia's infidelity and contemplates death as an answer to his distress.[51] At first he imagines only his own death but later turns to the idea of killing his unfaithful partner. The Propertian lover fantasizes about his own death on other occasions as well, mostly as a way to test Cynthia's feelings or punish her for her cruelty.[52] But this passage is unusual for its anger and vengeful quality turned outwards as well as inwards against himself.

The poem reads like a stream of consciousness. In lines 1–6, the narrator first begs that he himself might be killed (*me iugula*, 4).[53] Then he grows more reflective (7–10), realizing that all things change (*omnia vertuntur*, 7). Finally (11ff.) he becomes angry and hostile towards Cynthia about the terrible way she treated him. He imagines his own death as a form of revenge, but suddenly thinks of the story of Antigone and Haemon, in which both lovers die. He envisions himself

47. See Konstan 2006, 223–4, though see Kaster's review (2006) of Konstan for a more positive view of the evidence for jealousy.

48. See Woozley 1972.

49. On the Roman legislation, see Cantarella 1991.

50. Although this must remain speculative, I wonder if we are encouraged to see the death of the sparrow in Catullus c. 3 as a parody of a crime of passion. The bird is described as a poetic rival in c. 2 (he sings exclusively to the mistress), and as a sibling rival in c. 3 (he takes the poet's place in the mistress' lap, which has been compared to a mother's). The sudden death of the bird demonstrates the ability of the narrator to act aggressively towards anyone who interferes in his relationship with Lesbia, marking these poems as programmatic for both the erotic and invective poems that follow. For a contemporary example involving jealousy and a pet bird (not, one imagines, a frequent theme), see Glenway Wescott's *The Pilgrim Hawk*: "And during the loving fuss she made over the great bird on her arm, she kept shifting her eyes in his [her husband's] direction, imploring him to try to like it too. It might have been a baby, and he a lover; or was it the other way around?" (13).

51. James 2003b, 218–20 rightly points out the little attention the passage has received.

52. Papanghelis 1987.

53. He may even address this wish to his rival, if *hostis* in the same line is any clue.

in the role of Antigone, characterized by her devotion and position of being misunderstood. Cynthia, like Haemon, should kill herself, too, an act of violence that would definitively prove her love and unite the two in death. The narrator has moved from a fantasy of his own death to that of a double suicide. Yet the very next lines make the description of Cynthia's death sound more vengeful:

> sed non effugies: mecum moriaris oportet;   25
>   hoc eodem ferro stillet uterque cruor.
> quamvis ista mihi mors est inhonesta futura:
>   mors inhonesta quidem, tu moriere tamen.

> But you won't escape: it's right that you die with me.
> Let both our blood drip from this same sword.
> Even though your death will be shameful for me,
> a shameful death indeed, nevertheless you will die.

The reference to escape (*effugies*, 25) sounds like a threat, as does the urgency in the rest of the line. The repetition of *inhonesta* in lines 27 and 28 also implies a crime and shame that would not stem from a suicide. And the suggestion that the lover would kill Cynthia comes up in another mythological example immediately following, that of Achilles and his loss of Briseis. The lover suggests that the pain of losing Briseis later led to rage and the murder of Hector. While the case of Antigone brought out the narrator's feelings of devotion and piety, this example brings out the feeling of betrayal in erotic love as a root cause.

Yet in the end, the narrator admits he is a lesser man than Achilles; presumably he is also unable to fill the shoes of an Antigone. The models from Homer and tragedy provide him with the means of fantasizing about a violent course of action as a form of revenge and an outlet for his sorrow. These are ultimately roles that he adopts and just as quickly discards. We have already seen the Propertian lover's propensity for adopting the pose of other literary characters in exploring the boundaries of jealousy and anger, in elegies such as 1.3 and 4.8, for example. The adoption of tragic and Homeric models leads the lover to adopt various *personae* and to examine the same situation from different perspectives. Propertius 4.8 is less a poem about actual violence and retaliation and more a poem about fantasizing about a course of action that the lover would never actually carry out. The elegiac lover represents his frustration as so great that he dreams that he could, like characters in tragedy or epic, act out in rage, perhaps kill himself or the woman who has deceived him so many times. But significantly he resists this impulse and admits that he cannot act like an Achilles or Antigone.

While he toys with the idea of violence against the mistress, in the end his behavior conforms to the idea of restraint, albeit with less success, which we have seen in the other examples.

Conclusions

Other studies have examined the use of violence in terms of the narrator's desire and power over the female or the elegist's attempt to remain pure of epic elements. In this chapter, I have focused instead on the natural connection between violence and jealousy, an association that draws attention to the elegiac narrator's restraint in contrast to his mistress' rash and reckless assaults. Although the narrators vehemently deny wanting to harm the mistress, they claim to be eager for her attacks on him, and the noisier the better. The late-night brawls, which involve broken furniture, bodily attacks, and angry cries, prove to the neighborhood how much the male lover is fought over. They are "on display," like the mistress' new clothes, and advertise something to the public that is advantageous to the lover even if they bring humiliation as well.

The restraint shown by the male lovers, however imperfect, reveals their relationship to other men, as well as to other genres and authorities. The distinction between the poet's sensibilities and those who are not as refined may well convey a difference about genres, between elegy, on the one hand, and comedy and epic on the other. Male aggression and violence belong naturally to epic poetry or comedy. When epic elements enter into the elegiac world, as in Propertius 1.3 or 4.8, the narrators domesticate and reduce them to harmless versions of the original: when fighting occurs in elegy, it is often a battle that takes place in a bed, not a field.

But in the case of a violent response to jealousy, what we find is not merely a playful twist or generic stand. The narrator's depiction of male and female attacks, whether carried out or just imagined, is a calculated affair that he hopes will establish his own depth of emotion and character but that in fact reveals his own compulsive jealousy and narcissism. According to his presentation, the mistress' blows reveal her true attachment to him. He feels the same inclination, but rejects the use of violence as rough and crude. His deliberation over whether or not to strike makes it sound as if he has benefited from philosophical teaching. Yet as we have seen in earlier chapters, the lover often appears to uphold philosophical or moral arguments, but for reasons all his own. He is someone who cherishes *fides*, though not in a married relationship. He is concerned about the loss of Roman values in a quest for gain, but his sphere is domestic, not public or political. He worries about the loyalty of family but does so on erotic grounds, not moral or legal ones. And so, too, in the case of emotional restraint. He does not give in to the impulse to strike his mistress but is obsessed with the physical evidence of the mistress' love, desiring her blows as a means of proof for himself and for others. He is willing to undergo the sort of things anyone else would want to avoid, namely the humiliation of being beaten like a slave or shamed publicly for some wrong. He is not an advocate of anger control, then, but he uses this position to promote his moral advantage over the mistress. For all the attention he seems to give her, the narrator is really most interested in himself.

5

The Lover as Poet

Trust and Distrust of Poets

I have now examined some of the general features of elegiac jealousy in all three of the elegists as well as Catullus. We have seen examples that ranged from the onset of jealousy to its full expression and cases that offered insights into both male and female experiences as represented by the poets. In Chapters 5 and 6, I turn to focus on just one of the elegists, Propertius, who has an interest in the uses of jealousy, both poetic and sociopolitical, that goes beyond what we find in other writers of Roman elegy. In this chapter, I examine the role of the reader in jealous triangles. One of the more obvious features of Roman elegy is its self-referential character. Not only is the narrator of this love poetry himself a poet, but his poetry is about love, too. Thus the Roman elegists are at once writing about amatory relationships and writing about writing about amatory relationships. The first-person perspective has, through its immediacy, misled some in the past to think that the Roman elegists were writing autobiographically about their own experiences. Even though incorrect, this view highlights to what extent their writing is about writing as well as about love.

More striking still is the way that actual literary relations and rivalries with other poets are woven into the narrative. Not only do Gallus, Lynceus, Bassus, and others appear in Propertian elegy as poets, but they "make the switch" to love poetry within narrative time.[1] They are moreover intertwined in the amatory narrative of the poems as well. Elegy's position as a genre is thus depicted vis-à-vis its rivals in terms of amatory relations, and, not surprisingly, these rivalries are enacted through the motifs of jealousy. The elegist's relation to

1. See Sharrock 2000 for an excellent discussion of addressees in Propertius Book 1. Gallus and Lynceus have received a great deal of attention in the literature: see, for example, Cairns' recent book on Propertius (Cairns 2006), which devotes Chapters 3–7 to the poet and Propertian character Gallus; and Miller 2004 and Keith 2008, each of whom discusses Gallus, Bassus, and Lynceus together. I, too, discuss these three poets together, but focus on jealousy and rivalry rather than the Epicurean and poetic dimensions that are emphasized in these other studies.

other authors as well as to his readers is thus linked to questions of loyalty and temptation, prowess and vulnerability, trust and distrust.

Until now, we have seen elegiac narrators distinguish these rivals from themselves in terms of values, profession, or status, as was the case for example with Cynthia's disdain for her vulgar rivals in Propertius 4.8 or the lover's description of himself as someone who would never hit his mistress in Tibullus 1.10. In this chapter, by contrast, I examine an outsider who shares many similarities with the jealous figure: the reader of elegy. However surprising it may seem at first, readers of elegy, both those internal and external to the text, are put in a special position vis-à-vis the jealous character, in ways that affect even our sympathy and critical judgment.[2] We may, that is to say, take an interest in the outcome.

There are, of course, many types of readers: internal and external, ancient and modern, sympathetic and hostile, with many further distinctions possible as well. In the first part of the chapter, I look at a very specific type of reader, an internal rival named within the poetry who hopes to be a love poet. This is someone, in other words, who poses a threat not only to the lover's status in the affair but also to his relationship to elegy. Elegies 1.5 and 2.34 of Propertius are the focus, as they illustrate the use of jealousy to indicate anxiety over the narrator's place in the hierarchy of love poets. Though often studied as evidence of homosocial desire, these poems in fact offer a picture of desire coexisting with rivalry and competition, without one giving way to the other.

The second part of the chapter then turns to external readers, stressing elements that are generic enough that they are common to many readers. Some of the processes represented in literary accounts of jealous behavior resemble those that we ourselves use in reading texts, especially the indulgence in visual imagination and fantasy to construct a scene or narrative. In addition, readers who are privy to the confessions of the jealous narrator are themselves drawn in to a relationship of trust and loyalty vis-à-vis the narrator. Like the jealous figure him- or herself, who obsesses over the signs of whom or what to believe, the reader of narratives about jealousy also struggles with issues of trust and plausibility. Some of these practices may be general features of reading, but the elegiac poets use them deliberately for a specific end in their treatment of jealousy.

---

2. There has been more work on this dimension of the reader's role in Catullus than in the elegists: see, for example, the work of Adler 1981, Pedrick 1986, Selden 1992, Fitzgerald 1995, and Wray 2001. For theoretical studies of the relationship between fiction and reader, in particular the question of our sympathy, cf. Robinson 2005, 143–53 and *The Journal of Aesthetics and Art Criticism* (62, 2004), especially the articles by Coplan, Devereaux, and Mullin. I have found W. Booth's *The Company We Keep: The Ethics of Fiction* (1988), especially chs. 6 and 7, to be particularly helpful for understanding the role of the reader discussed here.

Internal Readers: Love Poets as Rivals

By now we have seen many examples of how important jealousy is to the elegiac lover, both as a means of reasserting his claims on a beloved as well as for his poetic identity and reputation. Those elegies that concern infidelity or a rival portray not only jealous feelings but a desire to act upon the threat, the third part of my definition (see Introduction). Action of some kind seems imperative, whether it consists of verbal abuse like Cynthia's harangue in Propertius 1.3, or force and violence, as in cases like *Amores* 1.7. It comes as a surprise, then, to find a few cases in which narrators become jealous but then apparently drop the matter and move on. Someone or something has provoked their jealousy, but no attempt to regain the beloved or establish a claim is asserted. And narrators leave it unclear whether they have decided there never was any threat to begin with or if it is just better to ignore it. As I suggest below, they do satisfy the third criterion of my definition, that is, they feel it appropriate to establish their claim. They just fail to carry it out.

Sometimes this change of heart occurs when lovers are on the verge of punishing their beloved. The lover has a history with the beloved and hope of continuing their relationship, despite the current disappointment. Thus cases in which a lover fails to chastise a beloved are not entirely surprising, even if they are uncommon. In Tibullus 1.9, for example, the lover is willing to forgive his youthful beloved, Marathus, for what he considers a single act of infidelity. The situation is, as it turns out, more complicated: Marathus has been doubly unfaithful, deceiving the Tibullan lover with both members of a couple.[3] But even though the crime is made clear in the second line (*foedera per divos, clam violanda, dabas?*), the narrator-lover cannot help but beg the gods to forgive the boy (*parcite, caelestes*, 5).

So, too, the male lover in Propertian elegy shows himself on occasion capable of vacillation towards Cynthia's infidelities. In 1.8a, for example, Cynthia contemplates a trip with a soldier to Illyria. The poem begins with a series of insistent questions, similar to what we will see in Propertius 2.34, as to how Cynthia could even think of doing such a thing as leaving. Yet the lover cannot bring himself to be hostile to her, and hopes she will have a smooth journey (17–8) and winds conducive to bringing her safely home (13–4). This soothing approach works its magic, for in the very next elegy (1.8B), the news comes that Cynthia has decided not to go after all. The narrator's change of heart is a successful stratagem for making the beloved remain one's own, a response to jealousy not examined in the previous chapter.

---

3. See Murgatroyd's introduction to the poem (Murgatroyd 2001, 257), especially on Tibullus' enduring sympathy for Marathus. Booth 1996 offers an excellent treatment of 1.8 and its companion, 1.9.

In a last example, Propertius 2.5, the narrator again shows a shift from initial jealousy to tolerance. The poem begins with a harangue about Cynthia's reputation, known allegedly to everyone throughout the city. The narrator threatens departure and a new girlfriend (5–6) and urges himself to act while his anger is fresh (*nunc est ira recens, nunc est discedere tempus*, 9). Yet apparently he does not act quickly enough, for he ends up placating the beloved in the remainder of the poem. To soothe Cynthia's tantrum at his anger (this is in fact a response to a response), he promises he will never harm her physically. The worst he will do is reveal her infidelities in an epithet that captures her fickleness (28). He has not changed on the main point, only the appropriate form or extent of the response. Though the male lover ends up retaliating, he stops himself from full-scale revenge. More than this, he offers Cynthia some comfort and reassurance.

In two of the most striking instances of this phenomenon, however, Propertius 1.5 and 2.34, the limit on a jealous response seems different in three significant respects. To begin with, both Propertius 1.5 and 2.34 involve overlooking the crimes of a rival, not those of a beloved, where the strategic advantages of forgiveness would seem to be fewer and thus the inclination to preserve a relationship absent. The narrator's jealousy in Propertius 1.5 and 2.34 is also notably more hostile and aggressive than usual. Yet very quickly after expressing such heated feelings of jealousy, the narrator appears not only to give up his jealousy but to become sympathetic and supportive of his rival. We might think of the similar situation in Catullus 68, too, where initial anger and frustration turn in the end to acceptance and an avowal to bear jealousy in a mature way (lines 135–40).

Earlier interpretations of these elegies have argued that the identity of the rival is key to understanding this apparent swing from anger to acceptance. Francis Cairns identifies Lynceus as L. Varius Rufus and emphasizes the Epicurean elements in 2.34 that he sees as responsible for the narrator's change of heart.[4] Others, most recently Alison Keith, have argued that homosocial bonding between male characters can explain the shift from anger to forgiveness in 1.5 and 2.34 as well as Catullus 50. Lynceus and Gallus are portrayed as writers of love poetry themselves, and unlike the rival who is a soldier or politician, one can imagine at least the basis for a better understanding here. The references to love and aching desire thus refer to the experience of sharing not love, but poetry, with an audience.[5] I present these views in more detail below, before arguing that we need to balance this kind of interpretation with attention to the evidence of jealousy that persists along with the signs of camaraderie. What we have here is not a case of either/or: jealousy is at the root of any interest in the rival, and any feelings of desire depend in the first place upon rivalry, a rivalry

---

4. See Cairns 2006, 296–300.

5. Keith 2008, 116–7, and for earlier discussions, see Oliensis 1997, 159 and Miller 2004, 92–3.

that does not disappear. As I will show, a competitive and biting attitude characterizes the male characters' relationship throughout both elegies.

Propertius 1.5 is the first of a series of poems (1.5, 1.10, 1.13, 1.20) addressed to Gallus.[6] I have already studied this elegy in a different connection in Chapter 1, specifically its depiction of love as illness. Here, however, I examine instead how the theme of jealousy affects the relationship between narrator and reader. It appears, at least superficially, that Gallus is in love with Cynthia and wants to pursue her as a love interest. The narrator-lover is furious at this, as the vehemence of the opening imperatives and questions in lines 1–4 indicate:[7]

> *Invide, tu tandem voces compesce molestas*
> *et sine nos cursu, quo sumus, ire pares!*
> *quid tibi vis, insane? meos sentire furores?*
> *infelix, properas ultima nosse mala,*

> Envious man, restrain your hostile tongue
> and let us go along on our course as equals.
> What do you want, madman? To feel my fury?
> Unhappy man, you hasten to discover the greatest suffering.

This passage reveals the narrator's passionate fury. He inveighs against his rival using the vocative case three times, each time with a word beginning with *in-*: *invide, insane, infelix*. The repetition of this prefix underscores the narrator's hostility, and its negative import points to Gallus' lack of judgment in choosing to go after Cynthia. Other vocabulary in these lines also reveals the narrator's aggressive feelings towards Gallus, especially *molestas* and *furores*, while *mala* (4) constitutes a threat via the prediction of the suffering that awaits Gallus if he pursues this girl.

The narrator then continues along this same line of thought, offering Gallus a grim picture, based on his own experience, of what lies ahead should he become involved with Cynthia:

6. On the identity of this figure, Camps 1961 and Butler and Barber 1933 are hesitant to link him to Cornelius Gallus. King 1975/6, Cairns 1983, 83ff., and now Miller 2004, 93f. take the more reasonable position that we should see an allusion to the poet Gallus, despite the reference to nobility in lines 23–4 (the poet Gallus was an *eques*). See also the discussions in Ross 1975 and Oliensis 1997, 161.

7. Note that in his Loeb edition, Goold transfers the first couplet to the end of 1.4. I believe it belongs with 1.5, which on my reading is just as much about competition as 1.4, if not more. In any case, given the careful arrangement of poems in Augustan poetry books, the couplet may look back as well as forward.

non tibi iam somnos, non illa relinquet ocellos;
     illa feros[8] *animis alligat una viros.*
a! mea contemptus quotiens ad limina curres,
     cum tibi singultu fortia verba cadent
et tremulus maestis orietur fletibus horror   15
     et timor informem ducet in ore notam
et quaecumque voles fugient tibi verba querenti,
     nec poteris, qui sis aut ubi, nosse miser!

She will not let you sleep, she will not let you close your eyes.
She single-handedly straps down even fierce men with her anger.
Ah, how many times will you run scorned to my door,
when your brave words will dissolve into a sob,
and trembling, shaking and mournful weeping will overtake you.
Fear will trace ugly stains upon your face,
and whatever words you want to say will elude you.
You won't be able to know, poor wretch, who or where you are.

The list of ailments amounts to a dismal picture of suffering, one that we might again read as a warning to Gallus, though it is not a punishment or form of revenge.

Amidst the rage, however, the narrator in 1.5 also begins to show signs of pity and understanding. He applies terms normally used for himself to Gallus: *insane* in line 3, but especially *miser*,[9] in both lines 5 and 18. At the end of the poem, after forecasting a life full of sleepless nights, tears, trembling, and disorientation, the lover offers Gallus a pledge of fellowship and commiseration:

non ego tum potero solacia ferre roganti,
     cum mihi nulla mei sit medicina mali;
sed pariter miseri socio cogemur amore
     alter in alterius mutua flere sinu.   30

I won't be able to bring you any solace when you ask me,
since I have no medicine for my own troubles.
Yet equally miserable, we will bear this common love together,
and take turns weeping in each other's breast.

8. Heyworth 2007a prints *ferox* instead, which may be preferable given the emphasis on men's weakness in this poem.
9. A hallmark of the love-poet's *persona* from the very beginning: cf. *miserum me* in Prop. 1.1.1.

The lover cannot cure Gallus or himself (28), but he does offer to share his burden with him insofar as they suffer from the same illness. Now, instead of angry or threatening vocabulary, we find instead an awareness of the two men's similar plight. The repetition of words like *pariter, socio amore* (29), *mutua*, and *alter in alterius* (30) emphasizes how much they have in common. Where once the narrator and Cynthia were described as *pares* (2), now it is the Propertian lover and Gallus who will share their experiences (*pariter*, 29). The common interest in Cynthia draws lover and rival together, and the angry jealousy we saw initially appears to dissolve into sympathy. By the end of 1.5, the lover no longer seems to insist on his claim to exclusive attentions and consequently does not desire to make any retaliatory response.

I will qualify this reading of Propertius 1.5 below, but first I want to examine another poem that exhibits a similar pattern of jealousy that apparently turns to support. In Propertius 2.34, the final poem of the second book, the lover again seems willing to set aside his jealousy for the sake of male camaraderie. The intruder Lynceus has not merely expressed an interest in Cynthia, he has actually laid hands on her. Forgiveness seems most unlikely at the start of the poem, where the lover erupts in an angry attack (2.34.9–14):

> *Lynceu, tune meam potuisti, perfide, curam*
>   *tangere? nonne tuae tum cecidere manus?*   10
> *quid si non constans illa et tam certa fuisset?*
>   *posses in[10] tanto vivere flagitio?*
> *tu mihi vel ferro pectus vel perde veneno:*
>   *a domina tantum te modo tolle mea!*

> Lynceus, you traitor, how could you touch my girl?
> Didn't your hands fall away at the very thought?
> What if she had not been so loyal and faithful?
> Would you have been able to live with such a crime?
> Kill me with either knife or poison, only get away from my mistress!

The pointed insistence of *perfide* in line 9 and the slew of questions that follow show that the lover is well aware of Lynceus' violation and angry about its implications.

Yet immediately following this passage, the narrator shifts from fury to pardon (15–20):

---

10. Heyworth 2007a prints *tu* for *in*, but this does not change the meaning of the line, though it does create a stronger alliteration of "t."

te socium vitae, te corporis esse licebit,   15
te dominum admitto rebus, amice, meis:
lecto te solum, lecto te deprecor uno:
rivalem possum non ego ferre Iovem.
ipse meas solus, quod nil est, aemulor umbras,
stultus, quod stulto[11] saepe timore tremo.   20

I allow you to be a friend in life and death,
I make you master of all my possessions.
All but my bed, I beg you: stay away from my bed.
I can't endure even Jupiter as a rival.
When I'm alone, I'm afraid of my shadow, though it's nothing,
and like a fool, I often tremble at foolish fears.

Instead of *perfide* (9), the narrator now addresses Lynceus with *amice* (16).[12] Instead of all the attention on the rival that we saw in the earlier passage (note the emphasis on *tu* and *te*, 13–7), the narrator shifts focus to himself, blaming the foolishness that causes him to think that even something so insubstantial as his shadow could be a rival (19–20). The lover mocks himself, as if to say: "I couldn't help myself, it's just the way I am. This has to do with me and my weakness, not you." Distrust has become so habitual for the lover that he takes himself to task rather than blame Lynceus for his actions. Yet when he calls himself *stultus* in line 20, the use of this term elsewhere suggests he may be posing rather than offering a sincere admission.[13]

The attitudes expressed towards the rival in Propertius 1.5 and 2.34 may seem substantially different from what we have witnessed in other Propertian elegies about jealousy. As mentioned earlier, the more tolerant and forgiving touch has been explained by others as deriving from a shared evaluation of the importance of love and love poetry. Gallus and Lynceus have both "made the

---

11. Heyworth 2007a suggests *falso*, but see n. 13 below on the importance of *stultus* in this context.

12. Cairns 2006, 302–19 offers an Epicurean reading of the poem and the shift from anger to forgiveness. Crucial for his view is the identification of Lynceus with the tragic poet L. Varius Rufus (cf. Cairns 2004, 306–8 and Cairns 2006, 296–300).

13. See the discussion of *stultus* in Chapter 2. Cairns 2006 discusses the word in the context of his Epicurean reading of the poem and sees it as self-deprecating (305). I see it instead as the adoption of the kind of language the narrator's adversary might have chosen to describe him, a view that will then be refuted as the narrator shows himself more knowledgeable about the emotions in the course of the elegy. Something similar occurs in Catullus 68, too, where *stultus* is used not for the phlegmatic person, but for the one who gets too heated up. It may seem as though Catullus applies the term critically and without either the inversion or the refutation I see at issue in Prop. 2.34. Yet Catullus' resolution in lines 135–40 to tolerate his jealousy suggests that this poem fits the same pattern.

shift" not just to Cynthia, but to love poetry. Lynceus has only recently become a literate sort: until the occasion of the poem, we learn, he has led an austere life (*vitae severae*, 23) preoccupied with philosophy and astronomy. But all that has ended now. The narrator welcomes his friend into the world of love, asking what good these other pursuits will be to him now: *quid tua Socraticis tibi nunc sapientia libris/proderit aut rerum dicere posse vias?* (27–8). This rival has changed camps, both in his personal life and his career. Once the poet-lover realizes that Lynceus is inexperienced in both respects, he slips into the role of teacher and wants to help rather than obstruct his friend's project.

In Propertius 1.5, the name Gallus also points to a poetic figure involved with the writing of love poetry. Though he cannot be identified definitively with Propertius' elegiac predecessor, Cornelius Gallus, the character's association with love and his connection with the erotic myth about Hylas in elegy 1.13 make it difficult *not* to think of the poet by that name.[14] An influential interpretation of Propertius 1.10, also part of the group of poems about Gallus in Book 1, takes the spying incident described there not as a voyeuristic scene, but as a reference to the poets' reading each other's work.[15] That is, when the narrator expresses his joy after watching Gallus in the act of "making love," he is actually only "reading" a poetic description of love and lovemaking. In this way, the poem is not actual spying or an invasion of privacy, but rather the sharing of poetry between two men writing in the same genre.

This view once again stresses the literary dimensions of the poem, and makes Propertius and Gallus writers and readers of the same genre. The elision between love and love poetry, lover and writer/reader about love would then suggest why this sort of rival does not provide a threat. Both 1.5 and 2.34 are tolerant of Gallus and Lynceus' transgressions precisely because their only "crime" lies in reading the speaker's poetry, not in stealing his girlfriend. If we adopt this approach, an interest in the rival seems to obscure or even rule out the presence of jealousy. Yet as I suggested above, the two coexist throughout: the interest in the rival only arises because of jealous feelings, and these never go away. Since both amatory and literary rivalry are present simultaneously in these poems, we need to understand the way in which they are intertwined and dependent on each other. For this reason, we should not privilege the literary dimension over the competitive one, however uncomfortable it may be to confront the depiction of the lover's jealousy.[16]

Interest in the rival and jealousy often go hand in hand. Jealousy over a beloved may occur not out of any true desire for the beloved, but in order to grow closer to the apparent rival. Freud describes this motive in his third category of jealousy, the "delusional" or "paranoid" type, which derives from homosexual

14. See n. 6 above.

15. For a history of the view and its proponents, see Keith 2008, p. 121, n. 13. See also Sharrock 2000, 271–2 and Miller 2004, 78.

16. Keith 2008, 119–20 and 133–4.

attraction.[17] Jealous feelings of this kind are not so much caused by fear that a beloved is lost to another, but develop rather as an excuse to explain a fascination with the rival. Yet the positive feelings would not survive without the structure of rivalry and competition that initially drew the lover's attention.

Even in cases where homosexual attraction is not the original impetus, characters that begin as rivals end up finding things they value in common. Fascination can develop because of an identification between the two parties.[18] As already suggested in Chapter 2, jealousy pushes one to think about a perspective other than your own. After all, rivals obviously have the same taste, at least in love (or love objects). They may be curious about each other, insofar as they also both appeal to the same person, and wonder in what ways are they similar, or what one has that the other lacks. The curiosity or even friendship that results, however, is a pointed one, for it has competition at its root.

Two important studies point to the different emphases I have been discussing. Eve Sedgwick's influential book, *Between Men*, examines homoerotic desire in literature, cases where a beloved functions merely as a means of bonding between two men. She is concerned in the works she examines with repressed homosexual desire and the inability of this desire to extend to women. This kind of interest is clearly present in the Catullan and Propertian examples at issue, where the female mistress is an occasion for the interaction and attraction between men. But Sedgwick does not bring out the idea of competition that I see as crucial to the examples of love elegy examined in this chapter, as her focus is mainly on the erotic feelings experienced by the two men.

An earlier work by René Girard (1961) is more relevant to the examples of Latin poetry I examine here. In his study of mimetic desire, *Mensonge romantique et vérité*, Girard emphasizes the competitive features of literary triangles in authors ranging from Cervantes to Shakespeare. Girard describes a fascination with the rival that arises not because of one's own desire, but because of another's.[19] In other words, it is a rivalrous desire to have what another has that dictates one's

---

17. Cf. Freud 1922, 225–32, and also White and Mullen 1989, 139. Freud calls the first two types competitive or normal, and projected. For a discussion of views on the difference between normal and pathological (often identified with delusional jealousy), see White and Mullen 1989, 175–8, and Baumgart [1985] 1990, ch. 4.

18. See Graham Greene, *The End of the Affair*, p. 152: "On the afternoon before, Henry had wavered. He had telephoned asking me to come over. It was odd how close we had become with Sarah gone. He depended on me now much as before he had depended on Sarah—I was someone familiar about in the house. I even pretended to wonder whether he would ask me to share the house when once the funeral was over, and what answer I would give him." We also find good examples of male bonding in film, e.g., Truffaut's *Jules et Jim* or Dorris Dörrie's *Männer*, where rivals for one woman either are or become friends.

19. Girard 1961; see the critique of his view, in particular its focus on male desire, in Lloyd 1995, 21–2.

own choices. This distinction between desire according to oneself and desire according to another is especially suggestive for the Roman examples at issue. Gallus and Lynceus may very well be interested in Cynthia not because of anything having to do with her, but rather because another lover has her or because another writer has created her in his poetry, and this provokes competitive feelings. This added element of competition is essential, for it suggests that rivalry does not give way to homosocial interest, but rather that homosocial interest would not exist without the ongoing presence of competition.

In light of this relationship between male friendship and jealousy, we need a new perspective. In 1.5 and 2.34, jealousy brings the two rivals together, but they remain rivals nonetheless, both in sexual and poetic terms. Hostility and competition linger beyond the expression of their male solidarity, and the lover's speech in both poems reveals that he cannot completely put aside the threat posed by the rival. Their ongoing rivalry manifests itself in three features we have seen as typical in elegies about jealousy: the lover's close attention to visual detail, references to superior status, and the use of threats.

Suspicious Monitoring

I start with the emphasis on visible manifestations in Propertius 1.5. Recall the earlier discussion in Chapter 1 and the long list of bodily changes the Propertian lover predicts for Gallus: sobs (14), shaking (15), fearful expressions (16), and confused looks (16–7). These signs mark the lover's illness, as we have already seen, and also the parallel positions of the two men who will both experience these symptoms. But there is more going on here than a description of lovesickness. The detailed list of Gallus' symptoms the narrator provides reflects the obsessive attention a jealous lover pays to any visual clue of infidelity. Every aspect of his condition is perceptible from the outside. The lover's watchfulness for visible manifestations of lovesickness reveals how closely Gallus is being scrutinized and how vulnerable the narrator is to the mistress' whims. Any mark of the same suffering that he himself has undergone is a telltale sign that Gallus is lovesick himself and thus has become intimate with Cynthia in the same way as the narrator has. The creative fantasy that constructs a rival and sees a threat in every man shows how easily the jealous figure can be thrown off balance. This is all the more likely in a case where the lover is searching for his very own symptoms in someone else. He knows exactly what to look for and how to interpret it when he finds it.[20]

The curiosity of the narrator in 1.5 about Gallus' condition also brings us back to the spying episode in 1.10 and the meta-poetic reading discussed earlier.

---

20. On recognizing that someone is suffering from one's own symptoms as lover, see Callimachus *AP* 12.71 and 12.134 and the discussion in Gutzwiller 1998, 216–7.

Although an attractive reading, it does not take account of the significance of the actual spying in the poem and its relation to jealousy. The sight of Gallus making love may be a metaphor, but it is not merely a metaphor. A jealous lover determines his rival's advantage over him through actual observation. The sexual dimension in this case, watching another man in the act of making love, is at least as relevant to the two men's relationship as the literary one. The narrator wants his revenge for Gallus' intrusion against him, described just five elegies earlier. He wants to show that he, too, is highly engaged with all of Gallus' activity, both in love and in love poetry. The hostility and invasiveness described in the poem cannot simply be erased, for it is a vital part of the two men's relationship, as least as the narrator wants to depict it. In Propertius 1.10, as in 1.5, whatever homosocial attraction there is between the two men, it does not override all tensions and signs of competition.

Boasts and Threats

Another sign of hostility in both Propertius 1.5 and 2.34 is the way the narrator alludes to the rival's inferior status. He does this, I argue, as a means of establishing his own superiority in love and love poetry. This diminishment of the rival is not new. In 3.15, for example, Cynthia's rival, Lycinna, was compared via the Dirce myth to a handmaiden, suggesting her inferior social status. In 4.8, the inferior status of Cynthia's rivals enrages her, and she asserts herself by playing the role of Odysseus, the legitimate husband, in contrast to these invasive intruders.

The Propertian narrator also manhandles inferior rivals and takes pains to express his dominant status over the newcomer to the world of love and love poetry. Considered against the pattern of jealous behavior we have seen so far, the language in 1.5 and 2.34 starts to sound less welcoming and more threatening. If we return to the lover's closing words in Propertius 1.5, we find that, despite the use of *mutua* and *pariter*, lines 27–32 also contain a threat:

> *non ego tum potero solacia ferre roganti,*
>   *cum mihi nulla mei sit medicina mali;*
> *sed pariter miseri socio cogemur amore*
>   *alter in alterius mutua flere sinu.*   30
> *quare, quid possit mea Cynthia, desine, Galle,*
>   *quaerere: non impune illa rogata venit.*

> I won't be able to bring you any solace when you ask me,
> since I have no medicine for my own troubles.
> But equally miserable, we will bear this common love together,
> and take turns weeping in each other's breast.

Wherefore, stop asking what my Cynthia is willing to do, Gallus.
Once you've asked her, you won't get off scot-free.

The lover makes sure to emphasize that Gallus' suffering will be extremely
unpleasant. This passage does not, or not merely, describe mutual suffering, but
reflects an attempt to hold onto his place and diminish that of his rival. The narrator states that, however great his experience, ultimately he will not be able to
help Gallus: *non ego tum potero solacia ferre roganti,/cum mihi nulla mei sit medicina
mali* (27–8). Whatever else this may say about love or how to read poems about
love, the lover's medical prognosis is full of foreboding and intimidation. Like
the use of myth to express a threat in Propertius 3.15, in 1.5 a picture of sickness
and decline is directed at warning the rival to stay away. The message is hostile,
even if the narrator eschews a direct attack.

The anxiety this reveals is particularly poignant given that the narrator has cre-
ated a striking role reversal in 1.5. If the Gallus referred to is indeed meant to evoke
Cornelius Gallus, then it is Gallus who should uphold the dominant position, with
Propertius his follower. And we would expect that as his follower, Propertius would
be labeled the inferior. Yet in 1.5, the places of the two love poets have been inverted.
In an Oedipal twist, the narrator depicts Gallus rejoicing in the former's work as if
Gallus, not Propertius, were the newcomer to love elegy. Because the poem comes
so early on in Propertius' first book, it is tempting to read this as a desire to represent an aggressive stand about his place among his predecessors in the genre.
Indeed, later on in the collection, in 2.34, Gallus is restored to his rightful place
among earlier love poets (91), as if there, at the end of Book 2, the narrator has
grown confident enough to name his important predecessors. The elegies that I
have been discussing thus refer to social and literary hierarchy to suggest that,
despite any apparent similarities between lover and rival, the rival needs to remem-
ber what a novice he is, and by analogy how experienced his adversary is. Jockeying
for position is crucial for a poet trying to establish his place in the tradition.

In Propertius 2.34 as well, the motions towards understanding and friendship with Lynceus are also accompanied by a threat and a reminder of the lover-
poet's superiority. This elegy is full of references to rivalry and hierarchy that are
both erotic and poetic.[21] The lover asserts his dominance as a teacher of love, an
attempt to gain the upper hand even after accepting Lynceus as an erotic poetic
colleague. He explicitly uses the language of domination in lines 47–50:

> *sed non ante gravi taurus succumbit aratro,*   47
> *cornua quam validis haeserit in laqueis,*

21. Lines 45–55 are rearranged by editors, but the sequence of thought is not important for my
point here, that the lover touches on anger he had supposedly put aside. See also Heyworth 2007b,
273, who is doubtful about restoring the correct order of lines.

nec tu tam duros per te patieris amores:
trux tamen a nobis ante domandus eris.

But the bull does not submit to the heavy plow
before his horns are caught up in strong ropes,
nor will you endure such challenges in love on your own.
Although fierce, you must be subdued by me first.

The lover also boasts about how far he has come on his own merits:

aspice me, cui parva domi fortuna relicta est   55
nullus et antiquo Marte triumphus avi,
ut regnem mixtas inter conviva puellas
hoc ego, quo tibi nunc elevor, ingenio!

Look at me, who received but a small fortune at home,
and who has no ancestor who won a triumph in ancient battle,
how I play king at a banquet among a multitude of girls,
through that talent for which I am now admired by you.

He claims he is admired (*elevor*) by Lynceus because of his innate talent and
boasts that he has not relied on either ancestry or fortune to boost his success.
In this way, his success will always outpace that of Lynceus, despite the support
of his family and connections. It is worth noting another possible meaning of
elevor, "I am diminished."[22] This would emphasize even more the rivalrous relationship the narrator has with Lynceus and the former's superiority at having
overcome a supposedly poor background and Lynceus' antagonism.[23] Either
way we define the verb, then, it supports the point that these lines concern rivalry, not friendship. Despite the apparent welcome the narrator of the poem
offers to this newcomer to the realm of love, he is careful to point out that he
has not overcome either his suspicions towards Lynceus or his competition
with him.

If it were not already clear that the poem is primarily concerned with the
issue of competition, lines 27–95 of 2.34 are entirely taken up with a comparison of genres. In congratulating Lynceus on having shifted his interests to
love poetry, the narrator first points out the advantages of this genre in comparison with philosophy and astronomy. As he goes on, he extols the pleasures
of elegy over tragedy (33–44) and then epic (45–50). From Homer he moves to

22. *OLD* s.v. 2.
23. Perhaps this explains why Gallus is given a noble background in 1.5, even though it does not
fit with what we know about the historical Gallus he most likely represents (see n. 6 above).

Virgil, and refers to the latter's opus in reverse chronological order in order to de-emphasize epic and highlight instead Virgil's interest in love in his early career. Love poetry will bring immortality to Propertius, just as it did to Varro, Catullus, and Gallus. Elegy is thus held out as a rival to epic poetry. While this triumph may seem to include Lynceus in the honor, in fact Lynceus' relative newcomer status shows that he had initially made the wrong choice by engaging in other genres, unlike the Propertian narrator who chose love poetry right from the start.

In the context of erotic and generic rivalry, it is also worth considering Propertius 1.4, the poem to the iambic poet Bassus, which is often analyzed together with 1.5.[24] The situations of 1.4 and the other two elegies are not exactly parallel, since Bassus does not appear to be a rival in the way that Gallus or Lynceus is. The complaint against Bassus is not that he tries to steal Cynthia away, but rather that he wants to introduce the Propertian lover to other women. Cynthia is furious at the suggestion, but her lover maintains a neutral front and returns to Bassus in order to report Cynthia's angry threat: she will spread such nasty rumors about Bassus that no girl will ever want to date him again (17–22).

Cynthia's angry reaction stems from jealousy at the thought of her lover involved with other women. And yet the representation of her hostility is also an exercise in literary *aemulatio*. As others have pointed out, what better subject for a poem addressed to an invective poet than a poem insinuating slander?[25] Immediately following comes 1.5, a poem about love addressed to a love poet. While the rivalry in 1.5 involved the two love poets, the rivalry in 1.4 entwines Bassus and Cynthia, who are both interested in the lover and who are willing to hurt each other in order to control the male lover. The portrayal of jealous outrage and literary rivalry here parallels the complexity of the jealous reaction in 1.5, where literary camaraderie and a sense of threat also go hand in hand. What matters here is not either the characters' anger or their tolerance, but rather the way in which these coexist within a single poem.

---

24. On the pair of poems, cf. the detailed analysis of Cairns 1983 and Miller 2004, 91–3. Cairns points to certain similarities between the position of Bassus and Gallus (63): "The prospect awaiting Bassus in 1.4 is thus similar to the one that awaits Gallus in 1.5: they will both become *exclusi amatores* (cf. 1, 5, 20), Bassus being excluded by all *puellae*, Gallus specifically by Cynthia (29)." Cairns goes on to point to Cynthia's anger in both elegies as another link between the two elegies. See also Keith 2008, 117–8.

25. This is the case Suits 1976 makes for 1.4: "Propertius seems to be threatening, then, to play the iambist against Bassus" (88). See, however, Cairns 1983 for a critique and modification of this view (80–2).

And indeed this is exactly what is going on in Catullus c. 50, mentioned earlier as one of the poems that has been read in light of literary relationships. Here, too, competition is just as important as *amicitia*.[26] The greater part of the poem consists of the narrator outlining the various delight and fun he and his friend, Licinius, shared as they composed poetry together, a pleasure that is described in sexual terms.[27] But this does not last through the final lines of the poem. In line 20, the Catullan narrator refers to Nemesis, the goddess of revenge, and his threat that she will strike if Licinius rejects his prayers (18–21). The allusion to a possible winner and loser thus underscores the continued presence of competition and anxiety over the poem's reception, no matter how playful the poet's tone might initially appear.

In Propertius 1.5 and 2.34, the poet uses jealousy to develop expectations of *fides* that rest not merely on the mistress but on the internal reader as well. Gallus and Lynceus are recent converts to love poetry and should be ideal readers. In fact, however, the poet-lover cannot entirely rid himself of the anxiety that they will steal his ideas or be competitors for a place in the hierarchy of love poets in Rome. What he wants from them is not unlike what he desires from his mistress: a shared evaluation of the importance of love and human relations over status, power, and ancestry. By choosing to love Cynthia, Gallus and Lynceus recognize the attractions of the lover's poetry and seem to share his values. But they go too far in their enthusiasm. The lover must worry that they are trying to outdo him and threaten his position. And as a result, he, too, becomes competitive, though apparently with some reluctance, as the apologetic strand in the poems we have examined suggests. Even as the lover himself grows more secure as he moves from Book 1 to Book 2, the expectations of, and disappointments from, his audience do not change. The loyalty missing from the lover's erotic relationship is missing from the relationship with his internal readers as well. This creates a bleak picture not unlike the one we will see in the next chapter, where the absence of *fides* is represented as pervasive in Roman society.

The representation of characters like Gallus and Lynceus constitutes one kind of audience for Propertius' elegies. They offer what looks like a more enthusiastic reception with which to balance Cynthia's typically negative reaction, even if ultimately we have seen that it, too, is fundamentally problematic. We can take 1.5 and 2.34 as representing yet another expression of the narrator's jealous obsession. From his paranoid perspective, the interest shown by other poets is not just a sign of his growing fame, but a threat to his success. Despite the demonstration

---

26. The juxtaposition of Catullus cc. 50 and 51 is surely significant. The structure of c. 51 involves three people, two of them focused on a third, and is therefore more suggestive of a jealous triangle than a straightforward love experience (*contra* Konstan 2006, pp. 240–41). The poem is also dominated by gazing and observing, a common feature of poems about jealousy. Perhaps most crucially, in Catullus c. 51, as in Propertius 1.5 and 2.34, the poem combines jealousy over the beloved with a special, almost admiring relationship to the rival.

27. Cf. lines 8–15 and the erotic words and images there (e.g., *incensus*, 8, *furore*, 11, etc.).

of his growing powers and security as a poet, he remains pathologically insecure, suspecting that everyone is out to steal his mistress from him. This blend of confidence and insecurity, success and threat, is intended to encourage our sympathy for someone who sees himself as treated unfairly despite, or because of, his talent. The narrator also hopes to win us over by representing others' conversion to the power of love poetry. He describes Gallus and Lynceus as recent converts[28] and makes their awakening happen "while we watch." By describing Gallus and Lynceus' switch to love poetry within narrative time, it is suggested that we, too, should be won over by love's authority. If we do not become writers of love poetry ourselves, at the very least we ought to be eager readers. This brings us to the subject of the external readership and the second part of this chapter.

External Readers: Vicarious Participants in Jealousy

I turn now to another kind of reader, not one who is inscribed into the text like Gallus or Lynceus, but rather one who stands outside it. How, one may ask, is this kind of reader affected by jealousy in the text? Certainly neither you nor I is capable of provoking the elegiac lover's jealousy, and it would be very surprising if we became jealous as a result of reading about elegy. Yet I argue that several structural and thematic features of elegy establish connections between the experience of the lover and the reader that put the two in parallel positions.[29] These sorts of features inevitably raise questions that involve the paradox of fiction—that is to say, how we can have emotions about characters or events that we know are fictional.[30] How can we be moved by what we know does not exist? The question, which centers not on whether we respond, but why and whether it is irrational, has generated a large debate. For our purposes, a solution to that problem is unnecessary. What is more relevant is that many readers do respond this way, and more importantly, in the case of jealousy, that they respond in a highly sympathetic way that is then steadily undermined as our suspicions grow, in keeping with the jealous narrator's own feelings of doubt.

---

28. Compare Damisippus in Hor. *Sat.* 2.3, who is depicted as a "recent covert" to philosophy and someone with only limited understanding of the ideas he is attracted to. For the elegists, the emphasis is not so much on deep versus superficial understanding as on experience versus naïveté.

29. See also other studies connecting the narrator and reader in Augustan literature: Lee-Stecum 2000 on Tibullus and Nagle 1988 on love triangles in the *Metamorphoses*. Lee-Stecum's approach is especially relevant: he argues that the reader is a "double of the poet/lover" in the search for stability. He connects this with issues of gender and power, however, and not the emotions or common processes experienced by both the jealous figure and the reader, as I do here. Valladares 2005 also discusses the shared position of "reader/viewer" and "lover" in Propertius 1.3. On the shared position of narrator and reader in other literature about love, see Nussbaum 1990, 8–9.

30. See n. 2 above.

In what follows, I explore two dimensions of this parallel experience between narrator and reader. To begin with, I return to the role of visualization in effecting jealousy, this time from the perspective of the reader. It is not only the jealous figure who creates pictures in his head; readers do this as well, and this habit aligns us with the one undergoing jealousy in ways that are at times surprisingly close.[31] Second, a reader shares in the anxiety over *fides* felt by the elegiac couple, though again from a different perspective.[32] While the lovers worry over whether they know everything they should about the other's devotion and loyalty, we readers of elegy, too, worry over whether or not we are being told an accurate version of events. For reasons already mentioned—the lack of any corroborating evidence, the tendency to hear a story from just one side, the narrator's confessional style that works on our sympathy—we are often left in a state of *aporia* about whom or what to believe. Both of these strategies, the creation of visual images and a skeptical view towards the information we are given, initially encourage identification with the narrator. Yet in the end, I argue, we choose a more critical distance, since ultimately we would not like to seem at all like a person as suspicious and impetuous as the elegiac lover.

Visualization and Identification

The first correspondence between lover and reader shows up in the way in which jealous characters use visual clues and fantasy as fodder for their jealous thoughts. Visualization of the beloved is a hallmark feature of jealousy, whether the lover pores over events in pursuit of clues about infidelity or creates a fantasy about the beloved in the throes of infidelity.[33] Although we have seen many examples of this dimension of jealousy by now, we can add others to the list as well. Take, for example, Propertius 2.19, where Cynthia is away in the countryside, absent from the lover's view and thus vulnerable to rivals. The narrator consoles himself with the thought that his mistress is in a rural setting, and thus at a distance from all the men who would normally try to seduce her. He feeds himself comforting pictures of her engaged in harmless activities appropriate to the setting: looking out at the fields, participating in the sacrifice of a kid, even

---

31. On creating pictures as we read, see Booth 1988, ch. 10 "Figures that 'Figure' the Mind: Images and Metaphors as Constitutive Stories."

32. See Lloyd 1995, xi–xii on jealousy as a "strategy both readerly and writerly." I found this idea to be very promising and similar to the kind of approach I am trying to suggest about elegy.

33. In addition to the some of the examples discussed in Chapter 3, see Graham Greene's *The End of the Affair*, p. 74: "That was the worst period of all: it is my profession to imagine, to think in images: fifty times through the day, and immediately I woke during the night, a curtain would rise and the play would begin: always the same play, Sarah making love, Sarah with X, doing the same things that we had done together . . ."

mimicking a country dance (7–16). But any apparent reassurance provided by Cynthia's stay in the country is reversed at the end of the poem.[34] In fact, Propertius cannot rid himself of his worries that her name is voiced by an *assidua lingua* (31).[35] The innocent tasks he imagined her performing thus fail to displace entirely the narrator's fears that what she is really up to is the same thing she does in Rome itself, just without the need to hide it as before.

The elegists also include the representation of artistic scenes and familiar Roman monuments, as we have seen in both Propertius and Ovid. Although I have alluded to these before, I now want to emphasize a new element: the way that talking about visual or material art aids our own visualization as readers. In alluding to such scenes, the poets highlight how the jealous mind is filled with fantasies and images of paintings, buildings, and the physical setting for infidelity. I choose two examples already familiar from earlier chapters in order to highlight these "readerly" features: Propertius 1.3 and 4.8.

In the first of these, 1.3, there is to begin with a certain amount of detail that is meant to put the feared scene "before our eyes." The male lover watches a sleeping Cynthia, whose tossing and turning make him imagine that she is dreaming of making love with another man. When Cynthia wakes up, she too relies on what she sees before her to draw her conclusions: the lover's garlands, drunken state, and fatigue lead her to accuse him of having spent what was supposed to be *their* evening making love to someone else.

Both characters also use visual fantasy to heighten their jealousy. I have already said that the male lover takes Cynthia's restlessness to indicate her dreams about another man. *Vano auspicio* in line 28 below suggests there is no other man, but the lover indulges himself in creating a picture of Cynthia's infidelity:

> *et quotiens raro duxti suspiria motu,*
> > *obstupui vano credulus auspicio,*
> *ne qua tibi insolitos portarent visa timores,*
> > *neve quis invitam cogeret esse suam:*   30

and whenever you sighed and gave an occasional shudder
I froze, trusting in an empty sign,
lest some dream be bringing you unfamiliar fears
or someone be forcing you to be his against your will.

---

34. Note, too, that the narrator mentions that he will go hunting (*ipse ego venabor*, 17) before joining Cynthia; on the implications of hunting (never an innocent activity in elegy), see Green 1996.

35. I read *metuam* in this line instead of *mutem*, which makes little sense in the context. See Camps 1966a and Richardson 1977 *ad loc.* and cf. Papanghelis' proposal of *iactem* (in Heyworth's apparatus criticus [2007a]).

Yet this visualization is complicated by the preceding lines. There the lover tells us he himself attempted the very thing he fears from a rival. He is the one who disturbs Cynthia's sleep with sexual advances; he is the one she rejects (21–6). The male lover has in effect put himself into the shoes of his rival, and imagines a new role and thus a different connection with Cynthia.

The lover's interest in playing the rival was in fact insinuated in the beginning of the elegy, where the poet-lover compares his sleeping mistress to three mythological women, Ariadne, Andromede, and a Maenad, popular subjects of private wall paintings in Pompeii and perhaps Rome as well, and thus more imagery to fill a reader's mind.[36] As we saw in Chapter 2, the Propertian lover sees himself as the rescuer of Cynthia as well as the one who abandoned her. He wants to play the roles of both lover and rival, to feel jealousy but also be the cause of it, and to enjoy both aspects in a relationship with Cynthia. He sees both of them in different roles, and the switch from one to another, even within a single elegy, forces readers to constantly readjust their understanding of the character in appearance, motive, and behavior.

In alluding to familiar artistic scenes, the poet highlights how the jealous mind is filled with pictures, a connection he explores elsewhere as well with respect to Roman art. By describing these pictures in words, he draws his readers in as well, forcing us, too, to look or gaze at what he is compelled to, leading us to his own perspective of the jealous figure within the text. The male lover thus engages in a significant amount of fantasy. He imagines Cynthia as herself and as other women, as sexually available but also his own. He pictures himself simultaneously as her rescuer, his own rival, and her Odysseus, come home to her at last.[37] This list reveals the jealous character as an inventor of stories, but it also shows to what extent he is an interpreter or reader as we are. As our engagement with art makes it easier to enter his jealous perspective, the lover also explores his jealousy by engaging with art and literature. His presentation of scenes both artistic and literary seems intended to provide some help towards understanding the dynamics of the jealous experience.

Turning to Cynthia, we find that she has an imagination as active as that of the male lover and reader. When she awakens and lays eyes on her lover, her first words reveal that she has constructed an entire story out of thin air, based solely on his appearance:

> 'tandem te nostro referens iniuria lecto   35
>   alterius clausis expulit e foribus?
> namque ubi longa meae consumpsti tempora noctis,
>   languidus exactis, ei mihi, sideribus?

36. See the excellent discussion of Valladares 2005.
37. See Valladares 2005, 228, where she also describes the shifts in the narrator's role, though she goes on to interpret these in terms of gender role reversals.

Has the rejection of another driven you out of shut doors
and brought you back to my bed?
For where have you spent the long hours of the night that was supposed
    to be mine,
you who return exhausted when the stars have run their course?

Cynthia does not merely accuse him of having been with another. She embellishes: there must have been a fight, there must have been slammed doors. She conjures up a narrative to account for the visual detail inherent in *languidus* (38), his sexual exhaustion. The jealous Cynthia is also a storyteller, then. And she is a reader, too. In portraying herself as an abandoned female, she does not identify with the women who were named in the poem's opening but chooses instead to model herself on Penelope at the same time that she uses the standard complaint of the male lover. She casts herself as the faithful one, waiting at home, spinning and singing songs. She appeals to what we have all read in order to illuminate her own experience.[38] These jealous characters, themselves fictive, create their own narratives that then refer to other stories and works of art.

Propertius 4.8 also draws attention to the role of seeing in stimulating both male and female jealousy. Cynthia has left the house under false pretenses and has clearly made a date with another man. The male lover responds by inviting two girls over, but Cynthia will surprise all of them when she returns home earlier than expected. The elegy as a whole unfolds vividly like a drama at which we have been made present. Cynthia's flamboyant departure is described as a *spectaclum* (21), a word that captures the emphasis on both seeing and being seen in this elegy.[39]

The lines involving the narrator and the two girls (35ff.) indicate in careful detail the seating arrangement, glasses used, and quality of the flame, thus allowing the reader to recreate the scene in his or her own mind. The male lover would have seen all this, but he also engages in some visual fantasy. Apparently unable to concentrate on the entertainment provided by the two girls, he confesses that his thoughts wandered to where Cynthia had gone: *Lanuvii ad portas, ei mihi, totus eram* (48). If other poems are a guide, this is not a ruse but instead a well-worn habit, as the lover regularly imagines Cynthia in her absence and fantasizes about her infidelity. When Cynthia goes to Baiae in 1.11, for example, the lover spends ten lines dreaming up what she may be doing there, especially hoping that she is not listening to another man's seductive whispers (lines 9–18).

But the jealous character is of course not the only one creating images. Someone who enjoys fiction indulges this love of images, just as the jealous person

38. See Fantham 2006, 189 on Propertius' mythological choices: "Boucher has noted that . . . Propertius draws largely on the classic heroines of Homeric tragedy and Apollonius; these would be what his public had read or heard or seen, so that a phrase or even a mere epithet could evoke remembered texts or images without need for narrative."

39. See the emphasis on both Cynthia and the lover as spectacles in O'Neill 2005, 260–5.

obsessively manufactures them. Even without explicit comparison to works of art, descriptive language induces us to visualize images in our heads. We cannot help but picture scenes such as Cynthia's return from the dead (Propertius 4.7), Cynthia dressed up in Eastern luxuries (Propertius 1.2 and 1.15), or the fight between and her and the lover described in Propertius 3.8. The same can be said of Tibullus' idyllic landscapes that conjure up an escape to the Golden Age, or Ovid's description of Corinna and himself at the theater, fighting over his apparent glances at other women. The fundamental features of the genre—the locked-out lover, his enslavement and battles, the scenes set in the bedroom, city, or countryside—all of these, too, force readers to conjure up a scene in their heads. And this is all the more true for the ancient audience: since many of these elegiac *topoi* derive from mime and New Comedy, ancient readers of elegy would have seen these very kinds of scenes performed on the stage.

The effect on us is only that much greater in poems where the poets specifically allude to the act of seeing or visualizing, as in the cases about jealousy and works of art, whether that means wall paintings (e.g., 1.3), portraits (e.g., 2.6, a poem I discuss in the next chapter), or monuments (e.g., 2.31 and 2.32). In these cases, the role of seeing and interpreting visual images is explicit. But it is not only that we are made to see what the lover sees. When jealous lovers use pictures to fuel their jealousy, this process is analogous to our use of pictures while reading. We mostly create pictures for increasing our understanding and pleasure while reading, while jealous figures may have a variety of different reasons for doing so. It could be simply their imagination or a sharing of fears. There could also be a feeling of violation or a desire to see "justice done." Insofar as readers participate in the pleasures of generating mental images, they do not initially tend to take a critical stance toward excessive emotion that would have been unacceptable by Roman and philosophical standards, as I discussed in Chapter 1.

Doubts and Suspicions

A second process that jealousy and reading share is that both subsequently trigger skepticism about the information we take in.[40] As with the role of visualization,

40. See Proust 1954, 3. 519: "C'est un des pouvoirs de la jalousie de nous découvrir combien la réalité des faits extérieurs et les sentiments de l'âme sont quelque chose d'inconnu qui prête à mille suppositions. Nous croyons savoir exactement ce que sont les choses, et ce que pensent les gens, pour la simple raison que nous ne nous en soucions pas. Mais dès que nous avons le désir de savoir, comme a le jaloux, alors c'est un vertigineux kaléidoscope où nous ne distinguons plus rien." (*It's one of the powers of jealousy to reveal to us how the reality of external facts and the sentiments of the soul are something unknown that lends itself to countless conjectures. We think we know exactly what things are and what people are thinking, for the simple reason that we're unconcerned about them. But as soon as we have the desire to know, as the jealous person has, then we are looking through a vertiginous kaleidoscope in which we can no longer distinguish anything.*)

this feature is not something unique to elegy, but reappears in most narratives about jealousy. In novels such as Füst's *The Story of My Wife*, Sabato's *The Tunnel*, or Robbe-Grillet's *La Jalousie*, the grounds for the narrator's jealousy are never really confirmed.[41] These and other similar accounts dwell on the jealous person's imagined fears, often from a first-person perspective. Yet the validity of these fears is left open all the way through to the conclusion of the novel. The reader faced with internal inconsistencies and the lack of any corroborating evidence is forced to sift through the history and reconstruct it through clues and puzzles, just as a lover has to do with the beloved's behavior. This experience is illustrated most vividly in Robbe-Grillet's novel, where characters are identified only by letters and a single scene recurs repeatedly throughout the novel without explanation. The point is not, it seems, to settle the question of whether the jealousy in a given case is well founded or not. It is instead to establish a particular relationship between the protagonist and the reader, one that is on a somewhat equal footing.[42] A reader may sympathize with or despise the jealous character, but in terms of the quest for confirmation and a desire to trust, the two roles are allied.

So, too, in the majority of cases involving elegiac jealousy, we never know whether there is any good basis for imagining that the mistress is in fact unfaithful in the poet-lover's absence or indeed whether either of them is as guilty as the other paints the situation. There is a perception of guilt on both sides, of course, but no independent evidence that the reader can use to make an assessment. In some examples, to be sure, we do encounter concrete evidence of rivals and probably infidelity, rather than merely depicted or imagined suspicions. But these often fly in the face of the asseverations of fidelity, leaving us to waver between claims and practice. Ultimately, the elegists will not proclaim or resolve the truth either about their mistresses or about themselves. There is a fundamental inability to know that promotes a deep skepticism and epistemological failure.[43]

41. It is significant that in Maupassant's *Pierre et Jean*, so long as we hear things only from Pierre's perspective, we are unsure whether or not he sees the situation clearly. But later his suspicions are in fact corroborated, something that almost never occurs when a narrative about jealousy is told entirely in the first person.

42. See the suggestive remarks of Booth 1988, 187: "our fullest friendships on this scale are with those who seem wholly engaged in the same kind of significant activity that they expect of us. Usually in the past such activity has included that most important of all 'reading' challenges, the interpretation of moral character . . . In tracing these efforts, we readers stretch our own capacities for thinking about how life should be lived, as we join those more elevated judges, the implied authors. We cannot quite consider ourselves *their* equals: they are more skillful than we at providing such exercises in moral discernment. But they imply that we might become their equals in discernment if we only practiced long enough."

43. On jealousy as a means of exploring skepticism, see the dissertation of Charlebois (2000). She sees the depiction of jealousy in Renaissance drama as representative of two separate crises, one having to do with issues of certainty arising as a result of the Protestant reform, and a second concerning gender and the male inability to understand female desire.

It is worth noting how different this situation is from the one we find in Catullus. In his poetry, the narrator is steadfastly faithful in the affairs with Lesbia and Juventius (unless we are to imagine him conducting both affairs simultaneously, something for which there is no evidence in the text). It is only the beloveds who are portrayed as deceitful: no intimations of guilt or even indecision stain the lover's portrait there.[44] In the elegiac poets, the narrators also adhere to the part of the wronged lover. Yet Propertius and Ovid give clues that this is not an accurate picture. While the lovers represent themselves as having been wronged by their mistresses, they do not always live up to the claims about their own loyalty, as we saw in Chapter 3. The Roman elegists thus force readers to become critical in assessing whom to believe and when. They may initially encourage us to be understanding about the jealous person's difficulties in trying to determine the beloved's loyalty. Propertius also gives the impression that jealousy is common and frequent, and this suggests that it is normal and part of the human condition, perhaps not the kind of thing, in other words, to try to fight against.

Ultimately, however, we lose unquestioning sympathy for a narrator who gives us reason to distrust him.[45] Although the reader can enjoy the characters' fantasies at a remove, it is also clear how debilitating they are. The questionable nature of a jealous person's suspicions, the mixing of genuine concerns and worries with inflated or hasty judgments, the self-serving and defensive justifications, all undermine the credibility of the jealous person's narrative and raise another kind of skepticism about the lover's evidence. Our difficulties with the lover's version of events come to reside with doubts about the lover or narrator himself, and there is frustration at the way in which we are left hanging without direction about whom or what to believe. This leads further to critical reflection and a distancing even from ourselves, who have through our initial identification with the jealous characters marked ourselves as susceptible to jealousy and suspiciousness as well.

This twofold response to jealousy derives in large part from the form in which it is presented. A brief comparison with a tale of jealousy in Ovid, *Ars Amatoria*

44. Poems like c. 76 are concerned to establish the lover's total and absolute commitment to Lesbia.

45. Compare McCarthy's description of competing responses among Plautus' audience (McCarthy 2000, 25–6): "Farcical comedy offers the chance to identify with someone whose low juridical status does not prevent him from controlling those around him and, more important, who can see through all the pretensions and high-minded claims of justice and right. But this fantasy is always limited by the fact that the social order reasserts itself in the end: the master regains control, even if he demonstrates that control by pardoning the slave. Conversely, the naturalistic mode reassures the audience members that their control over others is as it should be and is safe from any irresponsible challenges. But this mode itself is often enlivened by the cynicism and rebellion that trickery can offer."

3 and *Metamorphoses* will be useful here, both in summarizing the chapter and showing what is special about jealousy in elegy.[46] The tale of Procris and Cephalus shares many similarities with elegiac stories about jealousy. For example, we find that the senses and rumor again play a crucial role in arousing jealousy. The depiction of jealousy also reveals all the suspicions and fantasies that are common fare in elegy. But neither version builds the connections between reader and jealous figures that elegy does and hence does not draw out either our sympathy or any instructive critical response.[47]

In what follows, I use the version of the story in the *Metamorphoses* (7.675–862), which offers a more detailed account of the characters' emotional experience. Cephalus recounts the story of his marriage and its tragic end, a tale that once again concerns jealousy on both sides of the relationship (though in this case the progression begins with a goddess' jealousy). Soon after his marriage to Procris, the goddess Aurora tries to seduce Cephalus while he is on a hunting trip. When he can talk only about Procris and effectively rejects Aurora's advances, she lets him go, but not before planting in him seeds of doubt about his wife's loyalty. He returns home in disguise in order to test what Procris' response to another man would be. A mere hesitation on her part is interpreted as guilt, and the couple splits. They are eventually reunited, but several years later, when he goes out again on a hunting trip, Procris learns that her husband has been calling upon the breeze, Aura, in a flirtatious manner. The jealousy that initially almost destroyed the marriage now destroys Procris' life, as her husband mistakes her for a deer and kills her with the very spear she had given him upon their reconciliation.

The story includes many of the features of jealous behavior we have already seen: a lover's impersonation of the rival, the role of the senses in stimulating jealousy (especially hearing in this case), and jealousy experienced by both male and female characters. But why does Cephalus go hunting a second time? He seems unaware of how risky absence can be in love. And his flirtation with Aura, whose name sounds so much like Aurora, shows how little attuned he is to the potential everywhere for jealousy.[48] It is difficult to feel sympathy for this

---

46. *Ars Amatoria* III.687–746 and *Metamorphoses* 7.675–862. See Anderson 1990 and Gibson 2003, 359–60 on differences between the two versions. See also the studies of Tarrant 1995, Davis 1983, and Bowditch 2005, a feminist interpretation of the episode in the *Ars*.

47. We may feel sympathy for Procris, especially in the *Ars*; see Gibson 2003, esp. *ad* 723ff. But her blindness to her emotional state there also creates a distancing effect. See Nussbaum 1990, 280–1 on the importance of reflection if a work is to "convey knowledge of love": "The only text that could promote this sort of knowing would be a text that had the requisite combination of emotive material with reflection" (281).

48. On the ambiguity between aura/Aura, see Gibson 2003, 358 and Bowditch 2005. The latter also discusses this episode as one about reading and misreading, but her argument privileges the perspective of Procris and a female readership.

character, initially or later on, and not just because he causes pain and destruction, but because he is so unreflective. We may feel more compassion for Procris
and her undeserved suffering, though the symmetry of the lovers' mistakes—
first one, then the other takes their partner to be unfaithful—ends up not so
much distinguishing as assimilating the two characters. In the end, the story of
Procris and Cephalus does not encourage any identification between the characters' experience and our own as readers. The absence of a skeptical strain in
the narrative renders Procris and Cephalus completely gullible and susceptible
to suggestion and impulse. Instead of feeling that they are at least partially
justified in their responses, or that we are edified by our own realization of their
mistakes, it is easier to want to remain uninvolved in their destructive tale.[49]
Jealousy travels like a contagion from Aurora to Cephalus to Procris, and this
rather frightening dimension offers little encouragement for either our partici-
pation in the characters' experience or our understanding of jealousy.[50]

Conclusions

We have seen how important the elegiac features of jealousy are to eliciting a
response that is both compassionate but distanced. Without a clear emphasis on
any kind of development or self-reflection, we are less able to identify with the
jealousy of characters who otherwise endure the same predicament as those in
the elegiac affair. Elegy, like modern narratives about jealousy, provides a continuous tale of the relationship that allows time for establishing a connection with
the reader. As we saw in Chapter 1, elegy also has advantages over philosophy in
helping one cope with the emotions. We feel that we have come to know and
identify with elegiac characters, and thus the jealous person's plight resonates
with us even if he or she seems to be creating stories whose logic escapes us.

Reading about jealousy in elegy can have two very positive and healthy out-
comes. The extended treatment of jealousy across a body of poems lets us appre-
ciate more what certain emotions are like, even negative emotions, and from the
inside. In the end jealousy is about trust in those we love and whether it is well
placed. And that is an entirely legitimate concern, not a madness or sickness at
all. Secondly, even though the concerns are legitimate, there is a real question
about whether one has good grounds in a particular instance. Even though you

49. The lesson of the version in the *Ars Amatoria*, that women should not be credulous about
their man's infidelity, is so self-serving that it undermines the claim to instruct.

50. See also the interesting remarks by Booth 1988 about hierarchy in the author–reader relationship: "There is a sharp difference between authors who imply that we readers are essentially
their equals in the imaginative enterprise, because we are embarked on the same quest, and those
who suggest that we are either their inferiors or their superiors or that our path must be entirely
different from theirs" (184).

can be empathetic about what someone is worried about, you can also question whether they have a good basis for their worries. The benefit of both of these aspects of elegiac jealousy is that the reader can come to a better understanding of the cogency of jealousy as well as how to be judicious. In contrast with authors like Cicero and Lucretius, who urge us to regard passions like jealousy as sicknesses that require a philosophical cure, the elegists prefer that we understand jealousy, recognize its genuine and legitimate basis, but also have a healthy skepticism about our suspicions and fears and responses to them. And this is what we find in the next chapter as well, where a reader is encouraged to be skeptical of any kind of loyalty at all, whether in the spheres of love, religion, or politics.

6

What Jealousy Is About

Threats to Fides

Until now, my focus has been on erotic jealousy and literary rivalry, as well as the relationship of the external reader to the jealousy depicted in elegiac poetry. Jealousy is endemic to the kinds of relationships the narrator is involved in and is therefore one of the central themes of Roman love elegy. But the poetry is not simply about these love affairs and dalliances; the elegists think that jealousy is a symptom of a more pervasive problem in Roman society. In this final chapter, I examine Propertius' representation of *fides*, the expectation that, always in danger of being violated or unmet, lies at the heart of the characters' propensity for jealousy. The threat to *fides* in various realms ranging from the erotic to the familial, the civic, and the political, is evidence of more widespread problems and forms a larger concern of the representation of erotic jealousy.

I begin with an important antecedent that has sometimes been thought to contrast with elegy. Catullus' use of vocabulary such as *foedus, fides, pietas, amicitia,* and *beneficium* to describe the love affair with Lesbia is well known.[1] Particularly in c. 76, but also in a series of epigrams in the latter part of the corpus, the poet describes his feelings for Lesbia in terms borrowed from political and social relations at Rome.[2] This transfer of terminology has sometimes been seen as revealing a non-erotic dimension to the lover's feelings and the greater depth of his expectations of commitment.[3] But however much the Catullan lover stresses mutual obligation and loyalty by drawing on responsibilities from other aspects of Roman life, the point could equally go in the opposite direction, suggesting a judgment about the social and political realm through the lens of the romantic

---

1. Although often described as if something new, this blend of the erotic and the political was already present in Plautine comedy. See Konstan 1983, *passim* and esp. 151 on the use of this same vocabulary to describe an erotic relationship in the *Truculentus*.

2. Cf. e.g., Catullus cc. 72, 73, 75, 87.

3. See Lyne 1980, 23–6.

relationship.[4] But we need not decide this issue in Catullus here, for this possibility is explicitly realized in Propertius, who, at key junctures in his corpus, uses an absence of *fides* in the relationship as a way of speaking about a similar loss of trust in other spheres of life as well.[5]

Propertius uses the term *fides* more than the other elegists, with forms of the word appearing 32 times in his corpus as a whole.[6] The concept of *fides* also underlies many poems where the term itself does not appear, but where other vocabulary reinforces the significance of loyalty and trust. Roman elegy is full of language expressing the importance of pledges, promise, and oaths. Vocabulary such as *constans, certa* and *iniuria* is frequent, revealing the structure of expectations on which the relationship depends (cf. e.g., Prop. 1.18.23, 2.34.11, 3.8.19). The poets assimilate the elegiac affair to a type of marriage, even if they take pains in other places to distinguish the two kinds of relationship. In one crucial respect, the two are the same: the elegiac narrators have hopes for a single, everlasting love that resemble the idealistic goals of Roman marriage recorded in non-literary evidence.[7]

For example, the elegiac lover's expectations from the beloved resemble the idealistic claims put on Roman epitaphs for a deceased wife. These records show that a woman's chastity and loyalty were the most desirable qualities in a wife.[8] Even a quick glance at some examples of tombstones erected by husbands for their wives reveals the frequency of terms such as *fides, pudor, pia, pudica,* and *casta* to describe her, some of the very same words we find in Catullus' epigrams.[9]

---

4. See Ross 1969, Vinson 1992, and the persuasive treatment of this question in Skinner 2003, ch. 3.

5. See Bertaud's study of jealousy in the literature of Louis XIII for a similar suggestion. As she sums up in her conclusion (1981, 479): "La manière dont on définissait et considérait alors les diverses espèces de rivalité prouve en effet qu'elles relevaient, dans l'esprit de beaucoup, d'une seule famille de passions. Considérant que le besoin de posséder était fondamental chez l'homme, les moralistes logeaient à la meme enseigne l'amoureux qui voit dans sa maîtresse un bien qu'on peut lui voler, le roi qui refuse de partager son pouvoir avec ses conseillers, et le courtisan désireux de s'approprier, puis de conserver richesses ou honneurs" (*The way in which we define and evaluate different types of rivalry shows that in the minds of many people, they derive from a single family of emotion. Given that the possessive urge is basic to mankind, the moralists put in the same category the lover who sees his mistress as a good that someone wants to steal from him, the king who refuses to share his power with his advisors, and the courtesan who wishes to acquire, and then to keep, riches or honors*).

6. Boucher 1965, 99ff. gives a useful examination of the importance and use of *fides* in Propertius' poetry.

7. Recent work on the Roman family has emphasized the role of love and affection in the family: cf. e.g., Treggiari 1991 and Dixon 1991, and for a more negative view of the evidence, Garnsey and Saller 1987 and Bradley 1991.

8. For both epitaphs and wills the majority of evidence comes from what husbands have to say about their families rather than vice versa: see Lattimore 1942, 293–4 and Champlin 1991, 125.

9. See the examples in Lattimore 1942, 294–7, who does not, however, offer much interpretation, and also the 1st c. BCE *Laudatio Turiae* with its treatment by Horsfall 1983. See also now Ramsby 2007 on the parallels between the epigraphic and poetic material.

Wills, too, praise wives for their loyalty and might reveal the feelings of a spouse more honestly than epitaphs insofar as they were a less public document of the bereaved's feelings, though no doubt they still conformed to certain expectations.[10] Though children, not surprisingly, tend to come first in the list of heirs, wives are usually second in the list of family and are spoken of with great affection and devotion.[11] Not only does elegiac poetry use the same vocabulary of loyalty and chastity that we find in these documents, but male narrators describe their affair with all the props and elements of real marriage, alluding often to torches, marriage bed, and vows.[12]

The Importance of *Fides*

Fides is a concept that permeated many areas of Roman life, both private and public. In essence it represents the faith, trust, or confidence that individuals or states have in each other or in the gods, and as such involved obligations in the home (e.g., marriage), in the city (e.g., patronage and the duties of the senate), and abroad (e.g., diplomacy or war).[13] The demonstration of *fides* is meant to be reciprocated: it is part of an exchange in which there are expectations in return. So in the Catullan examples mentioned earlier, it is not simply that the lover proclaims the fulfillment of his own obligations to Lesbia. Rather, he points out what he has given her in order to show where she has failed him. Likewise in Roman comedy, where ethical terms occur repeatedly throughout the plays, the mutual expectations of reciprocal *fides* and *beneficium* are essential to driving the plot.[14] This vital connection to the storyline reveals the extent to which obligations needed to be met in order for a happy ending to eventuate, a requisite feature of all Roman comedy. *Fides* is particularly important in Plautus, especially plays like the *Aulularia, Bacchides*, and the *Captivi*. The question of *fides* between master and slave and captor and prisoner is central to the plots of the *Captivi* and *Bacchides*, respectively.[15] Yet moral labels in the play do not always get assigned in the way we expect: Greek characters whom we might expect to be deceitful in fact display the trustworthiness the Romans thought characteristic of themselves. The depiction of *fides* between individuals thus takes on a larger

10. See Champlin 1991: wills "are, most obviously, expressions of emotion: *testamenta, quibus omnem adfectum fateremur*," (8) and "Seldom do the actual documents that survive at any length omit some overt indication of the testator's feelings" (9).

11. See Champlin 1991, 120–6.

12. In e.g., Prop. 2.6.41–2, 2.7, 3.20: *foedera* and *iura* (15), *lex* (16), *pignora* (17), and *testis* (18).

13. Cf. Fraenkel 1916, Heinze 1929, Freyburger 1983 and also Freyburger 1986, which emphasizes the religious significance of *fides* as well.

14. As Konstan 1983 has shown (see his p. 17).

15. On *fides* in the *Bacchides* and *Captivi*, see the excellent articles by Owens 1994 and Franko 1995, respectively.

dimension that reflects upon national characteristics. Because the characters who show what is generally assumed to be a Roman virtue are in fact Greek, Plautus challenges his audience's expectations, thereby underscoring the value of *fides* itself.

In the *Aeneid*, loyalty in a personal relationship again represents issues of national identity, and here again there is a reversal of expectations. In the love affair between Dido and Aeneas, it is Dido who exemplifies loyalty and good faith, despite the legendary reputation of the Carthaginians as treacherous and perfidious. By contrast, the proto-Roman Aeneas is characterized by his deceptive and underhanded betrayal of Dido. As Starks has shown, ethnic stereotypes have been reversed so that *fides Punica* more aptly describes Aeneas than Dido.[16] In all these cases, *fides* marks a moral difference between the preservation of trust and duty and their violation through deception and betrayal.[17] More than just a story of unreciprocated love or the ill-treatment of a beloved, the love affair between Dido and Aeneas illustrates the way in which *fides* could be used to signal several different types of obligation, erotic and political, at once. The *Aeneid* and two Plautine examples thus suggest a poetic lineage for the elegists' interest in *fides* in addition to the role that it played in ordinary relations at Rome.

Surprisingly, in his study of the use of political vocabulary in Catullus' epigrams, Ross rejected the idea that the elegists used *fides* in a way that extended beyond the love affair itself:[18]

> *Fides*, too, occurs often in elegy, but again only in the sense of mutual trust, carefully unassociated with Catullus' metaphorical usage.... It must be enough merely to suggest that both the *foedus* and the *fides* between lovers in Augustan elegy are quite different from what they had been in Catullus, in spite of the superficial similarities in the way they are used; that in elegy they have been intentionally disassociated from their older technical usage, perhaps due to the more general sense in which the words were coming to be used, perhaps because the technical Roman sense of the terms was basically unpoetic; that they never occur in a metaphorical complex of terminology as they do in Catullus; and that the whole idea of *amicitia* is carefully avoided.

16. Starks 1999, esp. pp. 274–6 ("In Book 4, Vergil dramatically places opprobrious statements commonly used against Carthaginians in the mouth of Dido as weapons against Aeneas," p. 274).

17. *Fides* certainly had a moral dimension by Plautus' time, although Fraenkel 1916 and Heinze 1929 disagree about whether or not one was dominant in the earlier history of the word.

18. Ross 1969, 93f.

Though several studies of patronage and *amicitia* in the poets are sufficient to refute the more general claims here,[19] it is worth asking why Ross overlooked the wider significance of *fides* in Propertius' poetry, for example. We may not find a cluster of terms in the elegists as we do in even single poems of Catullus. But, as I hope to show, the elegiac narrator's allusions to historical or mythological scenes involving *fides* often develop out of a discussion of erotic jealousy, suggesting that the representation of trust in the love affair has broader repercussions.

I turn now to four examples from Propertius, all of which occur at important junctures in the first three books and which illustrate the ways in which the poet extends *fides* from the erotic relationship to more public connections at Rome. In the examples discussed here, the narrator will widen his focus from the sense of betrayal and loss that are fundamental to jealousy to include the civil wars, the mythology of Rome's origins, and life under Augustus.

The Range of *Fides*
Civil War (Propertius 1.21 and 1.22)

I begin with the end of the first book, where we find two poems, 1.21 and 1.22, that seem at first to have nothing at all to do with love or Cynthia. The narrator of 1.21 is a soldier fallen in the civil wars who speaks to a fellow soldier from beyond the grave and asks him to convey the news of his death. The next and very last poem of the book is a *sphragis*, an autobiographical note, again linked to the civil wars through the poet's identification of his birthplace. Both poems seem disconnected from the opening of the book, which had so clearly stated Cynthia and domination by love as its themes.[20] Yet I suggest that these two poems are in fact integrated with those that precede, precisely in regard to the absence of *fides* and the human costs when trust is not reciprocated.

In 1.21, friendship and marriage are brought together in an entirely new context, that of civil war. As mentioned above, a dead soldier, Gallus, asks a fellow soldier to convey the circumstances of his death to the man's sister, Gallus' betrothed. The death of Gallus severs the intended bond with the other family, as the network of obligations to fellow citizens can now no longer take place. Not only has the sister lost her love, but the whereabouts of his bones and the identity of his killer will also remain unknown. Loss of identity, once a casualty of

---

19. See Oliensis 1997 on *amicitia* and also the important discussion by White 1993, 88–91, who demonstrates parallels between the love poets' relationship with their mistress and with their social peers, including the common language of affection, the usual meeting place (the home), and the occasions for the poems (parties, gift-giving, etc.).

20. On the issue of coherence, see King 1975/6, Putnam 1976, and Nicholson 1988/9.

love, is now more significantly linked to the final stamp of death.[21] And instead of the hoped-for reciprocity of loyalty between lovers, here there is a morbid exchange that brings out only danger and grief: in return for the brother's safe return to his parents, he shall bring news of Gallus' death to his betrothed. Civil war marks the destruction of ties between brothers, families, and lovers.[22] Propertius 1.21 describes the costs of war through an individual's loss, and ties that loss to the larger bonds between comrades in war and members of a family and homeland.

In the next poem, the last in the book, the poet gives a short autobiography and identifies his Perusine origins by mentioning the civil wars (*discordia*, 5) that drove out her citizens. This information comes as a response to a series of questions posed by Tullus, asked apparently in friendship (*nostra semper amicitia*, 2). Yet as Putnam points out, we would expect a close friend to already know these details about the poet's origins.[23] The directness of the questions together with the indirectness of the answer suggests a dissolution of trust and signals that the civil wars have interfered with *amicitia* as well. The narrator depicts himself as a victim, though not of love's wounds this time. Like Catullus c. 101, the poem about the poet's dead brother, these two brief elegies of Propertius address personal loss of a different kind from what we see in the erotic elegies earlier in the book.[24] Yet the emphasis on intimacy, the body, and male friendship suggests a connection with the betrayals he suffers in love, only here the effects of devastation caused by civil war are far greater.[25]

Family and History (Propertius 2.6)

The previous examples, 1.21 and 1.22, dramatically shift the theme of the preceding elegies on infidelity in love to the subject of a loss of *fides* in civil war. Their position in the sequence of poems in Book 1 leads us to see ways in which the themes of loyalty and trust are central to both experiences. In Propertius 2.6, the narrator explores within a single poem the absence of *fides* in different spheres. The elegy begins with an outburst of jealousy: everything causes him to doubt Cynthia's loyalty. But jealousy over romantic betrayal swiftly moves to cover other ground.

21. See e.g., Prop. 1.5.18.

22. Cf. the association of war with a breakdown in family relations in Thucydides' description of the plague and the Corcyra stasis (*Peloponnesian War* 2.47–55 and 3.82–3).

23. Putnam 1976, 98.

24. Putnam 1976 also draws the connection between these poems and Catullus c. 101 (110–112).

25. See the suggestive remarks in Putnam 1976, 99: "The narrow world of a poet's heritage and personal relationships is expanded to embrace a far greater dimension of existence seen through events whose meaning Tullus might only dimly measure" and "One person's race, household gods, friendship expand into the whole land of Italy."

At the opening of the elegy, the desperate lover compares the flock of men surrounding Cynthia in adulation to a theater audience and Cynthia herself to the courtesans of New Comedy (1–4).[26] The comparison points to the influence of comedy on the construction of her elegiac character and the blend of erotic and familial love that is prominent in both this elegy and the plays of New Comedy.[27] Indeed, the elegy continues with a detailed list of the fears afflicting the jealous lover-poet, most of which derive from Cynthia's family connections:

> *me iuvenum pictae facies, me nomina laedunt*
> *me tener in cunis et sine voce puer;*   10
> *me laedet, si multa tibi dabit oscula mater,*
> *me soror et cum quae dormit amica simul:*
> *omnia me laedent: timidus sum (ignosce timori)*
> *et miser in tunica suspicor esse virum.*

The portraits of young men make me jealous, their names make me
    jealous,
an infant boy in the cradle makes me jealous.
I'm jealous if your mother gives you many kisses,
I'm jealous if your sister does, and when a girlfriend sleeps with you.
    Everything will make me jealous: I am fearful (forgive my fear)
and wretched, suspect that a man lurks in a woman's dress.

The lover's fears about Cynthia's wandering attentions result in the most unlikely paranoia. Paintings and family members—mothers, sisters, and even babies—provoke the lover's fears of being supplanted. The mere sight of any of these people or things close to the beloved is taken as evidence of her cheating. This unlikely list of rivals and the repetition of *me laedere* together suggest the torment and delusional character of the emotion. There are no reality checks; jealousy crosses every boundary, even if only in verbal hyperbole. The poem expresses the unboundedness of the lover's fears and sense of vulnerability. As part of his suffering, he suspects that every kind of affection presents the same kind of threat to his claims as a male erotic rival would. The lover asks his reader's forgiveness for this overwhelming fear and in so doing evades responsibility for his condition or any desire to change. Cynthia and her infidelity are portrayed as responsible for the lover's symptoms, which extend from suspicions about erotic love to familial love.

26. Lais and Thais were famous Athenian courtesans; the latter was the title character of a comedy by Menander (see Prop. 4.5.43). See James 2003a, 37.

27. The plots of New Comedy often depict a conflict between father and son over the son's love interest. On links between the female beloved in comedy and elegy, cf. Yardley 1972, Konstan 1994, 150–9, and James 2003a.

In general, jealousy leads to a fundamental breakdown in one's basic assumptions: the lover cannot be sure where the threat is coming from. All affection is rivalrous, competing and stealing affection he thought was his alone. The reference to ancestors' portraits in line 9 may be especially suggestive of the narrator's insecurity, as it likely refers to the practice of displaying ancestral masks in the *atria* of Roman homes.[28] We see here yet again the role of visual and aural evidence in provoking jealousy, whether those triggers are "real-life" or artistic. The portraits also mark the narrator's awareness of social class, as perhaps some anxiety about his place with Cynthia leads to feelings of inferiority about Cynthia's upper-class contacts.[29] Unlike Cynthia, who, as we saw earlier, was threatened by rivals of inferior status,[30] the male narrator here would then be expressing unease about those who are equals or even superiors. In fact, an awareness of status appears in the very next poem as well, where the narrator rejoices that he has escaped a law requiring him to marry: presumably some issue of class difference stands in the way of his being able to wed Cynthia.[31] If it is unclear whose rank was problematic, the emphasis on wealth and status in two successive poems is not. The reference to wall paintings later in the elegy (lines 27–34) may also point to the upper classes, who could afford to have more highly decorated homes. While Propertius has used art elsewhere to illuminate the initiation and development of jealous thoughts, here the particular references to features of noble houses points to the larger issues at stake.

We have some preparation, then, for the broad historical sweep that comes next,[32] where the lover goes on to argue that the corruption of trust has been present in Rome from the very start.[33] To make this case, he offers a list of examples, including among his evidence the Trojan war, the rivalry between Romulus and Remus, and the rape of the Sabine women, the standard steps usually given in the story about Rome's origins and growth:

> his olim, ut fama est, vitiis ad proelia ventum est,   15
>   his Troiana vides funera principiis;
> aspera Centauros eadem dementia iussit
>   frangere in adversum pocula Pirithoum.

28. On the *imagines*, see Flower 1996, esp. ch. 7, "Ancestors at Home."

29. Cf. Ovid *Amores* 1.8 for a similar assumption about the nobility of a rival.

30. Cf. Propertius 3.15 and 4.8, discussed in Chapters 2 and 4.

31. Cf. Suet. *Aug.* 34, Galinsky 1981 and Badian 1985. See also Treggiari 1991, who argues that it may have been the male lover's status, not Cynthia's, that posed the obstacle: "In considering why poets and their mistresses were debarred from marrying each other, we have tended to ask whether the woman was debarred because she was a courtesan. Perhaps we should be wondering instead whether Hostia was too high-born to marry a Propertius from Assisi, as Clodia or Metella would not have condescended to marry Catullus or Ticidas" (304–5).

32. Heyworth 2007b, 135 follows Ribbeck in suggesting that there are lines missing before line 15.

33. See Boucher 1965, 46 on the connection between jealousy and moral criticism.

cur exempla petam Graium? tu criminis auctor,
    nutritus duro, Romule, lacte lupae: 20
tu rapere intactas docuisti impune Sabinas:
    per te nunc Romae quidlibet audet Amor.

From these vices came wars, the story goes,
from these beginnings arose the destruction at Troy.
That same rough frenzy made the Centaurs break embossed cups in
    Pirithous' face.
Why do I seek examples from Greece? You are the source of the crime,
    Romulus, fed on the harsh milk of the she-wolf.
You taught how to rape the Sabine women with impunity:
because of you Love now dares whatever he wants at Rome.

Vitiis in line 15 has sometimes been taken to refer to unchastity or lewdness, but disloyalty makes better sense of both the examples and the context of the poem.[34] The presence of Romulus and Remus, for example, would not otherwise make sense in this list of stories. What links all these stories is the betrayal of trust that lies at their center, whether that be the theft of a spouse, as in the myth of the Sabine women, or the claims to a city, in the case of Romulus and Remus.

In sharp contrast to the usual portraits of early Rome as a more virtuous period, the poet implies with this list that the breaking of *fides* is part of Rome's heritage, and therefore belongs to his own pedigree as well.[35] Early Rome does not provide positive models of behavior, but rather an *aition* that serves to explain the origin and prevalence in contemporary Rome of murder, theft, war, and most of all the lack of any trust or fidelity in human relations. Propertius draws together jealousy in the earlier part of the poem with the absence of *fides* in the later section, creating a continuity between loss of *fides* in the private or personal, on the one hand, and the public and foundational, on the other.

As the poem reaches its conclusion, the narrator complains in familiar tones that he is an innocent victim of widespread infidelity. Yet he then reveals his own part in contributing to the decline in morals. In lines 27–34, he points his finger at painters, claiming that they corrupt contemporary houses with lewd

---

34. *His vitiis* is interpreted in various ways: Butler and Barber 1933 suggest unchastity; Richardson 1977 proposes that it means both man's pursuit of other men's women and his jealous protection of his own women; and Camps 1966a takes it to mean lewdness (i.e., predatory male admirers).

35. Cf. Edwards 1993, 42–7, with further examples. Lines 33–6 about the innocent old days, when no one had lewd paintings on their walls, undermines the earlier statement that jealousy has been around forever.

and provocative scenes.[36] To the lover's mind, scenes of love and adultery con-
tribute to infidelity by suggesting liaisons, and so encourage, perhaps even ini-
tiate and implicitly condone, them. Artists of all sorts are to blame for the
problem of infidelity, a reminder of the ancestral portraits mentioned earlier in
the poem. Like the painting of Zeus and Danaë in Terence's *Eunuch* that inspires
Chaerea to rape the *virgo*, a work of art can serve not only as an illustration of
infidelity, but its cause.[37]

The narrator's moral criticism of other artists raises questions about himself. It
is not simply that he is an artist, one particularly given to painterly tendencies in
his own poetry, or even that he reproduces verbally the very works of art he criticizes. Rather he, too, promulgates stories of his own about rivals, deception, and
infidelity in his poetry, much like the painters themselves. His own artistic activity
thus undermines his moral stance, and reminds us of the skepticism he provokes
in his readers about his credibility on erotic matters, something discussed in previous chapters. Is this meant to undercut the overt moral message, or is it simply
an attempt to take a moral turn despite having an imperfect past? The texts do not
allow us to settle this question. At the very least, the poet-lover is not represented
as someone who has a consistent message over which he has control. To the extent
that he turns to other stories about jealousy as a way of understanding his own, he
ends up provoking infidelity even where he hopes to attack it.

The many layers of 2.6 emphasize the pervasiveness and inevitability of betrayal, from the lover's own jealousy, to its roots in Greco-Roman culture, and then
finally to the artistic representations that keep the problem alive. They suggest
that the intimate space in which erotic jealousy takes place is just one facet of a
more widespread problem that elegiac characters encounter in their lives, whether
it is political or rhetorical, literary or visual. Propertius 2.6 recalls those epigrams
of Catullus that blur the lines between *fides* and *foedus*, when erotic bonds and
political ones become less clearly marked and distinct.[38]

In Propertius' case, the exploration of *fides* seems to move from intimate to
public, from the romantic affair to a larger network of relationships. Love is the

36.   *quae manus obscenas depinxit prima tabellas*
                       et posuit casta turpia visa domo,
                    illa puellarum ingenuous corrupit ocellos
                       nequitiaeque suae noluit esse rudis.   30
                 a gemat in tenebris, ista qui protulit arte
                    turpia sub tacita condita laetitia!
                 non istis olim variabant tecta figuris:
                    tum paries nullo crimine pictus erat.

See James 2003a, 39 and her n. 23, citing Clarke 1998 on the presence of erotic paintings in
all kind of homes, not just brothels.
37. Ter. *Eun.* 584–614.
38. See n. 2 above.

starting point for an examination of its origins in Roman culture. At the root of the problem is a lack of *fides*. The perception of infidelity is the trigger of erotic jealousy, but dwelling on the lack of trust leads to an awareness of problems in other relationships as well: within the household, in Greek or Roman mythology, and in the history of the beginning of the Republic. While 2.6 contains most of the symptoms of jealousy we have already discussed—fear at losing the beloved to even the most unlikely rivals, sympathy for the speaker's own jealousy when that speaker is the male lover, the emphasis on a list of visual evidence, and the role of art in stimulating jealousy—this poem extends these features to the larger social sphere in a critique that covers present-day Rome and even the entire Greco-Roman heritage from its beginnings.

Rome and the East (Propertius 3.13)

I turn now to Propertius 3.13, the central poem of the third book, which offers another example of infidelity and jealousy within the erotic relationship that looks towards suspicion and disloyalty in Rome at large. 3.13 is, on the face of it, about female fidelity and the role of money, two things often linked in elegiac poetry. The poem reads as a survey of marital *fides* in different times and places, stemming from the discussion of Galla's exemplary loyalty in the previous poem.[39] Yet while 3.13 purports to be about the loyalty of women, a closer look reveals that the real subject is *fides* more generally, and indeed, forms of the word appear four times.[40] The narrator traces the part played by *fides* from the two-person relationship to more extended connections with the outside world: between men and women; between men, nature, and the gods; between men and the state; and finally between seer/poet and audience.[41] In a fascinating twist at the end of the poem, the lover compares himself to Cassandra: like her, his words will be true, but not believed. By way of conclusion, the narrator moves the question of fidelity back to something more personal, the poet's relationship with his audience. Since the issue is communication and credibility, however, this level in fact concerns every relationship, private or public. The lover's claim

39. On the sequence of poems 12, 13, and 14, cf. Nethercut 1970 and Jacobson 1976; on the order of poems in Book 3 as a whole, see Putnam 1980.

40. *Infidum*, 23; *fida*, 24; *fides*, 49; *fides*, 61. See Grimal 1953, where he argues *fides* is the central theme of the fourth book; it is interesting to note its prominence already in the third. See also Gibson 2007, 48: "Accompanying the whole is an unstoppable flood of moralistic sentiment and vocabulary."

41. Camps 1966a (introduction to poem) notes the crescendo from "a typical sentiment of love-elegy" to "a discourse on a general theme . . . of national rather than erotic interest"; but I disagree that "the original cue is gradually allowed to be forgotten." Cassandra's infidelity to Apollo, even though unstated in the poem, shows how the theme of amatory infidelity remains present until the end, even as it expands to other types of relationships. See also Fantham 2006 on the convergence of private and public in both 3.11 and 3.13.

to be like Cassandra also contains a threat about the imminent doom awaiting us if we do not listen to his words. It is possible to find the adoption of this Homeric role as humorous or self-important (or both), but however we read it, the narrator's claim to be a seer and a voice protecting the welfare of a city marks this elegy's more expansive aims.

The poem opens with the thesis that the source of Rome's corruption is Rome herself. Instead of blaming the East for its luxury and lax morals, the problems begin with Rome itself, the same insinuation we found in 2.6.[42] Because the narrative of 3.13 involves some abrupt shifts in time and place, I begin with an overview of the poem's five sections. In the first of these, the narrator claims that women in Rome today have given in to a life of luxury and greed. The source of this high living is the goods brought in from the East: India, the Red Sea, Tyre, and Arabia (1–14). In the second section, we learn that fidelity exists in the East, as shown by the tradition of suttee and devotion by a *turba* of wives to a single husband (19–24). In the third section, the narrator offers a nostalgic glance backward in time, when the bounty of the countryside once provided harmonious relations between men and women (25–46). But now in another reversal, the fourth section proclaims that the lust for gold has banished piety, law, and shame (47–58). A list of historical and mythological exempla supports these claims, including the stories of Brennus, Polymestor, and Eryiphyla. The elegy concludes with the narrator requesting that others consider him a true seer for his country, even if, as with Cassandra, no one will believe his words (59–66).

This elegy, which begins with the narrower question of female fidelity, in fact goes on to undermine any notion of trust in human relations. The only place where one might have confidence in sincerity or commitment is a bygone world, and in fact some of the repetition of vocabulary in the beginning of the Golden Age section (25–46) and in the other more negative ones suggest that the narrator has his doubts even here. In what follows, I highlight just a few of the ways in which the narrator points to the breakdown of loyalty and trust.

To begin with, the charge of greed is made in the first section not only against women like Cynthia but married women as well, extending the discussion beyond that of infidelity within the affair. The themes and vocabulary of the first eight lines recall poems from the first two books representing a more intense stage of the affair with Cynthia.[43] But references to the chaste (*pudicas*, 9),

42. See Langlands 2006, 198 on early Rome's imperfections, with a focus on female *pudicitia*.

43. *Puellis, Venere,* and *querantur* (1–2) are paradigmatic of Propertius' earlier love poetry. The temptations of Eastern dyes and scents (5–8) are familiar from, for example, 1.2, 1.8B, 1.14, and 2.16, some of which I discussed earlier in terms of clothing as visual stimuli of jealousy. These lines read at first like a return to the sphere of Propertius' indulgent protests against Cynthia's extravagances in Book 1, away from the more brooding topics that tend to dominate Book 3: e.g., death (2, 5, 7, and *passim*), greed (4, 7, 13), infidelity (6, 12, 15), risk-filled travel (7, 12, 21, 22, 24/5).

women like Penelope (10), and *matronae* (11) show that in marriage, too, instead of the right kind of exchange of affection and devotion, what we find instead is a lust for gold.

The narrator seems to intend the next scene, describing the devotion of Eastern wives, as a contrast to what is missing in Rome. *Felix* introduces both this scene and the Golden Age passage (the first word of lines 15 and 25).[44] In the East, the narrator reports, the funerals of husbands (*Eois maritis*, 15) are uniquely blessed. A band of wives (*turba uxorum*, 18) stands around the burning pyre with flowing hair, and the women compete with one another to throw themselves on top of it. Yet the idea of many women competing over a single man is so exaggerated and anti-Roman that it is difficult to imagine a Roman husband finding this picture appealing.[45] As such, this picture can hardly be said to provide an optimistic case of marital *fides*.

The narrator next turns to *fides* between men and nature and men and the gods (25–50). The setting is the Golden Age, where gold and hence infidelity are absent. The only exchanges between men and women here are those of nature: bouquets of flowers and baskets of fruit (27–32). There is also *fides* between men and animals: the ram leads home the sheep of his own accord (39–40) and the altars of the gods and goddesses speak out spontaneously rather than in response to prayer or special request (41–6). Still, given the consistency between this inset and the preceding two, especially the references to female greed even in an age of abundance (see *furtive per antra* and *empta*, lines 33–4), the narrator's claims are once again undermined.[46]

Then, in an abrupt shift, the narrator moves away from this apparent utopia to Rome in the present day (51–8). While the narrator puts heavy emphasis on gold in lines 48–50, equally significant is the ethical vocabulary he uses in combination with the references to money:

> *at nunc desertis cessant sacraria lucis:*
> *aurum omnes victa iam pietate colunt.*
> *auro pulsa fides, auro venalia iura,*
> *aurum lex sequitur, mox sine lege pudor.*   50

> But now temples lie empty in deserted groves.
> Everyone devotes himself to gold without any respect.

---

44. Rothstein 1979, *ad loc.* distinguishes the two *felix* sections since the second is explicitly peaceful (*pacata*, 25) while the first contains military imagery. Cf. also *felix* in 3.12.15: *ter quater in casta felix, o Postume, Galla!*

45. See Cic. *TD* 5.27.78.

46. Note as well other verbal links between this section and others that are supposedly less *felix*, for example the forms of *praebere* in lines 7, 21, and 42. See also Clarke 2003, Ch. 5 on color imagery and the ways in which it dissolves some of the supposed distinctions made in the elegy.

Trust is driven out by gold, laws are sold for gold, law goes where gold goes,
and soon shame will be without regulation.

Through the lust for gold comes a devaluation of all moral behavior and law (see
iura, lex, and *lege* in lines 49–50 as well): *pietas, fides,* and *pudor* are pushed aside
in favor of wealth and what it can buy. If gold was formerly connected only with
the love affair, these lines reveal the spread of corruption to more fundamental
relations between men. And the historical and mythological exempla that follow
lend more support to this claim. Brennus' greed leads to an attack on the Temple
of Apollo, an assault against the deity.[47] When Polymestor kills Polydorus, the
young son of Priam, for his gold, he breaks the bond of trust by which he was
given the boy for safekeeping. And the story of Eriphyla and Amphiaraus
involves a wife's betrayal of her husband, for she gives up the location where he
was hiding to Polynices for a bribe of golden bracelets.[48]

Finally, in the last stanza (59–66), the narrator tells us he will speak out and
serve as a true seer for his country. The basis for the narrator's claim is his
ability to speak the truth without anyone believing him: *certa loquor, sed nulla
fides* (61).[49] While he does not mention the reason why Cassandra lost her *fides,*
a punishment from Apollo when she refused to be his lover, the narrator attempts to convince us that he, too, deserves our faith, and that he has been
treated unjustly, a stance of victimhood that is by now familiar. Another parallel
between the narrator and Cassandra is the way both blame illicit love for the
downfall of a city. In 63–4, Cassandra names two factors responsible for the fall
of Troy: Paris and the horse. So, too, the Propertian narrator takes us from the
failure of *fides* between men and women to the loss of any kind of trust between
men, whether political, religious, or legal. What starts with marital infidelity
quickly spreads and undermines the city as a whole. Unlike the narrator's identification with Odysseus elsewhere, the adoption of this Homeric role is not
about resourcefulness, but about doom and failure. What is more, the responsibility is shifted from the speaker to those who heard her prophecy, an audience
who has failed to understand and believe the message. By taking up the pro-
phetic mantle of Cassandra, who tells the truth despite the audience's doubts
about it, the narrator raises skeptical worries much as he did in the passage in
2.6 about provocative paintings. It could possibly be that the narrator really is

47. Also mentioned in Propertius 3.13.51.

48. Cf. 2.16.29. In other versions of the story the bribe is usually a necklace, the one Cadmus gave
as a wedding gift to his bride Harmonia. Eriphyla provides a contrast to Evadne, for both women's
stories come from the "Seven Against Thebes" cycle, Evadne having shown the utmost devotion to
her husband, Eriphyla utter deceit.

49. On *fides* as a mark of the orator's sincerity, see Allen 1950b. See also the repetition of forms
of *verus* (*verus, verax,* and *veros*) in the final eight lines.

like Cassandra and gives voice to the truth despite the things that he says and does that undermine his own credibility. Alternatively, claiming to be Cassandra could just be more posturing on his part and a rhetorical attempt to claim credibility when his own is already seriously compromised. The conflict between the poet-lover's moral voice and his poetic practice can be read in either of these ways, and nothing in the poems allows us to resolve these worries decisively one way or another. Their overall effect is to leave us with a certain amount of skeptical distance.

Not only does the narrator's identification with Cassandra affect our reading of 3.13 itself, it also raises problems about the poems that come immediately before and after. Poem 3.13 begins with the repetition of an interlocutor's question: *Quaeritis, unde avidis nox sit pretiosa puellis/et Venere exhaustae damna querantur opes*, and this forces us to look back to the preceding poem for what might have prompted the question. The very last line of 3.12 concluded by claiming that the virtue of the Roman wife Galla surpassed even that of Penelope: *vincit Penelopes Aelia Galla fidem*, 38.[50] Yet in the body of 3.13, the narrator twice undermines the comparison between Galla and Penelope. In one couplet he makes us doubt the chastity attributed to Galla, suggesting that even the "locked-up chaste" and women wearing the disdain of Penelope can be tempted (*clausas pudicas*, 9 and *quaeque gerunt fastus, Icarioti, tuos*, 10).[51] In a second passage, he says that no women like Penelope or Evadne are to be found at Rome (23–4). By the time he gets to 3.13, the narrator hardly maintains the credibility of Galla's fidelity claimed at the conclusion of 3.12.[52] As for 3.14, it hardly supports the position on fidelity made so thoroughly in 3.13. There the narrator extols the advantages of Sparta, which offers open access to naked women. The wavering attitudes towards fidelity that we see in this sequence of poems underscore the difficulty of finding a person or a story one can trust. And this takes on a special urgency because of another dimension to his invocation of Cassandra. She raises issues not only about the narrator's credibility, but also the political fate of Rome. Cassandra's prophecies, although they originate from a love affair, directly concern the fate of Troy, a city that obviously has great symbolic importance for Rome. This underscores the risks involved, whatever we think of the poet-lover's authority.

---

50. Perhaps the question is raised by 3.12; just so, 3.10 begins *"Mirabar,"* and 3.11 *"Quid mirare,"* as though Propertius responds to himself in the previous poem. Cf. also 2.1 and 2.31, which open with *"Quaeritis"* and *"Quaeris,"* respectively; and Boucher 1965, 377. See also *Qualis* at the opening of 1.22, and the comments of Putnam 1976, 94–5. Perutelli 2006, 56 discusses the emphasis on a comparison between women rather than men.

51. On *clausas puellas*, see also 3.3.49; and on *fastus*, see 1.1.3, where it describes the lover's expression before he was touched by love.

52. Jacobson 1976 discusses Galla's dual nature as paragon of virtue and woman in need of protection, which he takes to imply her untrustworthiness (161–2).

The concern is not simply about conduct in love affairs, but the health and well-being of the country as a whole. Questions about whom or what to believe thus involve not only the success of a love affair or the trustworthiness of our narrator, but of Rome herself.

Conclusions

Jealousy is key to the poet's exploration of erotic and poetic trust and implicates even a modern reader in the problem of whether or not the narrator of a given poem speaks reliably. This leads a reader to the heart of the Propertian narrator's exploration of deceit and suspicion in human relations of all kinds. The examples I chose in this chapter illustrate an impressive extension of the problem of *fides* through a variety of different kinds of relationship. Their position at the beginning, middle, and end of Books 1, 2, and 3 demonstrates their significance to Propertius' own poetic project. At key junctures in his poetry books, the Propertian narrator draws out comparisons between infidelity in love and the absence of *fides* in other spheres: marriage, politics, religion, even the relationship between narrator and audience. The elegiac lover's vulnerability to infidelity in love is just one example of a more general feature of life in Rome at that time. However personal and private the emotions may seem and however much they are shaped here by more literary concerns, they illuminate issues of greater consequence in society at large.

Conclusion

A Genre Structured by Jealousy

I began this study by noting how appropriate elegy was for studying depictions of jealousy, in particular because of structural features such as the first-person voice of the poetry and the triangular configuration of its characters. I want to conclude by looking at some other features of elegy that are familiar elements of the genre, but which I suggest can be explained in large part because of elegy's fixation on jealousy. In other words, what we take to be some of the central characteristics of elegy are in fact closely tied to the representation of jealousy more generally. I will emphasize three areas in particular: the obsessive chronicling of the love affair, the pervasiveness of role-playing, and the significance of *fides* of various kinds. It is no accident that poems focused on erotic jealousy should bear these traits. Whatever the other influences on their depiction, the persistence and special development of these features of elegy are best explained by the role of jealousy.

To begin with, any narrative will to some extent create a record or an account of certain events. But two things are distinctive about the elegiac narrators' account of the love affair: the fixation on a small detail from which an entire imagined scenario is elaborated, and the repeated treatment of a single theme or encounter, played over and over again, though often varying the perspective or angle from which it is viewed. Both of these elements, I suggest, are characteristic of the jealous person's suspicions and jealous imagination. In the hands of a jealous narrator, a late arrival or image of a beloved in new clothes quickly develops into elaborate stories of deceit and betrayal, as we have seen. The direction of a lover's gaze can lead to an exhaustive catalog of every word a lover speaks and every change in appearance. Small clues like these lead to suspicions that the jealous person easily spins into an entire paranoid fantasy.

The repetition of certain formulaic scenes also reflects a jealous lover's need to revisit critical moments as a way of understanding (or justifying) his feelings. Elegiac narrators write frequently on the topics of illness, rejection, rumor, travel, or the slavery of love, and explore these topics from different angles, as they affect the narrator himself, the beloved, and/or the rival. The elegiac repertoire, which can often seem narrow, stems from a desire to run through significant incidents multiple times and carefully analyze the signs of infidelity, making sure that nothing has been overlooked or misunderstood.

Scholars have typically taken both these features, the chronicling of behavior and the repetition of set scenes, as stock elements of the genre. Then they worry about their lineage: almost every introduction to elegy begins with a discussion of its precedents, exploring the possible influence of Hellenistic poetry and New Comedy on the formation of these generic elements, ultimately concluding that to a certain extent these elements represent a new development in love poetry.[1] But what makes these kinds of scenes paradigmatic is that they depend upon jealousy: jealousy gives elegy its distinctive form. It is because the poems focus so centrally and persistently on jealous encounters that these characteristics of intense visualization and analysis infuse the poetry, features that are central in some of the best-known narratives about jealousy as well, for example Proust's *À la recherche du temps perdu* or Robbe-Grillet's novel *La Jalousie*. The elegiac narrator's compulsive need to gather data, build a story upon it, interpret and then re-interpret it shows to what extent jealousy drives the poet's account. Repetition is such a prominent feature of elegy not because of it has a limited number of tropes, but because jealousy is centrally about obsessively cataloguing and revisiting the fraught scenes as a means of understanding one's position in a triangular relationship.

A second feature of elegy that is again crucially tied to jealousy is the frequency of role-playing. As we have seen, the elegiac lover tries out many different poses. He adopts the role of victim but also teacher, a female but also male role, the voice of the love poet but also that of an epic or tragic hero. It is common to interpret these shifting roles as signs of rhetorical training or generic rivalry: arguing on behalf of different positions is natural given the Roman practice of *suasoriae* and *controversiae*, while the inclusion of epic motifs or characters shows the narrator's ability to explore weightier themes and transform them in a new context, even if in the end he rejects them as unsuitable or less interesting than the subject of his mistress.

---

1. We find a fairly standard line about the origins of Latin love elegy in the handbooks and major introductions to the genre: e.g., Luck 1959, ch. 2; Hubbard 1974, ch. 1; Conte 1994, 321-51; Booth 1995, xiii–xx; Miller 2002, 11–15. All of these studies approach the question in a traditional way, looking first at Greek precedents such as Antimachus' *Lyde*. Not finding a sufficient basis there, they then speculate that the innovations we find in Roman elegy must be due to Gallus, of whose work we possess only 11 lines. One obvious shortcoming of a conjectural approach such as this is that we have no way of confirming or denying it. It also does not offer us any further explanatory basis for understanding the genre. In the absence of clear precedents, however, we would do better to try to understand *why* the topoi of elegy that I have enumerated above (the triangular relationship between narrator, mistress, and rival, the use of the first-person voice, the mistress' infidelity, etc.) appear in conjunction with one another rather than with other features, and this is the key, I believe, that jealousy provides.

But imagining other roles is also natural to jealousy. In jealous fantasies, one imagines oneself in admirable roles as well as the victim's role. A jealous person feels vulnerable and threatened but also wants to reassert himself: thus we find both a focus on pain and what the lover suffers but also the ways in which he might vanquish and conquer these threats or demonstrate his worth to the beloved. Elegiac narrators indulge regularly in precisely this kind of compensation through imagination. Furthermore, in imagining himself as another, the narrator constructs motives and stories that may lead to even more role-playing, as he appropriates other narratives in order to understand himself and his affair in terms of the characters from familiar literature and art. More than simply an engagement with other literature, this is specifically an engagement with other stories that bear on the question of his jealousy. Jealous narratives incorporate other similar stories, and therefore elegy's legacy is just as important as its lineage. Instead of merely looking back to Hellenistic poetry, we should look forward to opera and Proust.

Finally, elegy also has a lot to say about *fides*. Although jealousy is a negative emotion, it illuminates something positive by way of contrast. People feel jealous when they believe that a certain *fides* or trust is threatened. In focusing on jealousy, then, the elegists are inevitably concerned about our bonds to others and the ways in which those bonds are at risk. As a natural extension of that concern, the elegists examine the ways in which trust in other realms, such as the social and political, is in danger as well. Thus while the narrator is fixated on his personal vulnerability, a result of the mistress' infidelity and deceitful behavior, his disillusionment is not limited to the erotic. Instead, it is just one facet of a more widespread problem with the absence of trust, which he traces to Rome's origins and the civil wars so as to imply that it is endemic to the culture.

Connecting the emphasis on *fides* and threats against it with jealousy explains a preoccupation that has often seemed out of place in the adulterous relationships found in elegy. But it also explains a further feature of elegy that has not always been appreciated, namely the ways in which issues of trust also arise between the reader and the narrative presentation. Like a mystery, narratives about jealousy force us to attend to the clues and try to determine for ourselves what has happened. This is often difficult: the grounds for jealousy are rarely substantiated or disproved, and suspicions persist without any final word. The ability of the jealous mind to invent and elaborate also contributes to the failure of any resolution. While we may be inclined to believe the narrator, who has opened up his heart to us and claims both loyalty and experience, we also grow disenchanted as the façade begins to crack. Unlike a mystery, however, there is no explanation at the end, no way to know for sure to what extent our main source of information has been dealing fairly or unfairly with us. Ultimately, this puts us in the position of being suspicious and vulnerable, too.

In some ways this may remind us of Catullus' poetry, where the absence of *fides* also damages different relationships, including those of love (e.g., poem 76), friendship (e.g., poem 15), and political leadership (e.g., poem 29). Catullus, too, reverses gender roles and uses myth as a way to explore personal experience through the stories of others. But Catullus' poetry does not build a relationship with the reader in the way that elegy does. We may read about the lover's doubts and disappointments there, but we do not share in the experience of doubt ourselves. By contrast, elegiac poetry develops a narrative whose elements depend on jealousy in order to make us insecure and uncertain. As the poems examined in Chapter 6 suggest, this is intended to make us identify not only with the jealous lover, but with anyone who has placed his or her trust in another: anyone who has done this is vulnerable and prone to suspicions. The plight of the jealous figure is not only that he cannot trust the beloved. He cannot trust anyone, and he conveys that experience to us not only by the content of his narrative, but by its form.

BIBLIOGRAPHY

Adler, Eve. 1981. *Catullan Self-Revelations*. New York: Ayer.

Albrecht, Michael von. 1977. *Römische Poesie, Text und Interpretationen*. Heidelberg: Stiehm.

Allen, Archibald W. 1950a. "Elegy and the Classical Attitude Toward Love: Propertius 1,1." *Yale Classical Studies* 11: 255–77.

———. 1950b. "'Sincerity' and the Roman Elegists." *Classical Philology* 45: 145–60.

Ancona, Ronnie, and Ellen Greene, eds. 2005. *Gendered Dynamics in Latin Love Poetry*. Baltimore: The Johns Hopkins University Press.

Anderson, J.K. 1985. *Hunting in the Ancient World*. Berkeley, Los Angeles, London: University of California Press.

Anderson, William S. 1990. "The Example of Procris in the *Ars Amatoria*." In *Cabinet of the Muses: Essays on Classical and Comparative Literature in Honor of Thomas G. Rosenmeyer*, edited by M. Griffith and D.J. Mastronarde, 131–45. Atlanta: Scholars Press.

Annas, Julia E. 1992. *Hellenistic Philosophy of Mind*. Berkeley: University of California Press.

Armstrong, David, Jeffrey Fish, Patricia A. Johnston, and Marilyn B. Skinner, eds. 2004. *Vergil, Philodemus and the Augustans*. Austin: University of Texas Press.

Da Assis, Machado. 2009. *Don Casmurro*. Translated by Helen Caldwell. New York: Farrar, Straus and Giroux.

Badian, Ernst. 1985. "A Phantom Marriage Law." *Philologus* 129: 82–98.

Bailey, Cyril, ed. 1922. *Lucreti De Rerum Natura*. Oxford: Oxford University Press.

Barnes, Jonathan, and Miriam Griffin, eds. 1997. Philosophia Togata: *Plato and Aristotle at Rome*. Vol. II. Oxford: Clarendon Press.

Barnes, Julian. 1992. *Before She Met Me*. London: Vintage.

Baron, Marcia. 2004. "Killing in the Heat of Passion." In *Setting the Moral Compass: Essays by Women Philosophers*, edited by C. Calhoun, 353–78. Oxford: Oxford University Press.

Barringer, Judith M. 2002. *The Hunt in Ancient Greece*. Baltimore: The Johns Hopkins University Press.

Barsby, John A., ed. 1973. *Ovid's* Amores. *Book I*. Oxford Clarendon Press.

———. 1974. "The Composition and Publication of the First Three Books of Propertius." *Greece and Rome* 21: 128–37.

Barton, Carlin A. 2001. *Roman Honor: The Fire in the Bones*. Berkeley: University of California Press.

Bartsch, Shadi. 2006. *The Mirror of the Self: Sexuality, Self-Knowledge, and the Gaze in the Early Roman Empire*. Chicago: University of Chicago Press.

Baumgart, Hildegard. [1985] 1990. *Jealousy: Experiences and Solutions*. Translated by M. Jacobson and E. Jacobson. Chicago: University of Chicago Press.

Ben-Ze'ev, Aaron. 2000. *The Subtlety of Emotions*. Cambridge: MIT Press.

Bertaud, Madeleine. 1981. *La Jalousie dans la littérature au temps de Louis XIII. Analyse littéraire et histoire des mentalités*. Genève: Droz.

Billault, Alain. 2009. "Remarques sur la jalousie dans les romans grecs antiques." In Bernard Pouderon and Cécile Bost-Pouderon, eds., *Passions, vertus et vices dans l'ancient roman*, pp. 171–84. Lyon: Maison de l'Orient de la Méditerranée-Jean Pouilloux.

Booth, Joan. 1991. *Ovid: The Second Book of the* Amores. Warminster: Aris & Phillips, Ltd.

———. 1995. *Latin Love Elegy. A Companion to Translations of Guy Lee*. London: Duckworth.

———. 1996. "Tibullus 1.8 and 9: A Tale in Two Poems?" *Museum Helveticum* 53: 232–47.

———. 1997. "All in the mind: sickness in Catullus 76." In *The Passions in Roman Thought and Literature*, edited by S.M. Braund and C. Gill, 150–68. Cambridge: Cambridge University Press.

Booth, Wayne C. 1988. *The Company We Keep: An Ethics of Fiction*. Berkeley: University of California Press.

Boucher, Jean-Paul. 1965. *Études sur Properce: Problèmes d'inspiration et d'art*. Paris: Éditions E. de Boccard.

Bowditch, P. Lowell. 2005. "Hermeneutic Uncertainty and the Feminine in Ovid's *Ars Amatoria*: The Procris and Cephalus digression." In *Gendered Dynamics in Latin Love Poetry*, edited by R. Ancona and E. Greene, 271–95. Baltimore: The Johns Hopkins University Press.

Boyancé, Pierre. 1960. "L'épicurisme dans la société et la littérature romaines." *Bulletin de l'Association Guillaume Budé* 4.1: 499–516.

Boyd, Barbara Weiden. 1997. *Ovid's Literary Loves. Influence and Innovations in the* Amores. Ann Arbor: University of Michigan Press.

Bradley, Keith R. 1991. *Discovering the Roman Family: Studies in Roman Social History*. New York: Oxford University Press.

Braund, Susanna Morton, and Christopher Gill, eds. 1997. *The Passions in Roman Thought and Literature*. Cambridge: Cambridge University Press.

Braund, Susanna Morton, and Glenn W. Most, eds. 2003. *Ancient Anger: Perspectives from Homer to Galen*. Cambridge: Cambridge University Press.

Breed, Brian W. 2003. "Portrait of a Lady: Propertius 1.3 and Ecphrasis." *The Classical Journal* 99: 35–56.

Bright, David F. 1978. Haec Mihi Fingebam*: Tibullus in his World (Cincinnati Classical Studies, Vol. III)*. Leiden: E.J. Brill.

Brown, Robert D. 1987. *Lucretius on Love and Sex: A Commentary on* De Rerum Natura *IV, 1030–1287 with Prolegomena, Text and Translation*. Leiden: E.J Brill.

Brunelle, Christopher Michael. 2005. "Ovid's Satirical Remedies." In *Gendered Dynamics in Latin Love Poetry*, edited by R. Ancona and E. Greene, 141–58. Baltimore: The Johns Hopkins University Press.

Burck, Erich. 1981. "Liebesbindung und Liebesbefreiung: Die Lebenswahl des Properz in den Elegien 1,6 und 3,21." In *Vom Menschenbild in der römischen Literatur II: Ausgewählte Schriften*, edited by E. Burch, 349–72. Heidelberg: Carl Winter Universitätsverlag.

Butler, H.E., and E.A. Barber, eds. 1933. *The Elegies of Propertius*. Oxford: Clarendon Press.

Butrica, J.L. 1994. "Myth and Meaning in Propertius 3.15." *Phoenix* 48: 135–51.

Buunk, Bram P., Alois Angleitner, Viktor Oubaid, and David M. Buss. 1996. "Sex Differences in Jealousy in Evolutionary and Cultural Perpsective: Tests from the Netherlands, Germany, and the United States." *Psychological Science* 7.6: 359–63.

Cahoon, Leslie. 1988. "The Bed as Battlefield: Erotic Conquest and Military Metaphor in Ovid's *Amores*." *Transactions of the American Philological Association* 118: 293–307.

Cairns, Douglas. 2003. "The Politics of Envy: Envy and Equality in Ancient Greece." In David Konstan and Keith Rutter, eds., *Envy, Spite and Jealousy: The Rivalrous Emotions in Ancient Greece*. Edinburgh: Edinburgh University Press, 235–52.

Cairns, Francis. 1972. *Generic Composition in Greek and Roman Poetry*. Edinburgh: Edinburgh University Press.

———. 1983. "Propertius 1,4 and 1,5 and the 'Gallus' of the *Monobiblos*." *Papers of the Liverpool Latin Seminar* 4: 61–103.

———. 2004. "Varius and Virgil: Two Pupils of Philodemus in Propertius 2.34?" In *Vergil, Philodemus, and the Augustans*, edited by D. Armstrong, J. Fish, P.A. Johnston, and M.B. Skinner, 299–321. Austin: University of Texas Press.

————. 2006. *Sextus Propertius: The Augustan Elegist*. Cambridge: Cambridge University Press.

Calhoun, Cheshire, and Robert C. Solomon, eds. 1984. *What is an Emotion? Classic Readings in Philosophical Psychology*. New York: Oxford University Press.

Camps, W.A., ed. 1961. *Propertius Elegies Book I*. Cambridge: Cambridge University Press.

————. 1966a. *Propertius Elegies Book III*. Cambridge: Cambridge University Press.

————. 1966b. *Propertius Elegies Book II*. Cambridge: Cambridge University Press.

Cantarella, Eva. 1991. "Homicides of Honor: The Development of Italian Adultery Law over Two Millennia." In *The Family in Italy from Antiquity to the Present*, edited by D.I. Kertzer and R.P. Saller, 229–44. New Haven: Yale University Press.

Castner, Catherine J. 1988. *Prosopography of Roman Epicureans from the Second Century B.C. to the Second Century A.D.* Frankfurt am Main: Peter Lang.

Caston, Ruth Rothaus. 2006. "Love as Illness: poets and philosophers on romantic love." *Classical Journal* 101.3: 271–98.

Caulfield, Sueann. 2000. *In Defense of Honor: Sexual Morality, Modernity, and Nation in Early-Twentieth-Century Brazil*. Durham: Duke University Press.

Champlin, Edward. 1991. *Final Judgments: Duty and Emotion in Roman Wills, 200 B.C.–A.D. 250*. Berkeley: University of California Press.

Charlebois, Elizabeth Anne. 2000. *The Jealous Zealot: Faith, Desire, and Epistemology in English Renaissance Drama*. Ph.D., English, Northwestern University, Chicago.

Clarke, Jacqueline. 2003. *Imagery of Colour and Shining in Catullus, Propertius & Horace*. New York: Peter Lang.

Clarke, John R. 1998. *Looking at Lovemaking: Constructions of Sexuality in Roman Art, 100 BC–250 AD*. Berkeley: University of California Press.

Clay, Diskin. 1973. "Sailing to Lampsacus: Diogenes of Oenoanda, New Fragment 7." *Greek, Roman and Byzantine Studies* 14: 49–59.

Cohen, David. 1991. "The Augustan Law on Adultery: The Social and Cultural Context." In *The Family in Italy from Antiquity to the Present*, edited by D.I. Kertzer and R.P. Saller, 109–26. New Haven: Yale University Press.

Conte, Gian Biagio. [1991] 1994. *Genres and Readers: Lucretius, Love Elegy, Pliny's Encyclopedia*. Translated by G.W. Most. Baltimore: Johns Hopkins University Press.

————. 1994. *Latin Literature: A History*. Translated by Joseph B. Solodow, revised by Don Fowler and Glenn W. Most. Baltimore: The Johns Hopkins University Press.

Coplan, Amy. 2004. "Empathic Engagement with Narrative Fictions." *Journal of Aesthetics and Art Criticism* 62:2, 141–52.

Copley, Frank O. 1947. "*Servitium Amoris* in the Roman Elegists." *Transactions of the American Philological Association* 78: 285–300.

Crohns, Hjalmar. 1905. "Zur Geschichte der Liebe als 'Krankheit.'" *Archiv für Kulturgeschichte* 3: 66–86.

Crommelynck, Fernand. 2007. *The Magnificent Cuckold*. Translated by Ben Sonnenberg and Amiel Melnick. New York: Segue Foundation.

Curran, Leo C. "Vision and Reality in Propertius 1.3." *Yale Classical Studies* 19: 189–207.

Cyrino, Monica S. 1995. *In Pandora's Jar: Lovesickness in Early Greek Poetry*. Lanham: University Press of America.

Davis, Gregson. 1983. *The Death of Procris. "Amor" and the Hunt in Ovid's* Metamorphoses. Rome: Edizioni dell'Ateneo.

Davis, Kingsley. 1935/6. "Jealousy and Sexual Property." *Social Forces* 14: 393–405.

DeBrohun, Jeri Blair. 2003. *Roman Propertius and the Reinvention of Elegy*. Ann Arbor: University of Michigan Press.

Deuse, Werner. 1990. "Dichtung als Heilmittel gegen die Liebe. Zum 11. Idyll Theokrits." In *Beiträge zur Hellenistischen Literatur und Ihrer Rezeption in Rom*, edited by P. Steinmetz, 59–76. Stuttgart: Franz Steiner Verlag.

Devereaux, Mary. 2004. "Moral Judgments and Works of Art: The Case of Narrative Literature." *Journal of Aesthetics and Art Criticism* 62:1, 3–11.

Dion, Jeanne. 1993. *Les passions dans l'oeuvre de Virgile: Poétique et philosophie*. Nancy: Presses Universitaires de Nancy.

Dixon, Suzanne. 1991. "The Sentimental Ideal of the Roman Family." In *Marriage, Divorce, and Children in Ancient Rome*, edited by B. Rawson, 99–113. Canberra: The Australian National University.

Dunn, Francis M. 1985. "The Love Reflected in the *Exemplum*: A Study of Propertius 1.3 and 2.6." *Illinois Classical Studies* 10: 233–59.

Edmonson, Jonathan, and Alison Keith, eds. 2008. *Roman Dress and the Fabrics of Roman Culture*. Toronto: University of Toronto Press.

Edwards, Catherine. 1993. *The Politics of Immorality in Ancient Rome*. Cambridge: Cambridge University Press.

———. 1996. *Writing Rome: Textual Approaches to the City*. Cambridge: Cambridge University Press.

Enk, P.J., ed. 1962. *Sex. Properti* Elegiarum Liber Secundus, vol. 2. Leiden: A.W. Sijthoff.

Erler, Michael. 1992. "Orthodoxie und Anpassung: Philodem, ein Panaitios des Kepos?" *Museum Helveticum* 49: 171–200.

Evans, S. 1971. "Odyssean Echoes in Propertius IV.8." *Greece and Rome* 18.1: 51–53.

Fantham, Elaine. 1972. *Comparative Studies in Republican Latin Imagery*. Toronto: University of Toronto Press.

———. 1986. "*Zelotupia*: A Brief Excursion into Sex, Violence, and Literary History." *Phoenix* 40: 45–57.

———. 1989. "Mime: The Missing Link in Roman Literary History." *The Classical World* 82: 153–63.

———. 2006. "The Image of Woman in Propertius' Poetry." In *Brill's Companion to Propertius*, edited by H.-C. Günther, 183–98. Leiden: Brill.

Faraone, Christopher A. 1999. *Ancient Greek Love Magic*. Cambridge: Harvard University Press.

Farrell, Daniel M. 1980. "Jealousy." *The Philosophical Review* 89: 527–59.

Fear, Trevor A. 2000. "The Poet as Pimp: Elegiac Seduction in the Time of Augustus." *Arethusa* 33.2: 217–40.

Fedeli, Paolo, ed. 1980. *Sestio Properzio: Il primo libro delle elegie*. Firenze: Leo S. Olschki.

———. 1985. *Properzio: Il libro terzo delle elegie*. Bari: Adriatica Editrice.

———. 1994. *Propertius: Elegiarum Libri IV*. Stuttgart: Teubner.

Fitzgerald, William. 1995. *Catullan Provocations: Lyric Poetry and the Drama of Position*. Berkeley: University of California Press.

———. 2000. *Slavery and the Roman Literary Imagination*. Cambridge: Cambridge University Press.

Flower, Harriet I. 1996. *Ancestor Masks and Aristocratic Power in Roman Culture*. Oxford: Clarendon Press.

Fögen, Thorsten. 2009. "Tears in Propertius, Ovid and Greek Epistolographers." In *Tears in the Graeco-Roman World*, edited by T. Fögen, 179–208. Berlin: Walter de Gruyter.

Ford, Ford Madox. 1999. *The Good Soldier*. Oxford: Oxford University Press.

Fraenkel, Eduard. 1916. "Zur Geschichte des Wortes *Fides*." *Rheinisches Museum für Philologie* 71: 187–99.

Franko, George Fredric. 1995. "*Fides*, Aetolia, and Plautus' *Captivi*." *Transactions of the American Philological Association* 125: 155–76.

Frede, Michael. 1986. "The Stoic Doctrine of the Affections of the Soul." In *The Norms of Nature: Studies in Hellenistic Ethics*, edited by M. Schofield and G. Striker, 93–110. Cambridge: Cambridge University Press.

Fredrick, David. 1997. "Reading Broken Skin: Violence in Roman Elegy." In *Roman Sexualities*, edited by J.P. Hallett and M.B. Skinner, 172–93. Princeton: Princeton University Press.

———, ed. 2002. *The Roman Gaze: Vision, Power and the Body*. Baltimore: The John Hopkins University Press.

Freud, Sigmund. [1922]1955. "Some Psychoanalytic Neurotic Mechanisms in Jealousy, Paranoia and Homosexuality." In *The Standard Edition of the Complete Psychological Works of Sigmund Freud* (Vol. 18), edited and translated by J. Stratchey, 221–32. London: The Hogarth Press.

Freyburger, Gérard. 1983. "Venus et Fides." In *Hommages à Robert Schilling*, edited by H. Zehnacher and G. Hentz, 161–67. Paris: Société d'édition Les Belles Lettres.

———. 1986. *Fides, Étude sémantique et religieuse depuis les origins jusqu'à l'époque augustéenne (Collection d'Études Anciennes)*. Paris: Les Belles Lettres.

Füst, Milan. 1989. *The Story of My Wife: The Reminiscences of Captain Storr*. Translated by Ivan Sanders. New York: Vintage.

Gaisser, Julia Haig. 1977. "Tibullus 2.3 and Vergil's Tenth Eclogue." *Transactions of the American Philological Association* 107: 131–46.

Galinsky, Karl. 1969. "The Triumph Theme in the Augustan Elegy." *Wiener Studien* 3: 75–107.

———. 1981. "Augustus' Legislation on Morals and Marriage." *Philologus* 125: 126–44.

———. 1988. "The Anger of Aeneas." *The American Journal of Philology* 109.3: 321–48.

Garnsey, Peter, and Richard P. Saller, eds. 1987. *The Roman Empire: Economy, Society and Culture*. Berkeley: University of California Press.

Gebhardt, Ulrich C.J. 2009. *Sermo iuris: Rechtssprache und Recht in der augusteischen Dichtung*. Leiden: Brill.

Gibson, Roy K., ed. 2003. *Ovid: Ars Amatoria Book 3 (Cambridge Classical Texts and Commentaries 40)*. Cambridge: Cambridge University Press.

———. 2006. "Ovid, Augustus, and the Politics of Moderation in *Ars Amatoria* 3." In *The Art of Love: Bimillenial Essays on Ovid's Ars Amatoria and Remedium Amoris*, edited by R.K. Gibson, S. Green, and A. Sharrock, 121–43. Oxford: Oxford University Press.

———. 2007. *Excess and Restraint. Propertius, Horace & Ovid's* Ars Amatoria. London: Institute of Classical Studies.

Gill, Christopher. 1997. "Passion as Madness in Roman Poetry." In *The Passions in Roman Thought and Literature*, edited by S.M. Braund and C. Gill, 213–41. Cambridge: Cambridge University Press.

———. 2004. "Reactive and Objective Attitudes: Anger in Virgil's *Aeneid* and Hellenistic Philosophy." In *Ancient Anger: Perspectives from Homer to Galen*, edited by S. Braund and G.W. Most, 208–28. Cambridge: Cambridge University Press.

Girard, René. 1961. *Mensonge romantique et vérité romanesque*. Paris: Éditions Bernard Grasset.

Giuffrida, Pasquale. 1940. *L'Epicureismo nella letteratura latina nel I secolo a.C.* Torino: G.B. Paravia & C.

von Goethe, Johann Wolfgang. 1989. *The Sorrows of Young Werther*. Translated by Michael Hulse. London: Penguin.

Gold, Barbara K. 1993. "'But Ariadne Was Never There in the First Place': Finding the Female in Roman Poetry." In *Feminist Theory and the Classics*, edited by N.S. Rabinowitz and A. Richlin, 430–56. New York: Routledge.

Goldhill, Simon. 1991. *The Poet's Voice: Essays on Poetics and Greek Literature*. Cambridge: Cambridge University Press.

Goldie, Peter. 2000. *The Emotions: A Philosophical Exploration*. Oxford: Clarendon Press.

Gonzalez-Crussi, F. 1988. *On the Nature of Things Erotic*. London: Harcourt Brace Jovanovich.

Goold, G.P., ed. 1990. *Propertius, Elegies*. Cambridge: Harvard University Press.

Gosling, J.C.B. 1973. *Plato*. London: Routledge & Kegan Paul.

Gow, A.S.F., ed. 1952. *Theocritus*. Cambridge: Cambridge University Press.

Graver, Margaret, ed. 2002. *Cicero on the Emotions: Tusculan Disputations 3 and 4*. Chicago: University of Chicago Press.

———. 2007. *Stoicism and Emotion*. Chicago: The University of Chicago Press.

Green, C.M.C. 1996. "Terms of Venery: Ars Amatoria I." *Transactions of the American Philological Association* 126: 221–63.

Greene, Ellen. 1999. "Travesties of Love: Violence and Voyeurism in Ovid *Amores* 1.7." *Classical World* 92.5: 409–18.

———. 2000. "Gender Identity and the Elegiac Hero in Propertius 2.1." *Arethusa* 33.2: 241–61.

Greene, Graham. 1991. *The End of the Affair*. London: Penguin.

Griffin, Miriam. 1989. "Philosophy, Politics and Politicians at Rome." In *Philosophia Togata: Essays on Philosophy and Roman Society*, edited by M. Griffin and J. Barnes, 1–37. Oxford: Clarendon Press.

Griffiths, John Gwyn. 1990. "Love as a Disease." In *Studies in Egyptology Presented to Miriam Lichtheim I*, edited by S. Israelit-Groll, 349–64. Jerusalem: The Hebrew University.

Grimal, Pierre. 1953. *Les intentions de Properce et la composition du livre IV des "Elégies"*. Brussels: Latomus.

Grossman, David. 2006. *Her Body Knows: Two Novellas*. Translated by Jessica Cohen. New York: Picador.

Grzywacz, Margot. 1937. *'Eifersucht' in den romanischen Sprachen. Ein Beitrag zur Kulturgeschichte des Mittelalters*. Bochum: H. Pöppinghaus.

Guillais, Joelle. 1991. *Crimes of Passion: Dramas of Private Life in Nineteenth-Century France*. New York: Routledge.

Gutzwiller, Kathryn J. 1998. *Poetic Garlands: Hellenistic Epigrams in Context*. Berkeley: University of California Press.

Harris, Christine R., and Nicholas Christenfeld. 1996. "Gender, Jealousy and Reason." *Psychological Science* 7.6: 364–66.

Harris, William V. 2001. *Restraining Rage: The Ideology of Anger Control in Classical Antiquity*. Cambridge: Harvard University Press.

Harrison, S.J. 1988. "Deflating the *Odes*: Horace, *Epistles* 1.20." *The Classical Quarterly* 38.2: 473–6.

———. 1994. "Drink, Suspicion and Comedy in Propertius 1.3." *Proceedings of the Cambridge Philological Society* 40: 18–26.

Heinze, Richard. 1929. *"Fides."* *Hermes* 64: 140–66.

Henderson, A.A.R. 1979. *P. Ovidi Nasonis, Remedia Amoris*. Edinburgh: Scottish Academic Press.

Heyworth, S.J., ed. 2007a. *Sexti Properti Elegos*. Oxford: Oxford University Press.

———. 2007b. *Cynthia: A Companion to the Text of Propertius*. Oxford: Oxford University Press.

Hinds, Stephen. 1987. "The Poetess and the Reader: Further Steps towards Sulpicia." *Hermathena* 143: 29–46.

———. 1998. *Allusion and Intertext: Dynamics of Appropriation in Roman Poetry*. Cambridge: Cambridge University Press.

Horsfall, Nicholas. 1983. "Some Problems in the 'Laudatio Turiae.'" *Bulletin of the Institute of Classical Studies* 30: 85–98.

Hubbard, Margaret. 1974. *Propertius*. London: Duckworth.

Hubbard, Thomas K. 1986. "Speech, Silence, and the Plays of Signs in Propertius 2.18." *Transactions of the American Philological Association* 116: 289–304.

Hupka, Ralph B. 1981. "Cultural Determinants of Jealousy." *Alternative Lifestyles* 4: 310–56.

Hutchinson, Gregory. 2006. *Propertius: Elegies Book IV*. Cambridge: Cambridge University Press.

Inwood, Brad. 1985. *Ethics and Human Action in Early Stoicism*. Oxford: Clarendon Press.

———. 1997. "Why Do Fools Fall in Love?" In *Aristotle and After*, edited by R. Sorabji, 57–69. London: Institute of Classical Studies, University of London.

———. 2005. *Reading Seneca: Stoic Philosophy at Rome*. Oxford: Clarendon Press.

Jacobson, Howard. 1974. *Ovid's Heroides*. Princeton: Princeton University Press.

———. 1976. "Structure and Meaning in Propertius Book 3." *Illinois Classical Studies* 1: 160–73.

James, Sharon L. 1997. "Slave-rape and Female Silence in Ovid's Love Poetry." *Helios* 24: 60–76.

———. 2003a. *Learned Girls and Male Persuasion: Gender and Reading in Roman Love Elegy*. Berkeley: University of California Press.

———. 2003b. "Her Turn to Cry: The Politics of Weeping in Roman Love Elegy." *Transactions of the American Philological Association* 133: 99–122.

Joyce, James. 1992. *Dubliners*. London: Penguin.

Kahan, Dan M., and Martha C. Nussbaum. 1996. "Two Conceptions of Emotion in Criminal Law." *Columbia Law Review* 96.2.

Kaster, Robert A. 2005. *Emotion, Restraint, and Community in Ancient Rome*. Oxford: Oxford University Press.

———. 2006. "Review of David Konstan, *The Emotions of the Ancient Greeks: Studies in Aristotle and Classical Literature*." *Notre Dame Philosophical Reviews*.

Kaufhold, Shelley. 1997. "Propertius 1.3: Cynthia Rescripted." *Illinois Classical Studies* 22: 87–98.

Keith, A.M. 1994. "*Corpus Eroticum*: Elegiac Poetics and Elegaic *Puellae* in Ovid's *Amores*." *Classical World* 88: 27–40.

———. 2008. *Propertius: Poet of Love and Leisure, Classical Literature and Society*. London: Duckworth.

Kennedy, Duncan. 1993. *The Arts of Love: Five Studies in the Discourse of Roman Love Elegy*. Cambridge: Cambridge University Press.

Kenney, E.J., ed. 1961. *P. Ovidi Nasonis* Amores, Medicamina Faciei Femineae, Ars Amatoria, Remedia Amoris. Oxford: Oxford University Press.

Kershaw, Allan. 1983. "A! and the Elegists: More Observations." *Classical Philology* 78: 232–3.

Khan, H. Akbar. 1968. "Sea-Symbolism in Propertius I, 11." *Acta Antiqua Academiae Scientiarum Hungaricae* 16: 253–6.

———. 1969. "Image and Symbol in Catullus 17." *Classical Philology* 64: 88–97.

King, Joy K. 1975/6. "Propertius' Programmatic Poetry and the Unity of the '*Monobiblos*.'" *Classical Journal* 71.2: 108–24.

Knorr, Ortwin. 2006. "Horace's Ship Ode (*Odes* 1.14) in Context: A Metaphorical Love-Triangle." *Transactions of the American Philological Association* 136: 149–69.

Knox, Peter E. 1986. *Ovid's* Metamorphoses *and the Traditions of Augustan Poetry*. Cambridge: Cambridge Philological Society.

———. 1995. *Ovid, Heroides: Select Epistles*. Cambridge: Cambridge University Press.

Koch, Bernhard. 2006. *Philosophie als Medizin für die Seele: Untersuchungen zu Ciceros Tusculanae Disputationes*. Stuttgart: Franz Steiner Verlag.

Konstan, David. 1983. *Roman Comedy*. Ithaca: Cornell University Press.

———. 1986. "Love in Terence's *Eunuch*: The Origins of Erotic Subjectivity." *The American Journal of Philology* 107.3: 369–93.

———. 1994. *Sexual Symmetry: Love in the Ancient Novel and Related Genres*. Princeton: Princeton University Press.

———. 2001. *Pity Transformed*. London: Duckworth.

———. 2006. *The Emotions of the Ancient Greeks*. Toronto: University of Toronto Press.

Konstan, David, and Keith Rutter, eds. 2003. *Envy, Spite and Jealousy: The Rivalrous Emotions in Ancient Greece*. Edinburgh: Edinburgh University Press.

de Lacy, Phillip, ed. 1984. *Galen on the Doctrines of Hippocrates and Plato*. Berlin: Akademie-Verlag.

Lagache, Daniel. 1947. *La Jalousie amoureuse. Psychologie descriptive et psychanalyse*. Paris: Presses Universitaires de France.

Langlands, Rebecca. 2006. *Sexual Morality in Ancient Rome*. Cambridge: Cambridge University Press.

Lattimore, Richmond. 1942. *Themes in Greek and Latin Epitaphs*. Urbana: The University of Illinois Press.

Lazarus, Richard S., and Susan Folkman. 1984. *Stress, Appraisal and Coping*. New York: Springer.

Leach, Eleanor Winsor. 1966. "Propertius 1.17: The Experimental Voyage." *Yale Classical Studies* 19: 211–32.

Lee, Guy. 1982. *Tibullus: Elegies*. Liverpool: Francis Cairns.

Lee-Stecum, Parshia. 1998. *Powerplay in Tibullus: Reading Elegies Book One*. Cambridge: Cambridge University Press.

———. 2000. "Poet/Reader, Authority Deferred: Re-Reading Tibullan Elegy." *Arethusa* 33.2: 177–216.

Lindheim, Sara H. 1988. "Hercules Cross-Dressed, Hercules Undressed: Unmasking the Construction of the Propertian *Amator* in Elegy 4.9." *American Journal of Philology* 119.1: 43–66.

Lively, Genevieve, and Patricia Salzman-Mitchell, eds. 2008. *Latin Elegy and Narratology: Fragments of Story*. Columbus: Ohio State University Press.

Lloyd, Rosemary. 1995. *Closer & Closer Apart: Jealousy in Literature*. Ithaca: Cornell University Press.

Long, A.A. [1974]1986. *Hellenistic Philosophy: Stoics, Epicureans, Sceptics*. Berkeley and Los Angeles: University of California Press.

Long, A.A., and D.N. Sedley, eds. 1987. *The Hellenistic Philosophers*. Cambridge: Cambridge University Press.

Luck, Georg. 1959. *The Latin Love Elegy*. London: Methuen & Co.

Lutz, Catherine A. 1998. *Unnatural Emotions: Everyday Sentiments on a Micronesian Atoll & Their Challenge to Western Theory*. Chicago: The University of Chicago Press.

Lyne, R.O.A.M. 1979. "*Servitium Amoris*." *Classical Quarterly n.s.* 29: 117–30.

————. 1980. *The Latin Love Poets: From Catullus to Horace*. Oxford: Clarendon Press.

————. 1998. "Propertius and Tibullus: Early Exchanges." *The Classical Quarterly* 48.2: 519–44.

Machemer, G.A. 1993. "Medicine, Music and Magic: The Healing Grace of Pindar's *Fourth Nemean*." *Harvard Studies in Classical Philology* 95: 113–41.

Macleod, C.W. 1974. "A Use of Myth in Ancient Poetry." *The Classical Quarterly* 24: 82–93.

Maehler, Herwig. 1990. "Symptome der Liebe im Roman und in der griechischen Anthologie." In *Groningen Colloquium on the Novel III*, edited by H. Hofmann, 1–12. Groningen: Egbert Forsten.

Maleuvre, Jean-Yves. 1998. *Jeux de masques dans l'élégie latine: Tibulle, Properce, Ovide*. Louvain: Édition Peeters.

Maltby, Robert. 2002. *Tibullus: Elegies. Text, Introduction and Commentary. ARCA Classical and Medieval Texts, Papers and Monographs 41*. Cambridge: Francis Cairns Publications.

————. 2006. "Major Themes and Motifs in Propertius' Love Poetry." In *Brill's Companion to Propertius*, edited by H.-C. Günther, 145–81. Leiden: Brill.

Manning, C.E. 1994. "School Philosophy and Popular Philosophy in the Roman Empire." *Aufstieg und Neidergang der römischen Welt* 2.36.7: 4995–5026.

Manuwald, Bernd. 1990. "Der Kyklops als Dichter: Bemerkungen zu Theokrit, *Eid*. 11." In *Beiträge zur hellenistichen Literatur und ihrer Rezeption in Rom*, edited by P. Steinmetz, 77–91. Stuttgart: Franz Steiner Verlag.

Mathes, Eugene W., and Christine Verstraete. 1993. "Jealous Aggression: Who is the Target, the Beloved or the Rival?" *Psychological Reports* 72: 1071–4.

Maupassant, Guy de. 1979. *Pierre and Jean*. Translated by L. Tancock. New York: Penguin.

Mayer, Roland. 1986. "Horace's *Epistles* I and Philosophy." *American Journal of Philology* 107: 55–73.

————. 2005. "Sleeping with the Enemy: Satire and Philosophy." In *The Cambridge Companion to Roman Satire*, edited by K. Freudenburg, 146–59. Cambridge: Cambridge University Press.

McCarthy, Kathleen. 2000. *Slaves, Masters, and the Art of Authority*. Princeton: Princeton University Press.

McEwan, Ian. 1997. *Enduring Love*. New York: Anchor Books.

McGinn, Thomas A.J. 2003. *Prostitution, Sexuality, and the Law in Ancient Rome*. Oxford: Oxford University Press.

McKeown, J.C. 1979. "Augustan Elegy and Mime. *Proceedings on the Cambridge Philological Society* 25: 71–84.

————. 1989. *Ovid, Amores: Text, Prolegomena and Commentary in four volumes*. Vol. II. A Commentary on Book 1: Francis Cairns Publications, Ltd.

————. 1998. *Ovid, Amores: Text, Prolegomena and Commentary in four volumes*. Vol. III. A Commentary on Book 2. Leeds: Francis Cairns Publications, Ltd.

Mele, Alfred R. 2001. *Self-deception Unmasked*. Princeton: Princeton University Press.

Miller, P.A., ed. 2002. *Latin Erotic Elegy: An Anthology and Reader*. New York: Routledge.

————. 2004. *Subjecting Verses: Latin Love Elegy and the Emergence of the Real*. Princeton: Princeton University Press.

Milnor, Kristina. 2007. *Gender, Domesticity, and the Age of Augustus: Inventing Private Life*. Oxford: Oxford University Press.

Momigliano, A. 1941. "Epicureans in Revolt." *Journal of Roman Studies* 31: 151–7.

Morales, Helen. 2005. *Vision and Narrative in Achilles Tatius' Leucippe and Clitophon*. Cambridge: Cambridge University Press.

Moritz, L.A. 1968. "*Difficile est longum subito deponere amorem*." *Greece and Rome* 15: 53–8.

Most, Glenn W. 2005. *Doubting Thomas*. Cambridge: Harvard University Press.

Mowat, Ronale Rae. 1966. *Morbid Jealousy and Murder: A Psychiatric Study of Morbidly Jealous Murders at Broadmoor*. London: Tavistock Publications.

Muecke, Frances. 1994. "Philosophy at the Sabine Farm (Hor. *Satires* 2.6.59–76)." *Journal of the Australasian Universities Language and Literature Association* 81: 81–92.

Mullen, Paul E. 1993. "The Crime of Passion and the Changing Cultural Construction of Jealousy." *Criminal Behavior and Mental Health* 3: 1–11.

————. 1996. "Editorial: Jealousy and the Emergence of Violent and Intimidating Behaviours." *Criminal Behavior and Mental Health* 6: 199–205.

Mullin, Amy. 2004. "Moral Defects, Aesthetic Defects, and the Imagination." *Journal of Aesthetics and Art Criticism* 62:3, 249–61.

Murgatroyd, Paul. 1975. "*Militia amoris* and the Roman Elegists." *Latomus* 34: 59–79.

————, ed. 1994. *Tibullus, Elegies II*. Oxford: Clarendon Press.

————. 1995. "The Sea of Love." *Classical Quarterly* 45: 9–25.

————. 2001. *Tibullus I: A Commentary on the First Book of the Elegies of Albius Tibullus*. London: Bristol Classical Press.

Musurillo, Herbert. 1967. "The Theme of Time as a Poetic Device in the Elegies of Tibullus." *Transactions of the American Philological Association* 98: 253–68.

Myers, K. Sara. 1996. "The Poet and the Procuress: The *Lena* in Latin Love Elegy." *Journal of Roman Studies* 86: 1–21.

Nabokov, Vladimir. 2010. *Lolita*. London: Penguin.

Nagle, Betty Rose. 1980. *The Poetics of Exile: Program and Polemic in the* Tristia *and* Epistulae ex Ponto *of Ovid*. Brussels: Latomus.

————. 1988. "A Trio of Love-Triangles in Ovid's *Metamorphoses*." *Arethusa* 21: 75–98.

Nethercut, W. R. 1970. "Propertius 3.12–14." *Classical Philology* 65.2: 99–102.

————. 1980. "Propertius 2.18: 'Kein einheitliches Gedicht . . .'" *Illinois Classical Society* 5: 94–108.

Neu, Jerome. 1980. "Jealous Thoughts." In *Explaining Emotions*, edited by A.O. Rorty, 425–63. Berkeley: University of California Press.

Nicholson, Nigel. 1988/9. "Bodies without Names, Names without Bodies: Propertius 1.21–22." *Classical Journal* 94.2: 143–61.

Nussbaum, Martha C. 1988. "Non-Relative Virtues: An Aristotelian Approach." *Midwest Studies in Philosophy* XIII: 32–53.

————. 1990. *Love's Knowledge: Essays on Philosophy and Literature*. New York: Oxford University Press.

————. 1993. "Poetry and the Passions: Two Stoic Views." In *Passions and Perceptions: Studies in Hellenistic Philosophy of Mind*, edited by J. Brunschwig and M.C. Nussbaum, 97–149. Cambridge: Cambridge University Press.

————. 1994. *The Therapy of Desire: Theory and Practice in Hellenistic Ethics*. Princeton: Princeton University Press.

————. 1995. "Eros and the Wise: The Stoic Response to a Cultural Dilemma." *Oxford Studies in Ancient Philosophy* 13: 231–67.

O'Hara, James J. 1993. "Medicine for the Madness of Dido and Gallus: Tentative Suggestions on *Aeneid* 4." *Vergilius* 39: 12–24.

O'Neill, Kerill. 2005. "The Lover's Gaze and Cynthia's Glance." In *Gendered Dynamics in Latin Love Poetry*, edited by R. Ancona and E. Greene, 243–68. Baltimore: The Johns Hopkins University Press.

Oliensis, Ellen. 1997. "The Erotics of *amicitia*: Readings in Tibullus, Propertius and Horace." In *Roman Sexualities*, edited by J.P. Hallett and M.B. Skinner, 151–71. Princeton: Princeton University Press.

Olson, Kelly. 2008. *Dress and the Roman Woman: Self-Presentation and Society*. London: Routledge.

Owens, William M. 1994. "The Third Deception in *Bacchides*: *Fides* and Plautus' Originality." *American Journal of Philology* 115.3: 381–407.

Pao, Ping-Nie. 1969. "Pathological Jealousy." *Psychoanalytic Quarterly* 38: 616–38.

Papanghelis, Theodore. 1987. *Propertius: A Hellenistic Poet on Love and Death*. Cambridge: Cambridge University Press.

Parrott, W. Gerrod. 1991. "The Emotional Experience of Envy and Jealousy." In *The Psychology of Jealousy and Envy*, edited by P. Salovey, 3–30. New York, London: The Guilford Press.

Paschalis, Michael. 1986. "*Aut ego fallor aut ego laedor* (Ovid *Metamorphoses* 1.607–608). A Witty Tautology?" *Eranos* 84: 62–63.

Pease, Arthur Stanley, ed. 1935. *Publi Vergili Maronis Aeneidos liber quartus*. Cambridge: Harvard University Press.

Pedrick, Victoria. 1986. "*Qui potis est, inquis*? Audience Roles in Catullus." *Arethusa* 19: 187–209.

Pepe, George M. 1972. "The Last Scene of Terence's *Eunuchus*." *The Classical World* 65.5: 141–45.

Perutelli, Alessandro. 2006. *Ulisse nella cultura romana*. Firenze: Le Monnier Università.

Pichon, René. 1902. *De sermone amatorio apud Latinos elegiarum scriptiores*. Paris: Libraire Hachette.

Pigeaud, Jackie. 1981. *La maladie de l'âme: Étude sur la relation de l'âme et du corps dans la tradition médico-philosophique antique*. Paris: Société d'Édition "Les Belles Lettres."

Pinotti, P. 1988. *Publio Ovidio Nasone: Remedia Amoris*. Edizioni e saggi universitari di filologia classica 39. Bologna: Pàtron.

Pizzocaro, Massimo. 1994. *Il triangolo amoroso: La nozione di "gelosia" nella cultura et nella lingua greca arcaica*. Bari: Levante Editori.

Pohlenz, M., ed. 1982. *M. Tullius Cicero* Tusculanae Disputationes. Stuttgart: Teubner.

Polleichtner, Wolfgang. 2009. *Emotional Questions: Vergil, the Emotions, and the Transformation of Epic Poetry. An Analysis of Select Scenes*. Trier: Wissenschaftlicher Verlag Trier.

Postgate, J.P., ed. 1980. *Tibulli Aliorumque Carminum Libri Tres*. Oxford: Oxford University Press.

Preston, Keith. 1916. *Studies in the Diction of the* Sermo Amatorius *in Roman Comedy*. Ph.D., Classics, University of Chicago, Chicago.

Proust, Marcel. 1954. *A la recherche du temps perdu*. Paris: Librairie Gallimard.

Putnam, Michael C.J., ed. 1973. *Tibullus: A Commentary*. Norman: University of Oklahoma Press.

———. 1976. "Propertius 1.22: A Poet's Self-Definition." *Quaderni Urbinati di Cultura Classica* 23: 93–123.

———. 1980. "Propertius' Third Book: Patterns of Cohesion." *Arethusa* 13.1: 97–113.

———. 1990. "Anger, Blindness and Insight in Virgil's *Aeneid*." In *The Poetics of Therapy: Hellenistic Ethics in its Rhetorical and Literary Context*, edited by M.C. Nussbaum, 7–40. Edmonton: Academic Printing and Publishing.

———. 1998. *Virgil's Epic Designs: Ekphrasis in the Aeneid*. New Haven: Yale University Press.

Quinn, Kenneth. 1973. *Catullus: The Poems*. New York: St. Martin's Press.

Rabbow, Paul. 1954. *Seelenführung: Methodik der Exerzitien in der Antike*. München: Kösel-Verlag.

Raditsa, Leo Ferrero. 1980. "Augustus' Legislation Concerning Marriage, Procreation, Love Affairs and Adultery." *Aufstieg und Niedergang der römischen Welt* 2: 378–339.

Ramsby, Teresa R. 2007. *Textual Permanence: Roman Elegists and the Epigraphic Tradition*. London: Duckworth Academic and Bristol University Press.

Rankin, H.D. 1968. "A Note on Catullus 17." *Latomus* 27: 418–20.

Reynolds, R.W. 1946. "The Adultery Mime." *The Classical Quarterly* 40: 77–84.

Richardson, Jr. Lawrence, ed. 1977. *Propertius, Elegies I–IV*. Norman: University of Oklahoma Press.

Richlin, Amy. 1981. "Approaches to the Sources on Adultery at Rome." In *Reflections of Women in Antiquity*, edited by H.P. Foley, 379–404. New York: Gordon & Breach.

Robbe-Grillet, Alain. 1957. *La Jalousie*. Paris: Les Éditions de Minuit.

Robinson, Jenefer. 2005. *Deeper than Reason: Emotion and its Role in Literature, Music and Art*. Oxford: Oxford University Press.

de la Rochefoucauld, Francois. 1977. *Maximes et réflexions divers*. Paris: GF Flammarion.

Ross, David O. 1969. *Style and Tradition in Catullus*. Cambridge: Harvard University Press.

———. 1975. *Backgrounds to Augustan Poetry: Gallus, Elegy and Rome*. Cambridge: Cambridge University Press.

Rothstein, Max. 1979. *Die Elegien des Sextus Propertius*. New York: Garland.

Rudd, Niall. 1959. "Colonia and her Bridge: A Note on the Structure of Catullus 17." *Transactions of the American Philological Association* 90: 238–42.

Sabato, Ernesto. 1988. *The Tunnel*. Translated by Margaret Sayers Peden. New York: Ballantine Books.

Salzman-Mitchell, Patricia B. 2005. *A Web of Fantasies: Gaze, Image and Gender in Ovid's* Metamorphoses. Columbus: The Ohio State University Press.

Saylor, Charles. 1967. "*Querelae*: Propertius' Distinctive, Technical Name for his Elegy." *Agon* 1: 142–9.

Schadewaldt, Hans. 1985. "Der *Morbus amatorius* aus medizinhistorischer Sicht." In *Das Ritterbild in Mittelalter und Renaissance*, edited by H.S. Herbruggen, 87-104. Düsseldorf: Droste Verlag.

Schofield, Malcolm. 1991. *The Stoic Idea of the City*. Cambridge: Cambridge University Press.

Scourfield, J.H.D. 2003. "Anger and Gender in Chariton's *Chaereas and Callirhoe*." In *Ancient Anger: Perspectives from Homer to Galen*, edited by S. Braund and G.W. Most, 163-84. Cambridge: Cambridge University Press.

Sebesta, Judith Lynn, and Larissa Bonfante, eds. 1994. *The World of Roman Costume*. Madison: University of Wisconsin Press.

Sedgwick, Eve. 1985. *Between Men: English Literature and Male Homosocial Desire*. New York: Columbia University Press.

Segal, Charles. 1990. *Lucretius on Anxiety and Death*. Princeton: Princeton University Press.

Selden, Daniel. 1992. "*Ceveat lector*: Catullus and the Rhetoric of Performance." In *Innovations in Antiquity*, edited by D. Selden and R. Hexter, 461-512. London: Routledge.

Sharrock, Alison. 2000. "Constructing Characters in Propertius." *Arethusa* 33.2: 263-84.

———. 2002a. "Gender and Sexuality." In *The Cambridge Companion to Ovid*, edited by P.R. Hardie, 95-107. Cambridge: Cambridge University Press.

———. 2002b. "Ovid and the Discourse of Love: the Amatory Works." In *The Cambridge Companion to Ovid*, edited by P.R. Hardie, pp. 150-62. Cambridge: Cambridge University Press.

———. 2005. "Those Who Can, Teach: Ovid's *Ars Amatoria* and Contemporary Instructional Writing." In *Wissensvermittlung in dichterischer Gestalt*, edited by M. Horster and C. Reitz, 243-63. Stuttgart: Franz Steiner Verlag.

Skinner, Marilyn B. 1987. "Disease Imagery in Catullus 76.17-26." *Classical Philology* 82: 230-3.

———. 2003. *Catullus in Verona: A Reading of the Elegiac Libellus, Poems 65-116*. Columbus: The Ohio State University Press.

Smith, Kirby Flower. 1913. *The Elegies of Albius Tibullus: The Corpus Tibullianum*. New York: American Book Company.

Solmsen, Friedrich. 1961. "Propertius in His Literary Relations with Tibullus and Vergil." *Philologus* 105: 273-89.

Sommariva, G. 1980. "La parodia di Lucrezio nell' *Ars* e nei *Remedia* ovidiani." *A & R* 25: 123-48.

Sontag, Susan. 1979. *Illness as Metaphor*. New York: Vintage Books.

Sorabji, Richard. 1997. "Is Stoic Philosophy Helpful as Psychotherapy?." In *Aristotle and After*, edited by R. Sorabji, 197-209. London: Institute of Classical Studies, University of London.

———. 2000. *Emotion and Peace of Mind: From Stoic Agitation to Christian Temptation*. Oxford: Oxford University Press.

Sousa, Ronald de. 1987. *The Rationality of Emotion*. Cambridge: MIT Press.

Stahl, Hans-Peter. 1985. *Propertius: "Love" and "War." Individual and State under Augustus*. Berkeley, Los Angeles and London: University of California Press.

Stanford, W.B. 1963. *The Ulysses Theme: A Study in the Adaptability of Traditional Hero*. Oxford: Blackwell.

———. 1980. *Greek Tragedy and the Emotions: An Introductory Study*. London: Routledge & Kegan Paul.

Starks Jr., John H. 1999. "*Fides Aeneia*: The Transference of Punic Stereotypes in the *Aeneid*." *The Classical Journal* 94.3: 255-83.

Stearns, Peter N. 1989. *Jealousy: The Evolution of an Emotion in American History*. New York: New York University Press.

Stemmler, Theo, ed. 1990. *Liebe als Krankheit: 3. Kolloquium der Forschungsstelle für europäische Lyrik des Mittelalters*. Mannheim: Gunter Narr Verlag.

Suits, Thomas A. 1976. "The Iambic Character of Propertius 1.4." *Philologus* 120: 86-91.

Tanner, Tony. 1979. *Adultery in the Novel: Contract and Transgression*. Baltimore: The Johns Hopkins University Press.

Tarrant, R.J. 1995. "The Silence of Cephalus: Text and Narrative Technique in Ovid, *Metamorphoses* 7.685ff." *Transactions of the American Philological Association* 125: 99-111.

Tennenhouse, Leonard. 1989. "Violence Done to Women on the Renaissance Stage." In *The Violence of Representation: Literature and the History of Violence*, edited by N. Armstrong and L. Tennenhouse, 77–97. London: Routledge.

Thomson, C.F.S., ed. 1997. *Catullus*. Toronto: University of Toronto Press.

Tolstoy, Leo. 2005. *The Kreutzer Sonata and Other Stories*, tr. David McDuff. London: Penguin.

Toohey, Peter. 1992. "Love, Lovesickness, and Melancholia." *Illinois Classical Studies* 17: 265–86.

Tov-Ruach, Leila. 1980. "Jealousy, Attention, and Loss." In *Explaining Emotions*, edited by A.O. Rorty, 465–88. Berkeley: University of California Press.

Tränkle, Hermann. 1960. *Die Sprachkunst des Properz und die Tradition der lateinischen Dichtersprache*. Wiesbaden: F. Steiner Verlag.

Treggiari, Susan. 1991. *Roman Marriage: Iusti Coniuges from the Time of Cicero to the Time of Ulpian*. Oxford: Clarendon Press.

Tupet, Anne-Marie. 1976. *La magie dans la poésie latine: Des origines à la fin du régne d'Auguste*. Paris: Société d'Édition "Les Belles Lettres."

Valladares, Hérica. 2005. "The Lover as Model Viewer: Gendered Dynamics in Propertius 1.3." In *Gendered Dynamics in Latin Love Poetry*, edited by R. Ancona and E. Greene, 206–42. Baltimore: The Johns Hopkins University Press.

Verducci, Florence. 1985. *Ovid's Toyshop of the Heart: Epistulae Heroidum*. Princeton: Princeton University Press.

Vinson, Martha P. 1992. "Party Politics and the Language of Love in the Lesbia Poems of Catullus." In *Studies in Latin Literature and Roman History VI*, edited by C. Deroux, 163–80.

Volk, Katherina. 2010. "Aratus." In *A Companion to Hellenistic Literature*, edited by J.J. Clauss and M. Cuypers, 197–210. Chichester: Blackwell.

Weir, Susan. 1992. "*Crimes passionnels*: Gender Differences in Perceived Justification for Murder in the Face of Marital Infidelity." *The Irish Journal of Psychology* 13.3: 350–60.

Wells, Stanley, and Gary Taylor, eds. 1988. *The Oxford Shakespeare: The Complete Works*. Oxford: Oxford University Press.

Westcott, Glenway. 2001. *The Pilgrim Hawk: A Love Story*. New York: The New York Review of Books.

Wheeler, Arthur Leslie. 1910. "Propertius as *Praeceptor Amoris*." *Classical Philology* 5: 28–40.

Whitaker, Richard. 1979. "The Unity of Tibullus 2.3." *Classical Quarterly* 29: 131–41.

White, Gregory L., and Paul E. Mullen. 1989. *Jealousy: Theory, Research and Clinical Strategies*. New York: The Guilford Press.

White, Peter. 1993. *Promised Verse: Poets in the Society of Augustan Rome*. Cambridge: Harvard University Press.

White, Stephen A. 1995. "Cicero and the Therapists." In *Cicero the Philosopher: Twelve Papers*, edited by J.G.F. Powell, 219–46. Oxford: Oxford University Press.

Wierzbicka, Anna. 1999. *Emotions across Languages and Cultures: Diversity and Universals*. Cambridge: Cambridge University Press.

Williams, Bernard. 1997. "Stoic Philosophy and the Emotions: reply to Richard Sorabji." In *Aristotle and After*, edited by R. Sorabji, 211–3. London: Institute of Classical Studies.

Williams, Gareth. 2010. "Apollo, Aesculapius and the Poetics of Illness in Ovid's *Metamorphoses*." In *Papers of the Langford Latin Seminar, Fourteenth Volume (ARCA 50)*, edited by Francis Cairns and Miriam Griffin, 63–92. Cambridge: Francis Cairns Publications.

Williams, Gordon. 1980. *Figures of Thought in Roman Poetry*. New Haven: Yale University Press.

Woozley, A.D. 1972. "Plato on Killing in Anger." *Philosophical Quarterly* 22: 303–17.

Wray, David. 2001. *Catullus and the Poetics of Roman Manhood*. Cambridge: Cambridge University Press.

Wyke, Maria. 1987. "Written Woman: Propertius' *scripta puella*." *Journal of Roman Studies* 77: 47–61.

———. 1989. "Reading Female Flesh: *Amores* 3.1." In *History as Text: The Writing of Ancient History*, edited by A. Cameron, 111–43. London: Duckworth.

Yardley, J.C. 1972. "Comic Influence in Propertius." *Phoenix* 27: 134–9.

Zetzel, James E.G. 1996. "Poetic baldness and its cure." *Materiali e discussioni per l'analisi dei testi classici* 36: 73–100.

INDEX